INSPIRING WOMEN TODAY

THE INSPIRING WOMEN TODAY SERIES

Inspiring Women Today
Three True Stories of Real Women, Vol. A
(Full color, released August 2019)

Inspiring Women Today
True Stories of Real Women, Vol. 1
(Black and white, released March 8, 2021)

Inspiring Women Today
True Stories of Real Women, Vol. 2
(Black and white, to be released March 8, 2022)

To find out about releases, events, and insider news, visit IWT online today and subscribe:
www.InspiringWomenToday.com

INSPIRING WOMEN TODAY

TRUE STORIES OF REAL WOMEN, VOLUME 1
WITH A FOREWORD BY KRIS RADISH

Erin C. Mahoney • Denise Duncan • Diane Diaz Rodriguez • Audrey Boland • Gail Fay • Christina DeBusk • Stella Ssemakula • Kristina Savka • Lisa Johnson • Ali Pilling • Sophal Chhay Benefield • Claudia Frustaci • Betsy Jordan • Michelle Hubbard • Lauren Clemett • Belinda Jane Dolan

Written and Compiled by Rodney Miles Taber

POWERS PRESS
An Imprint of Bimini Books

Copyright © 2021 by Rodney Miles Taber
All rights reserved.
Published by Powers Press, an imprint of Bimini Books

No part of this book may be reproduced in any manner without written permission except in the case of brief quotations embodied in critical articles and reviews.

Although the author and publisher have made every effort to ensure that the information in this book was correct at press time, the author and publisher do not assume and hereby disclaim any liability to any party for any loss, damage, or disruption caused by errors or omissions, whether such errors or omissions result from negligence, accident, or any other cause. Forms and agreements are included for your information only.

For information about special discounts for bulk purchases or author interviews, appearances, and speaking engagements please contact:

Rodney Miles Taber
www.inspiringwomentoday.com
rmiles@inspiringwomentoday.com

First Edition

Written, compiled, cover, and book design by Rodney Miles:
www.RODNEYMILES.com
Cover image: 3Motional Studio / Pexels

For my great-grandmother, Hannah,

For my grandmother, Jeannette,

For my mother, Ronna,

For my daughter Fallon

And for Dawn

"I know of no greater happiness
than to be with you all the time,
without interruption,
without end."

—Franz Kafka

"Men cannot stop the Third World War. It is not in their cells. But women can. A man can love a child, but he doesn't go through the labor pain. The solutions on this Earth are not in the hands of men. The solutions on this Earth are in the hands of the woman, in the psyche of the woman."

—YOGI BHAJAN

in·spire

verb

1. fill (someone) with the urge or ability to do or feel something; create (a feeling, especially a positive one) in a person; animate someone with (such a feeling).

2. breathe in (air); inhale.

Origin: Middle English enspire, from Old French inspirer, from Latin inspirare 'breathe or blow into' from in- 'into' + spirare 'breathe'. The word was originally used of a divine or supernatural being, in the sense 'impart a truth or idea to someone.' —Google

CONTENTS

Foreword by Kris Radish xvii
Preface xxi
Introduction 1
[1]   The Good Stuff by Erin C. Mahoney 5
[2]   False Evidence Appearing Real by Denise Duncan 19
[3]   Good Grief by Diane Diaz Rodriguez 31
[4]   Mexico by Audrey Boland 43
[5]   Hats and Scarves and Stuff Like That by Gail Fay 63
[6]   A Little Kindness by Christina Debusk 77
[7]   Women & Children First by Stella Ssemakula 89
[8]   Out of Hiding by Kristina Savka 97
[9]   The Holistic Approach by Lisa Johnson 109
[10] The World is Your Oyster by Ali Pilling 123
[11] Hearts of Cambodia by Sophal Chhay Benefield 137
[12] Intensive Care by Claudia Frustaci 153
[13] Keys of Leadership by Betsy Jordan 163
[14] Scared and Sacred by Michelle Hubbard 173
[15] Audacious by Lauren Clemett 183
[16] Clarity by Belinda Jane Dolan 201
Inspire Women Today 218
Women / Future Conference 219

FOREWORD

BY KRIS RADISH

"Life is a grand adventure, and if you hesitate or surrender, you might miss seeing the most beautiful bird ever, the loveliest sunset, or the best kiss of your life."

—KRIS RADISH

SOMETIMES WHEN I am feeling sorry for myself, I pause for a few moments, turn my head so I am looking behind me at the past, and then I shrink in embarrassment at my ridiculous parade of emotions. My sisters from the past lived lives of hardship, change, struggle and commitment that always make my own problems fade quickly.

I have always found inspiration in learning about past lives but it's also beyond true that women today are as inspiring, memorable, and remarkable as those women who keep an eye on us from their grace filled positions in our history books and hearts.

Inspiring Women Today is a testament to the tenacity and power of the female spirit. Author Rodney Miles is a man who has been blessed with a parade of women in his life who have inspired him in ways that other men should note. His own mother, wife, and daughter have helped define the shining slice of divine feminine that all men possess, but not all recognize or honor. He has honored the women in his life by celebrating those whose lives and words follow in this lovely and inspiring book.

The women you are about to read about have struggled with everything from dyslexia and emotional and physical abuse to drug addiction and cancer. They have tried and failed. They have fallen down and gotten back up again. They have lost children, been discriminated against, shoved to the side, treated as if they don't matter and have risked everything to become whole and recognized as they honor the true callings of their own hearts. Their journeys will inspire you as they have inspired me.

The female spirt is a wise and wild element that can be trampled but never broken. It is true that knowing you are not alone during a tough time can help save your life and these stories, these brave and wonderful women, these sharing hearts, will help you find your own strength to move forward

The women in the following pages are not just survivors but also heroines. I have spent my life working to inspire women, and very smart men, and I know that Inspiring Women Today will move you to new places and help you see that no matter what you are going through, you are not alone, and that yes, you can survive and move forward.

Blessings from my own female heart to yours.

Always,

Kris Radish

Saint Petersburg, Florida
October, 2020

About Kris Radish

KRIS RADISH is an American best-selling author, award-winning journalist, and nationally syndicated columnist. She has written three works of non-fiction, twelve novels, and has appeared on several national television shows. Her work focuses on self-empowerment and often celebrates female friendships, hope, and optimism.

www.KRISRADISH.com

PREFACE

Interviews as Art & Inspiration

> "When we tell our stories we change the world. I know that sounds dramatic, but I believe it. We'll never know how our stories might change someone's life."
>
> —BRENÉ BROWN
> *I Thought It Was Just Me*

WHY DOES A *man* create a series of books celebrating women? Because women have always played enormous roles in my own life, and because nature in its stunning intelligence has bestowed gifts and abilities to women that enable them to do things often un-accomplishable by men.

These chapters are, for the most part, based upon interviews with each woman. As a ghostwriter these last ten years, I've found live interviews vital to creating content that matches an author's voice. With *Inspiring Women,* I removed most or all of my own questions and comments, then developed each chapter into a bit of a narrative, hoping to present each woman as she really is and speaks and feels, and at the same time hoping to tap the power of *story*. I was not shooting for high art or enduring literature, but candid experiences of remarkable people, and in *their own* voices. I find by presenting their stories in this way, I connect with them the most.

Their experiences each have something profound to teach, often simply by their living through what they have lived through, often by their courage ("But then, what else would someone do?")

they might say), often by the lessons they've taken from each challenge, and for sure, by their tragedies and their triumphs.

Each has been remarkable in their courage and willingness to share, knowing these stories will reach people who can use them and be inspired.

And each time I set about working on these chapters, some aspect of my own personality improved. Angst was replaced by a desire to be kind. Anxiety replaced by peace. Cynicism by hope. I got inspired. I got excited. I found strength and goodness in the world.

I hope they do the same for you.

Rodney Miles Taber
Cape Canaveral, Florida
March, 2021

INTRODUCTION

> "Sure, he was great, but don't forget that Ginger Rogers did everything he did—backwards and in high heels."
>
> —BOB THAVES, cartoonist

FOR WHATEVER REASON, I seem to have always enjoyed the company of and gravitated toward strong women. Even as a book collaborator over the last decade, my client list must be comprised 80 percent of women. So I wanted to celebrate women and once I had the basic framework for this project and announced it, the response was instant and energetic. And one of the things I enjoy most about a project like Inspiring Women Today is how as you conduct interviews common themes seem to bubble to the surface. They have for this, Volume A, as well as the larger Volume 1. Paying it forward is one of the themes, as you'll see. So is strength, both in small and large ways.

In these pages you'll find the joys, hopes, tragedies, triumphs, and wisdom each author has been brave and generous enough to share. My primary requirement for authors involved in this project has been candor, and the women involved really have been candid, often in such bold ways. I am truly grateful to each of them, because the hope is to create a series of books women of all ages and backgrounds can have whenever they need or might enjoy a dose of inspiration.

For example, I remember being nine years old, bouncing a kickball by our seven-story apartment building in New York (Staten Island) and hearing the ice cream man's chimes. I looked to our third-floor window and hesitated to call for my mom, because I knew money was tight. But on that day I didn't have to ask. The window opened and Mom leaned out, smiling under her red hair. My heart jumped at her smile. She waved. I put the ball down and waved back. She dropped a clear sandwich bag tied at the top, filled with change, and it landed in my hands with a crunch.

There was bound to be enough for me and my little brother, Aaron, and I saw him already among the kids surrounding the ice cream van in the middle of Lincoln Avenue.

I ran over, thinking, cherry Italian ice, and wondered what life was like for my mom. I remembered the fights that led to the divorce five years earlier. They used to fight in the kitchen when they thought we were asleep, and I used to sneak down from my bunk bed and out of my bedroom to watch from the safety of the stairs. Money seemed to be the problem, at least one of them. And I remembered her letting me climb into her bed when I was little, where she'd confide in me like an adult—it made us friends.

My mother, Ronna, moved us to those apartments because my aunts and uncles and even my grandparents lived in the same buildings and they would watch us when she was at either of her two jobs. I remember her up early, off to the train that took her to the Staten Island Ferry, which took her to Lower Manhattan where she got on and off of a bus and then walked blocks and boarded an elevator that lifted her to the 35th floor of One World Trade Center. And I remember her not appearing at home again until late at night, after her second job waitressing at Beefsteak Charlie's, in the frilly shorts they wore.

I also remember walks through Rockefeller Center at Christmas, tons of gifts below the tree each year, homecooked meals, private school and soccer league, and even an occasional vacation, usually around some family gathering somewhere. It was an incredible childhood. It pleased or worried me most of the time. And it was inspiring.

My mother would surprise me again when at sixteen I explained my girlfriend and I had "decided to make love" and she was now late with her period. There, on the sidewalk in Pompano Beach outside our rented townhome, Mom paused walking her dachshund, and got serious, but not mad. "Well," she said, "I can raise the baby as my own and when the time comes, we can let him or her in on things, so you two can still go to college." But the test came back negative and we all calmed down.

My mother had a special relationship with her grandmother, Hannah, who was very strong. As a young girl Hannah Sanger rode in a wagon out west to Nebraska where her parents claimed land—a homestead—where she watched them bake bread and play the accordion for the Native Americans that showed up. As a young woman herself, she ran the farm while her boys were fighting in World War II. When Hannah was older, in her nineties, my mother asked her, "Grandma, you did so much for us. How do we repay you?"

"You repay me by taking care of your children," she said.

INTRODUCTION

My mother is still there for me, and my wife has a similar story with her mother, Sandy—single mom, two jobs, warm holidays, and still there for her. Without my own wife, Dawn, this book would not exist—Heck, I might not exist! Together for 30 years, she is an amazing wife, mother, and still my best friend. She made reinvention of myself at 40 (as a writer) possible. Before that, she sold rugs with me on the side of the road, laid tile, remodeled and flipped houses with me, then built a massage therapy practice, closing it when her hand-crafted "dragon wings" (for bearded dragons) business took off.

When we had our daughter, Fallon, she just seemed to know what to do. She is a perfect mother, and Fallon a pure blessing of a daughter. I watch Fallon rise early, go to work, study hard, and enjoy a beautiful relationship with a brilliant young man. I watch her laugh with her friends and truly care about others.

I'm humbled and grateful for the women in my life. I sincerely hope you find reading these books and connecting with these amazing women as inspiring as I found interviewing them. Women have power and magic—they are sacred, and that includes you.

Please enjoy *Inspiring Women Today*.

INSPIRING WOMEN TODAY

[1]

THE GOOD STUFF

by Erin C. Mahoney

To my mother, Danielle Therese Isabelle.
I have so many broken stories of my youth and cherish
the fact that you wanted more for me.

"My coach said I run like a girl.
And I said if he ran a little faster he could too."
—MIA HAMM

I'M A CEO. I'm a bestselling author. I'm a motivational speaker. I am a very proud United States veteran. I'm a mother and a wife. I am the proof anything is possible!

I was delivering a keynote speech recently to raise money for a preschool. I talked about *had I gone to preschool, who knows?* I said to them, "I was a kid who did not go to preschool. I was raised by a single mother from the time that I was two, and I could not read to save my life. I could not blend sounds. I struggled with punctuation. Reading comprehension did not exist for me. I felt ashamed, stupid, and embarrassed all of my school years. I remember being in the third or fourth grade and praying the teacher would not call on me to read aloud for fear that I was going too slow or stumbling over my words. I remember feeling like I wanted to crawl under the desk or somehow disappear so no one would see me and learn that I had this big secret—I couldn't *read*."

Not too many people know that about me. This past year I did some cognitive neurology testing to better understand my struggles with reading and writing. Dyslexia, language disorder, reading disorder, and ADHD! I've lived with all of them my whole life, undiagnosed. I never dreamed I'd be a bestselling author. It's completely insane to me still! Not being able to read well was a *real* struggle for me—something I didn't always feel safe sharing. But I must be vulnerable and brave now.

MY MOM really struggled. She came here from Canada when she was in the first grade. She didn't speak a lick of English and she was left-handed. They sent her to Catholic school and she spent most of her grammar school years getting swatted with a ruler because she was writing with the "wrong" hand (and she was trying to learn a new language). She told me that much later in life. I know now that there were things that happened in her life that she saw happening to me. The difference was that no one helped her. When she saw me struggling to read, she was like, "No way," because she always wanted better for me. When I was in the first or second grade myself, she dragged me to a summer reading program. I went kicking and screaming. I hated it and felt stupid.

The program seemed very odd to my seven-year-old self. They would blindfold us and have us write on the chalkboard and draw lines and listen to commands. I would go home and tell my mother, "Mom, this is so stupid! We don't even read there. How am I going to learn to read?" But now I know it was something like Brain Gym or some of these programs where through movement they are stimulating the frontal lobe of your brain. Basically, different people have different sides of their brain that they use and they are comfortable with. I'm a creative person, I'm a big idea person—maybe not always so organized or systematic. Whatever they did worked, and by the end of the summer, I was reading a little better.

Recently I was going through some papers from my mom's house and I found a report card from the third grade. It said I was reading at a first-grade level. I found a fifth-grade report card and the notes from teachers made me feel sad. Teachers wrote about my struggles and how I wasn't meeting grade level, yet they pushed me along anyway. Back in the day I do not think they assessed kids like they do now. They did not know what to do or how to help me, so they just ignored it and kept sending me to the next grade level anyway.

I had an enormous amount of shame around it. I was embarrassed. I became the funny kid who would act out so I'd get kicked out of the classroom because of the fear. I was terrified they would call on me to read aloud and hey, *if you're not in the room, they can't call on you, right?* Or I was the fourth grader who was trying to get small enough to get under her desk. Intentionally making myself small had a cost later in life.

I think because of that challenge I learned to be very social. For a long time, I was trying to protect myself. I was terrified that others would figure out what a poor student I was. I figured if I was this bubbly, social person, then no one was going to be able to see the side of me that struggled, the piece of me that I did not love. I think, like my mom, I am a lover of people and an extremely hard worker.

I watched her work. I watched her come home from waitressing to raise my sister and me. Seventeen years of waitressing. She would be in the kitchen, and I didn't know at the time, but she would be in kind of a fetal position, she would unzip the back of her uniform and kind of curl up, and she would cry. Not in front of us. I would be sleeping but from time to time I would get up and see her like that.

"I'm just really tired," she would say.

Years later I found out she was trying to write bills. She was busting her tail all weekend and didn't know how she was going to pay the rent. There was a time when my aunt had to drag her to welfare, which she certainly qualified for and needed. My aunt had to drag her because she was an immensely proud woman. She would drive forty minutes out of town to the grocery and I would be like, "Why do we go so far? There's grocery down the street."

Later I learned it was because she didn't want anyone to see us paying with food stamps. She didn't want other kids to make fun of us. She wasn't going to have that. She gave up so much to raise us the best she could. I believe my mother never remarried because she never trusted another man around her daughters. She told us that later in life.

They say strong women come from absent fathers—or abusive, or asshole fathers. My dad would fall into all those categories. The abuse would be emotional. He was never there, and she raised us completely alone.

WHEN I WAS younger, I went into the military because I was afraid to go to college. *Who does that, right?* That was a pivotal point for me. I was only 17 years old, but I made a big decision all on my own. I started to discover my own worth and purpose. Like I said, I thought I was afraid of college, that I didn't belong there. College was a place where I would fail. I believed the military was a place where I could be successful. I knew I was physically strong and fiercely determined. It was an opportunity to feel good about myself. My mom kept telling me I *could* be successful.

Going into the military instead of college might terrify most people but I was *so* afraid of being embarrassed or worse—failing out of college—that it seemed like the perfect next move for me. For a long time I felt like I was *less than*—How could I possibly be successful? You go through those years where everyone in any social situation asks, "Where do you go to school?" when you're in your twenties, because it's a way to spark a conversation. *I didn't go to school, I didn't go to college,* so I immediately felt like I was out of those conversations. It wasn't until deep, personal development and learning about worthiness and self-love that I really started to see my own worth, see my own brilliance, allow things to just unfold.

But it wasn't easy.

I was in the Air Force and when you get to the rank of sergeant you can test for early promotion. Promoting early means more pay, more responsibility. You have a window of time where you must be nominated and then you go through a rigorous process of interviews and things like that in order to put the stripe on early. I was eligible and I was recommended. There were about 65 other candidates recommended on the base who went into this process. There were only two stars that were to be given early. Through that process you have to know everything from current affairs to military history. It's a lot of hard work. You go through multiple panels and numerous interviews. It is quite an ordeal.

I worked hard and I was focused. *I wanted this.* It made sense. I thought, *If I am here I might as well make as much money as I can and take on a leadership role to further my career.* It came down to a handful of people. In those final days we all had the sense that this process was winding down and they were going to announce who got the stripe, who got the promotion soon. I went into my final interview and I was asked a current affairs question. I knew the exact answer only because I had been on a treadmill around 5 a.m. that morning and saw it on the news. So, I killed the question! I had every detail and they were totally blown away.

When they made the announcement, I was one of the two recipients who earned early promotion. It was a big deal! At the time, there was a man in my life (now my ex-husband) who was supposed to be my biggest cheerleader. He had also been in the running for the stripe but he had been knocked out many rounds before. When I got home and shared my joy, he looked me right in the eye and he said, "You got that stripe because you were the prettiest one in the shortest skirt."

I will never, ever, forget that moment. I was hurt, heartbroken, and beyond disappointed. I had to make his comment my new motivation. I probably would have physically hurt him and ended up in jail or something, so I had to "process," and I made that the fire in my belly. There is this small spark in me at times and it turns into a raging fire with the right fuel! I asked myself, *How can I make that positive*? I am all about turning negative comments and energy on its head and making it positive, and his nastiness made me even more driven. Eventually I did divorce that asshole. Clearly he didn't know who he was dealing with and he couldn't keep up.

We all have to surround ourselves with people who feed us. I was in the minority when I went into the military. The ratio of men to women was 27 to 1. I was definitely in a man's world. Even as a veteran—I hate to admit it—it's still to some degree a good ole' boys club. They don't always want to hear a woman's voice, and when they do they want to label her. I like to say I'm driven and relentless and thoughtful, and they want to call me a bitch. It's okay! In my opinion I can care deeply for someone, but I don't need to give a shit what they think. I need to care about what *I* think, more.

I'm nobody's bitch, and we're going to keep fighting.

My mom for years fed me that information, "You can do anything." I watched her. She raised two girls completely on her own—financially, emotionally—and never stopped telling us we could be amazing. For whatever reason I know she lacked confidence herself, but she would breathe it into me and my sister every opportunity she had. She would laugh now. She passed away but I quote her so often in my speaking engagements, she would be like, "Are you kidding?" One of her quotes that comes up all the time for me is:

> "You can never get past anything
> unless you go straight through it."

I love that! It's wise and powerful just like my mom was. Her words and actions help me still! She taught me about staying focused. She taught me about hard work. She taught me compassion and the importance of integrity. She taught me to never quit! She believed in me always! I don't want to quit on myself, I don't want to quit on my kids. I never ever want another human being to feel the way I did as a kid. No child or adult should feel stupid, embarrassed, or ashamed because they might not learn as easily as someone else, or as quickly as a teacher believes they should. I needed help and more time to learn. It simply took me longer to understand what was being taught to me. *I was not and am not stupid.*

And I no longer feel ashamed or embarrassed.

I DON'T WANT to say we had nothing growing up, we never felt like that. My sister and I had Nike sneakers and Guess jeans, and it made us really cool in the eighties, but another one of my favorite quotes from my mom was, "You can't buy the good stuff." She *gave us* all the good stuff. She taught us about being kind. She taught us that when you don't have money to make donations, you give of your time, or you give your old clothes, but you help others. There are so many ways to be of service. She would say, "I'm giving you all the good stuff, the stuff that money can't buy." She gave us her time. She gave us her love and affection.

The good stuff.

Those are now the things I try to give to my family and in my business. It's only now that I know I went into the service because *I am a woman of service*. I was meant to serve. I love my country. That's why that was my destiny—It didn't really have anything to do with the fact that I felt I wasn't smart enough, I just needed to discover my own self-worth. I've always been pretty self-aware but realizing self-love and discovering your self-worth can be a slow process. It's not something that happens overnight or something you get after reading one or two books. For me it's about always being *in the practice*. Sometimes we lose it. We forget it. So in my life, I'm always in the practice of loving myself and staying in that vibration that says, "You are okay." I want others to know *they* are okay.

Girl Power was born from need. I didn't wake up one morning and say, "I'm going to start this business to empower girls and women." It started, really, when a very special little girl in my life was being teased and needed some help. Through that process of helping her she became brave and courageous, she navigated through unexpected obstacles. I will always be proud of her, because when you ask someone to be kind or to stop behaving a certain way, and when you try to stand in your power, it can be tricky to also be loving and kind. It's one thing to stand in your power; it can be very different to do it in a way that's loving and kind and to come from a place of abundance. But she did it! I talk all about it in my book, *Girl Power Guidebook*.

From that experience and part of my journey my company was born. I realized there are millions of girls who need to hear these messages—that you are enough, that you get to be unique, that you are loved at every stage whether it's about body image or self-confidence, whether it's being brave and courageous, or just being healthy overall. And now there's been so much work we just can't stop. It's not easy to continue sometimes, but I've made a promise to myself as well as the girls and women I serve in this work. Sometimes it's very easy to break promises we make to *ourselves*, but I'm determined not to do that. I'm not quitting on the girls or the women that need this work, whether it's through the *Girl Power* books or the Girl Power Go programs.

Girl Power Go has grown up. We still serve 1st through 8th grade and we're also serving high schools now. I have a team of certified instructors, so there are several tracks:

- One will be a business in a box. When a guidance counselor in Florida reaches out to me, for example, and they want to be a part of it and they want to teach Girl Power, they can purchase the content. With that they get the *Girl Power Guidebook* and a certain number of *Girl Power Journals*.
- They might also want to get training, so either I or one of my trainers might go down there.
- The last piece is consulting. We are bundling in things like one live call with me each month, where they can do a Q&A. Organizations can also learn everything that we have learned—how girls see themselves through self-portraits, for example.

Some girls when they first arrive in our class and do their beginning self-portrait, draw themselves the size of a raisin, but when they leave, their head doesn't fit on the page or they draw themselves with a cape. It's pretty powerful to witness the self-esteem transformations firsthand. To me those are measurable successes. And I love that work.

My vision has always been to empower girls and women. If people want to run with it and build their geographical territory by teaching this incredible program without reinventing the wheel, then they can do that. If I have a woman who teaches 3rd grade and she wants to empower 40 kids, I want to give her the tools and the support she needs to do that.

My third book, *Positive Vibes,* came about because I saw the power of writing books when we published the *Girl Power* books. I don't know if I would be on this journey as a speaker had we not done those first two books. Based on an in-person program I was doing, empowering women at the time, we created that gorgeous little book (*Positive Vibes for Women*) in just six short weeks. The first two books (*Girl Power Guidebook, Girl Power Journal*) took us two years, and *Positive Vibes* took us six weeks. Talk about a passion project! I believe *Positive Vibes* is just the first in a powerful series.

At one time, I could not spell! But now I'm this bestselling author. I have a great publisher and a person who helps me edit. My gift is the gift of voice, and we can have a phone conversation, and through my voice I can get my message out there in a way that doesn't require me to feel ashamed. I had to find a new way, and that's all part of my journey to worthiness. I know now that just because it took me longer to learn, where maybe I had to work a little harder or to find different tools to get the information and understand it, it didn't mean I was stupid.

When my editor found this out about me, he sent me this:

> "Einstein was slow in learning how to speak. His parents even consulted a doctor. He also had a cheeky rebelliousness toward authority, which led one headmaster to expel him and another to amuse history by saying that he would never amount to much. But these traits helped make him a genius. His cocky contempt for authority led him to question conventional wisdom. His slow verbal development made him curious about ordinary things—such as space and time—that most adults take for granted. His father gave him a compass at age five, and he puzzled over the nature of a magnetic field for the rest of his life. And he tended to think in pictures rather than words." (—http://content.time.com/)

I can laugh about it now because I can take my time and I can stand in that and I can say, "That doesn't make me *less-than*." In fact, for me, it makes me more powerful. Every time there are people who feel that pain and share that with me, whether it's a student in a second-grade class or an executive in an audience, I'll ask them all, "Is there anyone here who has struggled to read?" And the hands pop right up. Just by standing up and saying these things people come up to me from the back of the room after a speaking gig and say, "I was that kid, too." I get that, and I tell them I don't want any other human being to feel those things. I don't want any other little girl or any woman or anyone of any gender to feel like they're stupid because maybe it takes them a little longer to learn.

I wonder if I would have been spared all those painful years of being scared, feeling stupid and ashamed, had I had someone in the school system who cared enough to reach back and help me to learn. Thank goodness my mom dragged me to the summer reading program I hated! It is where I learned about the power of drawing self-portraits. It was much later that I learned what they tell us about how we see ourselves. So, today I am sharing my truth and my authentic self. I want to inspire others to share the beautiful essence of themselves. I believe there is good in every human being. Some would say I'm naïve, I'm crazy—Well, I'm going to keep believing, because that's what feels really good to me.

If by sharing this, if by me being vulnerable and owning that I could not read, and still sometimes kind of struggle, and if it makes someone else feel like they can relate or they don't have to feel those horrible emotions, then that's worth it. I'm willing to stand here and hold space for others.

I HAVE BEEN in tears these last three or four of days, which is so unlike me, and part of it is because I feel like I am trying to figure this thing out, *what does my business look like?* But at the same time, I have to realize that's part of being an entrepreneur. There's no roadmap. That's what takes the courage and the bravery. You have to be resilient and relentless. I learned some of that in the military, but I really learned that from my mom. She gave me the tools and the *good stuff*.

To quote Maya Angelou:

> "I've learned that people will forget what you said, people will forget what you did, but people will never forget how you made them feel."

I want people to feel better because they shared space and time with me or someone in my company and the mission that we're on. I think I learned these things from Mom. She could have had a big, fat pity party because my dad was absent, because he didn't help financially, because most of the time we didn't have any money, because my grandmother was, frankly, really kind of mean to her, but she didn't. She showed up to her life and I feel like her showing up the way she did set the tone for my own life. She showed up in a way that said, 'Put on Elvis Presley or the Spinners, put on your makeup, and let's have a dance party before I go to work, while she drank her Tab in the pink can.

Mom was my inspiration for so many things. I try not to hold on to things, I try not to hold a grudge. I try not to do things that don't serve me. If they make you feel like shit they take their toll, they eat away at you. There used to be guilt with that, but I think she would be really happy and really proud of me that I'm living to the fullest in most days. I'm trying to *breathe my kids in* and stop the chaos every once in a while, and say to myself, *Are you present and does this feel?*

We forget. We get so caught up in the *doing* that we forget we are actually supposed to *feel things*—and not just the things we are told we should do or feel. I tell people, "Stop *shoulding* on yourself!" It didn't feel good to tell myself I was less-than because I couldn't read anymore. It's about what's on the inside and what's in your heart. It's what your mouth says and the actions you take that make you whole. That's what I believe. That's what makes me whole, that my actions determine how I feel and how I make others feel.

The current struggle. We are re-branding *Erin C. Mahoney* as a company and it takes a lot of time and effort and finance. And what is that costing me with my kids? My kids are 16 and 18. So just like when I wrote *Positive Vibes for Women,* and I needed to stop missing my life, it's time for me to reassess again and say, "How do I make it all work?" but from a place that says what is most important to me, "What fills me with joy, what makes me present?"

To be totally transparent, I was worried about preparing this chapter for this book because the last three or four days have been really hard—like *crying hard*. I'm trying to figure out what the path and vehicle is to package the Girl Power content so that it will serve more across the globe. Then, I have this new brand emerging, this "Erin C. Mahoney," where I'm stepping fully into a career as a speaker and EFT Practitioner. It's like when you're birthing something new, it gets very frightening. It's like when we pushed the GO button on the *Guidebook*—

What if they don't like it?

Who am I to write a book?

I'm the girl who couldn't read!

Those broken stories and voices. That broken record starts to play and make you think you're not enough, so you always have to stay in the practice of seeing your value, to know there is always another path for getting somewhere.

I look at Steve Jobs and other people who are massively successful who traveled their own paths. I thought college was the only path that would make me successful and smart, right? Such bullshit! There are so many paths. For example, I love audiobooks! Between being on the treadmill and in my car, Rachel Hollis and *Girl, Wash Your Face* got me out of the pit this last week. I *can* read, but it's hard for me. I would much rather listen[1]. Yet today when I type and put what's in my

---

[1] Editor's Note: Today, listening to audiobooks *is* reading. Definitions are evolving. —RMT

heart into words it's beautiful magic. There are new ways to consume and create. I talk most of my text messages these days. I often "talk" the punctuation. It makes for lots of laughter with my closest friends. Where I used to feel stupid, embarrassed, and ashamed, now I feel simply fine. The *good stuff* is in me!

My kids inspire me today. They are incredible human beings. Compassionate and kind, smart and generous. I feel proud of that as a mom. I feel sad that my mom never got to know them. I share her wisdom and know they feel her presence in me. I'm enjoying this phase trying to be present and watching them grow.

I'm inspired by other women, standing up and doing what other people say they cannot. I'm inspired by watching others grow into who they are supposed to be. I'm inspired when people are fearless. Those are inspirational things to me.

I seek inspiration from Brené Brown. Rachel Hollis inspires me. Local women inspire me. I try to put myself in a space with other women who are reaching for the impossible. Part of Rachel Hollis's story is that she was 19 years old and landed this incredible job but she dropped out of college, it kind of wasn't her bag. For me that was super-relatable because she's doing what other people said she couldn't do. That's the fire that's in *me*. When someone says, "You can't," I say, "Watch Me!"

When I wrote my "Couch to 5k" program for runners, it was because someone sat across the table from me and said, "You can't do that. Do you know what a huge undertaking that is, to teach groups of non-runners to run?" I had been doing that for years but this person didn't know me. That individual poured gasoline on the fire within me! Thank you, doubter! Motivation and determination live there! *Watch and learn,* I thought.

"Well, let's go there and we will see," I said. We brought 89 non-runners to the start. I stood in front of this brave and courageous group and I said, "The work is done. It is not about the finish; it is about the fact that your ass is at the start! Many of you never dreamed you'd be here. I'm proud of you! Now go have fun. You have earned it! Savor this moment."

My mission, passion, and purpose are to help people get unstuck, to help others step into their full potential and power. Let us inspire as many human beings as we can from a place of acceptance, patience, and good old fashion love!

Step into the light and be who you are meant to be.

The world needs you!

CONTACT ERIN TODAY!

ERIN C. MAHONEY is a motivational speaker, leadership and empowerment expert, and best-selling author of three books. It is her life's work to inspire and motivate people to step outside of their comfort zone and live a life that has positive impact on the world. And, it is her personal mission to create a generation of present, powerful women who love themselves fully. She is the founder and CEO of Girl Power Go, an empowerment company that serves young women and girls globally.

Find out more and get in touch with Erin today!

Books:

Girl Power Guidebook for Parents and Instructors

Girl Power Journal: Be Strong. Be Smart. Be Amazing!

Positive Vibes for Women

Podcast:

Awaken the Warrior Woman Within

Online:

www.erincmahoney.com

www.girlpowergo.com

Email:

info@erincmahoney.com

[2]

FALSE EVIDENCE APPEARING REAL

by Denise Duncan

> "I will love the light for it shows me the way,
> yet I will endure the darkness because it shows me the stars."
> —OG MANDINO

IT'S BEEN QUITE a bumpy little ride, life in general. For lack of a better term, and with complete self-respect, I am one, *tough old broad.* (That could be the name of a book! I love it.) Some of the best times of my life were in my early childhood. I was the baby of the family, with one brother and two sisters. We were all born and raised in Southern California and our parents provided us with a fun-loving and stable family home. Life was wonderful until I turned 13 years of age, when—let's just play nice and say I was a "spirited" teenager. And oh, the hell I put my mom and dad through—the whole family, really. I still have deep regrets but I've learned if you don't forgive yourself, you can never truly heal or grow. But by the ripe, old age of 17 I was a full-blown drug addict. By 19 my parents admitted me to a psychiatric hospital, a drug rehab. And these were some of the darkest times of my life.

This "rehab" managed to get me off of street drugs but replaced them with psych drugs. After several months of this drug treatment, a couple of surgeries, and a medical drug catastrophe, I ended up in a deep psychotic state for an extended period of time. The scariest part of it all was when I didn't even recognize my own parents. *Oh man, was I ever in for the fight of my life!* My dear sister Cindy was the only one I could really recognize, so she put her own life on hold, stayed with me at the psych hospital, and helped to put her baby sister back together again. My love and gratitude for my family is immeasurable.

A couple of years after getting clean and working on myself to become an acceptable part of the human race and my family again, I met a wonderful guy with dreams of marrying him someday. He was in the Air Force and quite the catch for a girl with my past. Well, instead of this being the perfect fairytale I had hoped for, I ended up getting pregnant and he decided to leave. Despite that, having my daughter Amanda was the best decision I have ever made. She saved my life. It was never easy being a single mom, but oh my gosh, is she ever worth it! It's hard to believe she's already 32 years old. What an incredible woman she has grown to be. Without question, She is my greatest source of true love and pride.

Had I not been a drug addict at a very young age and gone through some of the things I've gone through, my dream would have been to go to college and be a newscaster, a journalist. Instead, I took the rough road, and believe it or not, I'm glad I did.

IN 1997 I FOUND myself doing payroll for 800 employees for a huge, huge water transmission pipe company. I used to drop my daughter Amanda off each morning with my parents at their house and I'd go to work. Amanda would have breakfast there and they'd drive her to school (she had a lunch card I had to budget for). My mom would pick her up after school and care for her until I got off of work. Mom would cook them all dinner and save a plate for me, which I would eat each night when I picked Amanda up. That was usually my only meal of the day. I was working twelve hours a day with no overtime since I was paid a salary—a small salary with benefits, so I could at least take care of my daughter. My parents were of the belief that if they gave me too much I would just take more, and I agree with that 100 percent. They charged me childcare and a portion for the food, and well they should have. It wasn't a large amount but enough to learn from—in fact, that's part of my tenacity to keep going. It never was a handout, and they were always there to help me when I needed them.

Soon after, my parents retired and decided to sell Watkins[2], sometimes at state and county fairs. While at the L.A. County Fair, they saw a live Kitchen Craft[3] cooking demonstration, and they met two of the company's top salespeople (David and Rebecca Monge). They told my sister Julie about it, and soon after she and her husband Alan signed up to sell Kitchen Craft cookware and started training. What did they have to

---

[2] Watkins Incorporated is a manufacturer of health remedies, baking products, and other household items. An independent sales force sells the products using various methods, including the Internet, person to person, trade shows, party planning, and fundraising. The company was founded by J. R. Watkins in Plainview, Minnesota, who began selling liniment in 1868 door-to-door in the southeastern part of the state. By the 1940s, Watkins was the largest direct-sales company in the world, but soon began to decline. —Adapted from Wikipedia

[3] Read the fascinating story of Kitchen Craft here: https://kitchencraftcookware.com/ourstory/

lose? They had four kids to raise and they needed to make more money. After they were in it for a year, they were insanely successful and went on their first incentive trip to the Bahamas.

When they got back, they said to me, "You know, DD (my whole family calls me DD), you would really be good at this." I was grossly underpaid at the pipe company and had my daughter to raise, so what did I have to lose? —other than the fact that I would have to pay all of my own travel expenses, it was a commission-only sales job, and I didn't know the first thing about sales! I decided to go for it anyway, with financial help from my family to get started. I was going to reach for the stars, make my family proud, and make a better life for my daughter and myself.

When I left my job at the pipe company, the only pair of shoes I had were a pair of steel-toed boots issued to me by my employer. (If you've met me, if you've seen me, that's not my style!) When I showed up for training in those steel-toed boots, my sister was like, "What are you wearing?"

"Well," I said, "it's the only pair of shoes I've got." Those were the shoes I trained in and lived with right up until I got a schedule to go out on my own and make it to the "big leagues."

My daughter Amanda and I were living in Southern California, in the high desert, in Apple Valley. My daughter was 12 or 13 and in seventh grade at the time. I guess I didn't realize what a horrible thing it would be for her, taking her out of school at that point, away from her home and friends. But I didn't decide to do this to live the lifestyles of the rich and famous, I did it so I could provide for *both* of us. I always saw to it that Amanda was provided for. I, however, was usually not, with the little income I had. So that first summer after training I told her, "You're going with." She wasn't happy. She wanted to spend the summer with her friends. "This is going to make our lives better," I said, "and eventually you're going to understand why we have to do this."

My sister loaned me a Ford Aerostar minivan. Kitchen Craft loaned me a cargo trailer (that was pretty beat up) because we needed the van to be our house for a while. I loaded the cargo trailer to the brim with my booth and supplies. Now, I had never hooked up or pulled a cargo trailer before—no big deal, right? I was riddled with *fear*. I put a twin mattress in the van, my mom sewed us curtains for the windows, and we hit the road.

I was given a first-year-rookie schedule, where I wasn't making any money. We were up in Yreka, California at the Red Acres Fair, and I was flat broke. I didn't have gas or food, or anything—I didn't even have food for the demonstrations. We were staying in a KOA campground, and I knew there wasn't money in the bank, so I wrote them a hot check. Now, the show prior to that, there was money coming in, but they used to FedEx our checks to our home addresses. A friend of mine up in Apple Valley was supposed to pick up my check and put it in the bank, but she didn't. It wasn't a big check, it wouldn't even have covered the overdraft fees in my checking account at that point, that's how bad it was. We hadn't eaten in two days and my daughter finally said to me, "Mom, I'm just *hungry*."

"Okay," I said.

My parents were full-time RVers, so I couldn't call them collect to ask for help, because all they had was a cell phone and I didn't have one (they were still expensive and uncommon, and mine had been turned off). We got in the van, so low on gas it was running on fumes, and I drove us to a 7-11. I walked in and looked at the gentleman behind the counter and told him, "Hi. My name is Denise—Denise Duncan, if you need to know all that. I'm going to walk over there and I'm going to take one pack of powdered donuts and one jug of chocolate milk for my daughter. We haven't eaten and I don't have any money, so I'm stealing them, and you have two options: You can turn a blind eye, or you can call the police, but that's what I'm doing. I'm really sorry, but I just have to do this." I went over and took them, and as I walked out, he winked and turned his back to me.

When I got in the van, Amanda said, "Mom! You just make everything better somehow! I don't know how you do it, but these aren't just for me, they're for us."

I looked at her and I said, "Honey, every one of those six donuts is yours. They've got your name all over them. Your momma's gonna be just fine."

We went to the local police station since I had no way of calling anyone for help. I went in an explained my circumstances, and the lovely gal at the desk phoned my parents for me. My dear dad once again came to my rescue and sent me enough money via Western Union for food and gas to get home. I was too tired to drive through the night, though, so we slept in a truck stop. Actually, my daughter slept in a truck stop that night. My eyes were wide open, because I was *petrified*.

After that, most people would have never, ever gone on to another show again. I had promised my daughter, "We're going to have a great time," and this was the outcome, right? No.

I believed in myself—and I think that's what I would want every woman to hear, louder than anything. It's nice to have a family that cares and is there to hold you up, and it's nice to have a significant other to hold you up and be a team, but for me, there is an "I" in "team." So, instead of giving up, I marched on. I went from taking my daughter away from home in the middle of summer to stealing food at a 7-11 and sleeping in a van at a truck stop to *success* I had just never imagined.

I was doing live demonstrations for the oldest, largest, stainless steel cookware manufacturer in the world. I did lengthy demonstrations that turned strangers into family in two hours and gave them the catapult to good health. That's what I did for a living. That's how I felt about it and I still do. I traveled all over the

United States. I would be gone sometimes a couple of months at a time from my daughter who was at a tender and very impressionable age. But I made a decision to do it for us both.

If my story seems strong, emotional, and maybe even hard to hear, the story of my mentor and dear friend Dave Hurley (owner of Kitchen Craft) is eight thousand times more difficult than mine. I saw such *conviction* in him and I believed it. I learned from him that you can overcome any and all of what life throws at you, as long as believe in yourself. If he could do it, well then, so could I.

Fear, to me, was being a single mom and not being able to pay the bills, not being able to keep a roof over our heads and keep Amanda fed. My daughter was a teenager and she believed she had to have that Roxy sweatshirt and designer tennis shoes to feel like she fit in. So, I made sure she had what she needed, and I made sure I provided for her, but at what cost to myself, right? But hey, I decided to have a child, and her dad decided to leave, so this is what we're going to do. Kitchen Craft taught me how to manage that. I learned I was always my own worst enemy in my head, always trying to "fix it," instead of just "doing it," and my favorite saying was (and is) "Clean out between your ears, girl! Otherwise, you will bring yourself down."

It was life changing when I started with Kitchen Craft and I went into a setting where I got this undying respect from complete strangers. When complete strangers treat you better than most people you call "friends," you find yourself learning more and more about yourself, and really, finding your own worth. Once I found my own worth, there was no holding me back. I was like, *Oh, my gosh, I'm so much more than I ever thought I was.* I had just never seen myself as being worth much.

That all changed when I could see what my peers saw in me and see the results of believing in myself as much as they did. It was the whole experience, the training (which was really more about life skills than selling cookware), and the sense of becoming a part of something that would make a difference in people's lives, as well as mine. And for the first time in my adult life, I finally felt like I was really good at something, and it made me feel valued! Truthfully, I'm the worst salesperson on the planet. I would *give it away* to everybody, but I was selling *hope*. It's the relatability and the love for people that I enjoy. And when you get to go back to those same venues year after year and your customers come and see you, they love on you like family.

Let's not forget this didn't happen overnight. The first five years of this kind of industry are going to make you or break you, and they break *everybody* long before we make it. It's true. But if you can just have the mindset that what you're doing is the right thing for you as a person, and that you can find a balance of self-joy in that, it will happen. Something happens where you get this innate ability to relate with people and for me that was my gratification, how much I enjoyed those people and how much those people enjoyed me. I knew I was in the right place. I had found my passion. It wasn't actually about massive monetary gain to me, which was probably my biggest self-employment failure. I was like, "Easy come, easy go." Success was never about having copious amounts of money. It's been about balance, and for me, about achievement, self-worth, and recognition. And I started to rise in the company.

I'll never forget my fifth year in the business. I was the keynote speaker at one of the conventions, and I was talking about the fear of being on the road by myself, and the fear of being away from my daughter and leaving her with my sister or her best friend's family—the fear of all of that, the *guilt* of all of that, even while I knew I was doing this for the betterment of my daughter, to be able to provide for her and our future. It's really a convoluted emotional thing to do, you know, stepping up and out of the box, stepping up and out of the comfort zone. And I was up there speaking when it all of a sudden hit me, and you could have heard a pin drop—

"Fear," I said, and I spelled it out: "F-E-A-R, fear, is nothing more than *false evidence appearing real*," which most of us have heard a million times by now, but at the time, I had never heard it. Yet it was what came out of my mouth. It wasn't in my little notes I was speaking from, but I said it, and I still remember what I felt:

Oh, watch out world, I'm coming for you! And once I figured out my *fears* were holding me back, I believed deeply I could achieve anything my heart desired!

The sincere recognition from this company was always a big part of what kept me going. That's just part of who I am. It really was for me, like, *Oh my gosh! I'm accomplishing things in my life!* When I earned my first Million Dollar Club trip (I had earned the annual incentive trips every year, but this was the first Million Dollar Club trip) there were only twelve of us who achieved that prestigious award that year.

We all went to New York for two days prior to embarking on—*oh my gosh*—the Queen Mary II. Remember my steel-toed boots? Well, we got to New York, we embarked on the Queen Mary II, and of course, this is all about the shoes I was embarking in. I had to look the part of the Queen Mary II. I had a red-and-white, polka-dotted scarf, blue pedal-pushers, a crisp white blouse and a pair of red wedge pumps like they used to wear in the '40s, with the little matching handbag. And I realized, *I was able to do that?* I had a 400-dollar *pair of shoes* to get on that ship in!—What?

Wow! I had arrived, and for a brief moment my shoes defined success for me. It didn't take me long to realize shoes really have very little to do with success or self-worth. (But I still adore those shiny little red shoes!)

We were on the Queen Mary II for seven days. We went to the QM2 island and got to hang out there for a day, but the trip was really all about enjoying the world's largest transatlantic ocean-liner across the great Atlantic Ocean. Things are different on a ship with the magnitude and prestige of the Queen Mary II. It's very, very old money and extremely wealthy people with a ballroom instead of a disco. (They did have a little disco on the back of the ship for the lower-class passengers, like me, Dave Hurley, and our cookware family.) Remember Rose and Jack from the movie, *Titanic*? Just sayin! [Laughter]

We all had a blast dancing the night away in that disco! Our days were spent relaxing and going to the spa, eating exquisite food, and enjoying the beauty of this magnificent ship! It was one of the best experiences of my life. And if that wasn't enough for a girl who was a single mom, who had been was sleeping in a van, who had been through the emotional warfare, drug addiction, and financial struggles I had been through, I was now in the Million-Dollar Club—the Diamond Club. I got a diamond ring, a leather jacket, and all of that recognition.

Wow, Just wow!

Once we got back to New York and disembarked from the QM2, our group of twelve got on a first-class flight to Boston for the second phase of our Million Dollar Club adventure. We stayed in beautiful suites at the world-famous Omni Parker House for three days. We toured the entire city and all of its history! Boston quickly became my favorite city in the U.S.! It was then time to meet up with the rest of our Kitchen Craft family for the "regular," annual incentive trip. They all flew into Boston and met up with the twelve of us as we hopped on a plane and flew to *Ireland*. All of this was *one trip*, we were gone for like three weeks.

When we landed in Shannon, Ireland, we got on a luxury, chartered bus and headed to our destination in Killarney. This was like my fifth incentive trip, maybe sixth. My first one was all over Europe—Italy, France, Spain, cruising the Mediterranean. But this was now the Million Dollar Club—nothing anybody with my background would have ever dreamed about. I would have never allowed myself to dream about stuff like this because it just wasn't attainable. We're told, "You've got to keep it real with yourself, remember that," or "Never set expectations too high, you'll just have disappointments." Remember that one? I would have never said, "I'm going on the Queen Mary II, then going to Boston, and finishing off the trip with a week in Ireland!"

Come on!

While we were in route to Killarney on the day of our arrival, we stopped at a real-life castle. There we had an authentic Irish breakfast. The castle was built in the 1600s. It was magical and amazing. We had porridge there—porridge! We all started singing the tune from the movie *Oliver*. And I'm thinking to myself, *Is this really happening, right now, in my life?* That night, all of us were so dog-tired after the long flight and everything we did that day, we checked into the hotel in Killarney and everyone was like, "Oh, please just let us sleep," as we did face-plants into our beds. *Ah, finally some rest!*

Not 15 minutes later the phone rang. It was Dave Hurley, our fearless leader! "Oh my gosh," he said, "did you know Michael Flatley's last Riverdance performance is tonight? Did you know tonight is the grand finale, right here in Killarney? I just bought us all tickets. You have one hour to meet up in the lobby." We jumped up, splashed cold water on our faces, and off we went! What an amazing experience that Riverdance was. It spoke to my soul and resides in my heart still today!

And our adventure was just getting started. Ireland is breathtakingly beautiful, and I was just about to experience it all! We saw the Gap of Dunloe[4], we did the Ring of Kerry[5], we kissed the Blarney Stone[6], we did all these things. We even spent our last night in Ireland at the world-class Adare Manor, where we had the entire 17th-century castle to ourselves for the night! What an insanely, magical, life-changing trip. I was pretty sure I was living a fairytale, and I was the one who earned it! All because I conquered my *fear* and believed in myself!

Can you imagine, that was just one of many trips? What about the trip on the four-masted schooner through the Greek Isles? Oh, and cruising the fjords of Norway, just to name a few.

Did the trips give me the motivation to go out there and sell, sell, sell? Well, they certainly didn't hurt, but the trips were never really about motivation to me. They were about *recognition*. My motivation was what the cookware *does for people*—it always was.

But the money didn't hurt, either!

WE ALL HAVE expectations of what we are "supposed" to be doing, isn't that right? We have things that are "expected" or "required" of us. But if you just step outside of that box, the outcome is really quite amazing. After you make a million in sales, you have to continue to make a million in sales. You quickly learn the highs and lows of the direct sales industry. Outcomes are often not what you'd like to have happen, but that's just the nature of the business.

When the economy crashed in 2008, the cookware industry was hit hard. And by 2009, I was one of the many that lost everything. It took me a few years to get back on my feet, but I never quit or gave up, and for the *next* five years the cookware industry flourished! In looking back, I realized I had a false sense of security

---

4 The Gap of Dunloe, also recorded as Bearna an Choimín, is a narrow mountain pass running north-south in County Kerry, Ireland, that separates the MacGillycuddy's Reeks mountain range in the west, from the Purple Mountain Group range in the east. —Wikipedia

5 The Ring of Kerry (Irish: Mórchuaird Chiarraí) is a 179-kilometre-long (111-mile) circular tourist route in County Kerry, south-western Ireland. —Wikipedia

6 The Blarney Stone (Irish: Cloch na Blarnan) is a block of Carboniferous limestone[1] built into the battlements of Blarney Castle, Blarney, about 8 kilometres (5 miles) from Cork, Ireland. According to legend, kissing the stone endows the kisser with the gift of the gab (great eloquence or skill at flattery). The stone was set into a tower of the castle in 1446. The castle is a popular tourist site in Ireland, attracting visitors from all over the world to kiss the stone and tour the castle and its gardens. —Wikipedia

and should have been a better steward of my money (*whoa,* what a defining moment!). By late 2014, I was seeing an all too familiar trend in the business, and I knew the road ahead was going to be a really rough one. So, after a 15+ year career with Kitchen Craft, I decided it was time for new endeavors. It was the hardest business decision I've ever had to make. It was like losing a piece of myself. I miss it, that part of my life. Mostly, I miss my cookware family (my customers) but the business and the income just weren't what they once were, and I couldn't hold on any longer.

Soon after, my husband and I separated and he filed for divorce. It was at that point in my life I thought, *I'm not going to experience that again. I have experienced that collapse several times in my adult life and this time I am just not going to allow it to happen again.*

After my marriage of seven years fell apart, I found myself questioning my own self-worth. I was losing myself and feeling broken all over again. The craziest part about our marriage is that it wasn't conventional. I mean, we essentially lived and worked in separate states, owned separate properties, and had separate bank accounts, which apparently didn't help us, because the demise of our marriage was all financial anyway. I watched the man I loved turn into someone I didn't even know. Oh man, did he get fierce once my money dried up and I was having to start a new business. But no matter what, it takes two to tango and we couldn't even agree to disagree! It was all just crazy and horrible!

Our divorce was finalized on February 16th 2018. I'm so relieved to be closing that chapter in my life. Life is way too short to spend it destroying each other. I've always been one to pull myself up by the boot straps, and keep marching on, but this divorce, it's been a toughie on me, that's for sure. I've decided to not let it define me, not now, not after all the hurdles I've overcome.

Today, I'm working on getting to know myself again, cleaning out between my ears, and constantly reminding myself to be proud of my life. I'm self-employed and I still love what I do for a living. I'm doing well financially. I'm healthy. I feel good. I'm even starting to date, (Oh my gosh, can you imagine, after like 15 years? *Whoa, how does this work now?* It's just awful!) But it sure does feel good to have a pulse again!

Life is always bound to change. Most women I know—myself included—don't like change. But if you learn to embrace it, change can be just what you need. So, I kicked myself into self-preservation mode, and decided it was time to downsize and get rid of my big, four-bedroom house. It was time to let go of all that stuff and start living a simpler life.

I now live in Mesa, Arizona, in snowbird country, well known for its five-star RV/park model resorts with endless amenities. I now own a 400-square foot park model (like a "tiny" house) that I got for next-to-no money in one of these cool resorts. I had it completely remodeled, put my style and pizzazz into it, and turned it into my own little Nantucket cottage. Cutest thing you've ever seen, and I'm mortgage free! Think that took some of the pressure off? You bet it did! It's exactly where I was meant to land.

I didn't go belly-up. I minimized. I bought myself a smaller new car and a nice little work van. I started my own business ten minutes from home, at the Mesa Marketplace. I have my very own storefront along with 1,500 other vendors selling their goods. I've been there for three and a half years now, selling a variety of products, including a healthy ceramic cookware—cookware is my *passion*, and I'm really good at it.

I refer to the "light at the end of the tunnel" all the time. My parents, my daughter, my dear friends are always like, "Man, that Denise? She just takes a licking and keeps on ticking. And when she walks in the room, she has a glorious smile—*But how? Why?*" I think my strongest quality is that I have never given up, that no matter how bad it gets, or how deep I have to dig, I refuse to stay there. I'm a true believer in the greater good. Period.

August 4th of this year will be my 35th anniversary of being clean. That's pretty heavy, huh? I very proudly call that my greatest achievement. And as far as what keeps me going, first is my faith. Second, my obligation as a parent to be present and mentally healthy for my only child, Amanda. Lastly, my dear parents. I need to be strong for them, and not let them down. They've been through enough. I want to be there for them, as they have always been there for me.

And I know my worth, I believe in myself. And whether you believe you can or you can't, you'd be right, either way.

About Denise Duncan

Denise is available as a keynote speaker!
To find out more and make arrangements, visit
www.INSPIRINGWOMENTODAY.com

[3]

GOOD GRIEF
BY DIANE DIAZ RODRIGUEZ

"Although the world is full of suffering, it is full also of the overcoming of it."
—HELLEN KELLER

I AM NO STRANGER to grief. I was four years old when I saw my first deceased person. She used to work in the household of my maternal grandparents, and I remember going down to the church with my mom. It wasn't a scary moment for me, though. In fact, I had an inner knowing that it was a sacred moment and a very special occasion. Now, I'm what most people recognize as a rainbow baby[7]. I grew up understanding I had a sibling who died as a baby whom I never met. And since the age of four I have experienced major losses about every two years up until the age of 33, whether it was death by illness, death by homicide, accidental death, traumatic death, infantile death—you name it, I was exposed to it. In my culture it was very acceptable to have funeral rituals and to participate with the elderly and neighbors who were sick, so it was something that was very normal and natural to me and I always gravitated toward those who were hurting.

---

[7] A rainbow baby "is a baby born after a miscarriage, stillborn, or neonatal death," Jennifer Kulp-Makarov, M.D., FACOG, explained to Parents.com. "It is called a rainbow baby because it is like a rainbow after a storm: something beautiful after something scary and dark." She adds, "It is an extremely emotional and devastating experience to lose a pregnancy [or baby]. To create a life or bring a baby into the world after such a loss is amazing like a miracle for these parents." —https://www.parents.com/baby/what-it-means-to-be-a-rainbow-baby-and-why-rainbow-babies-are-beautiful/

A lot of people don't talk about grief, or they think grief is only death, dying, and bereavement. That brings about a lot of *death anxiety*. My passion, my mission in life, is to bring about support for the grieving, and to empower ourselves to *companion* grief instead of avoiding it or participating in myths that we have been long conditioned into believing about grief. *Compassion* is one of the greatest gifts that we can give each other, and compassion is something that can be learned. Sympathy, empathy, and compassion are not the same things, and a lot of people have a misconception about them. But it doesn't have to be that way.

I WAS BORN in 1970 in New Jersey, a natural-born American citizen of Puerto Rican descent, and I was raised in South Florida, coming here at the age of seven or eight years old. In high school my whole idea was to join the military, but I got pregnant, and at that time they had just passed a law saying you could not join the military if you had dependents. Because I was in the delayed enlistment program, I had to drop out, and that was a whole different type of grieving in itself. I had to come to terms all of a sudden with the fact that I would not live my dream of becoming an officer, and I had to reinvent myself.

I got married, my (former) husband joined the military, and we left South Florida. (My first career was in accounting because that's what I was good at and that's what I studied in school. My certificate in financial studies served me well for my first twenty years.) We started our military career in Spain. We were young with two babies and poor, but it was amazing! The best place to live and be poor is in Europe. It was nice to be able to just jump in a car and do staycations anywhere you wanted to. We were stationed overseas for ten years.

In 1999, my father-in-law died, and we were getting ready to move back to the United States. After we did, my son Sergio was diagnosed with cancer just a month before his 9th birthday, when he was eight years old. At this critical time for me, I remember Oprah had a series on her TV show called *Honoring the Spirit*. It empowered me and gave me permission to do self-care, to not have to be everything for everyone all the time, because that was running me ragged and leaving me resentful. And I think that was the beginning for me of recognizing there was more to life than the constant hustle and bustle and just trying to survive. Being an A-type personality, I was very controlling and very perfectionistic, and she, Oprah, helped me relinquish some of that. So, I have to give a shout out to my girl, Oprah. It was the beginning of a transformation for me and I often tell people that I went from analyzing numbers to analyzing behaviors, to analyzing grief.

Parents don't want to bury their children. If your parents die, you become an orphan. If your spouse dies, you're a widow or a widower. But if your child dies, it's so taboo that there is no culture on Earth that has a name or a label for that. In that, there is a certain isolation and a certain stigma because people are very uncomfortable talking about a deceased child. No one wants to plan a funeral, no one wants to talk about a child dying, because that brings up the reality of their own children's mortality, or their own grandchildren's mortality. And in that I found I was able to provide my years of knowledge, my years of companioning, which I did normally and naturally to help people.

Even before I went into my current career full-time, I was an 11th Hour Volunteer[8]. When somebody is actively dying. I would provide respite care for family members so that as their loved one was dying; they could go to the bathroom or down to the cafeteria at the hospital and not worry that their loved one would die by themselves. Or, sometimes those passing didn't even have family and were just kind of alone, so I'd stay with them.

But it wasn't until my own son was diagnosed with cancer, relapsed from cancer, and died from cancer that I realized my calling was (and always had been) in grief, in bereavement, in supporting other people. As I was trying to get that support, I found there were a lot of professionals—doctors, even psychologists—who didn't know how to appropriately support me or my family while we were grieving because they were so uncomfortable with their own ideas and their own hang-ups.

After a two-and-a-half-year battle with cancer, Sergio died on April 4, 2002. He was 11 years old. To get through the loss, I became very aware of what was going on for me. I knew it was okay for me to feel the way I was feeling and that I didn't have to follow what other people said or expected of me about going through grief. I think that came from watching others grieving with people invalidating or trying to stifle their grief, and I knew there had to be a better way.

I became very comfortable with silence and stillness and I will often say that while my faith wasn't broken, it was shaken, and it was a time in my life of a lot of soul-searching, a lot of searching for meaning, a lot of understanding that I wasn't alone even though I felt very, very alone. Part of getting through that was honoring myself, respecting the process, and being willing to take a step back.

I realized there was a really big need to support people. There are times when becoming an expert in your own grief is what ends up being the healing and the "out" of living with that consistently. So, I went back to school in 2002. I took a sabbatical because we moved to the Florida panhandle, then we adopted two girls (a sibling group), so my focus changed for a little bit, but I eventually got a bachelor's degree in social psychology in 2011.

Today, I teach a lot of *mindful* grieving. After you've had a significant loss, you are usually either constantly doing busy work, in a sense avoiding the reality of what's going on (though you can't really avoid it), or you're stuck, staying in that consistent cycle of living the death story. I could have focused on how my son died and what led up to his death, but I chose to focus on his life, and not just making it about his death. I do believe with Sergio's care there were some mistakes made, but the empathic part of me knows that I did the best I

---

[8] https://www.gohospice.com/11th-hour-volunteering-keeping-vigil-patients-bedside/

could with what I had and those around me did the best they could with what they had. Was it perfect? Absolutely not. But being able to be open to that process really helped a lot of the healing. It's going on 17 years in April and there's still a lot of healing work for me. New grief will often bring up pieces of old grief.

After Sergio died, I was perfectly okay with the thought of not having more children, so I thought. I think one of the things that happens when you get tossed into a significant loss like death or the loss of a big relationship, you end up indifferent to having that thing happen again, you lose that sense of death anxiety. I no longer had death anxiety. It was just like, *Okay, I've seen death, I've witnessed death, I've held death in my hands, and if it comes, it comes.*

Part of me did want more children and the other part of me was okay if I didn't. So, when we looked at adopting the girls it was just one of those moments of synchronicity. Things aligned. My oldest biological daughter was 16 at the time. We started taking the adoption classes, and my (adopted) girls were wards of the state so they were in the foster care system. That kind of checked that box off for me, where I wasn't starting off new at 35, but at the same time, Dave and I were at the end of his military career, so we had built the home, we had a stable relationship, we were at that point in our lives where we could offer more. And why not? We had the means, we had the desire, and we decided to go ahead and adopt these girls.

Sergio taught me a lot in his first eleven years of life. If you're a parent I'm sure that by watching your child grow up, you have evolved, and you're probably a proud parent at that, just as I am about my kiddos. They teach us so much, not just about how they see the world, but how we see the world and how we end up adapting to it. So, Sergio taught me a lot about his life, but in his death, I learned so much more.

I would not have done this; I would not be the person I am without his dying. For me it was, *Okay, there's a reason for this, there's a reason for everything that happens.* And for others, they were like, "What possible reason could there be for a child to waste away for two and a half years and die from cancer? What possible reason could there be for God to need another soul up in Heaven?" It goes back to what we find meaning in, and I choose that I don't want my son's life to be in vain, and I sure as hell don't want his death to be in vain.

In his legacy, in honoring his life, in celebrating his life, I am taking those lessons and I am passing them on so that maybe somebody doesn't have to go through the pain or the burden exactly the way I did. Maybe a little bit of what I share is enough—even if it's for a moment—to give someone a sense of relief. And that's enough for me.

SOUTH FLORIDA—Coral Springs, Coconut Creek, Broward County—was my stomping ground growing up and I still go back and visit there frequently. Three weeks ago, I was down in the Parkland area because we were doing the communal trauma support training for the Parkland shooting[9]. We have that anniversary coming up, on the 14th of February.

When we are impacted by grief, we don't have a choice but to continue living life *changed*. Not that we want to, we're just kind of thrown into it and it's either sink or swim, it's do the best that you can. There are people who think they can stuff grief away but when they least expect it, it comes back up. One of my tag lines is "meaningful living despite everyday grieving." While we never fully get over grief, I believe we can grow from it. Does everybody? No. You have to be open to it because experiencing grief is vulnerable. Society tells us we have to be successful at everything we do, and that failure is not okay. Right?

But who gets to decide, who gets to define that? Well, *how do we learn if we don't fail?* If we don't fail and we don't analyze what went wrong, how can we grow from that? Grief is the same way. People don't want to lean into all that messy stuff because they're afraid they're going to get stuck in it, going to get judged by it, and like they're opening Pandora's Box.

And there's that misconception that you can't control it. Sometimes controlling and compartmentalizing, especially for our A-type personality people, serves you well in grief. You learn how to use those skills you already have for what it is that you need, and I'm of the belief that we all possess those skills innately. It's just that when we're in a crisis, when we're scared, when we're worried, when we are angry, we lose sight of that because our brains are naturally designed to help us survive. You often hear people say when they're angry, "I see blood! I see red!" When you go into that red zone, your brain is no longer making those connections to help you think

clearly. When you're in deep grief, you're in a life crisis, you're in an existential crisis.

So, what do you do? It depends on the person. There has to be a lot of validating. There has to be normalizing. Everything we think is abnormal becomes normal in grief. People don't want to hear that. People often say to me, "I feel like I'm going crazy, like I'm spinning out of control, like this tape recorder in my head (whether it's a voice, an image, a thought) doesn't want to stop." That's because our brains are wired to problem-solve. It's like a computer, it's going to try different things to fill in the blank. And when you feed it information, it no longer has to fill in the blank by itself.

When we learn about our nature like this and we learn a few techniques it can make big differences for us as well as those around us. I teach people who want to compassionately connect that the first thing is to remain present*:* "I'm really pissed off right now because this guys was being lewd with my wife. What did that mean to me?" Was it that you felt inadequate in being able to protect her or in being able to stop or control

---

[9] On February 14, 2018, a gunman opened fire at Marjory Stoneman Douglas High School in Parkland, Florida, killing seventeen students and staff members and injuring seventeen others. —Wikipedia

that situation? Was it that you were disrespected? Was it that this person had no respect for a married woman or a *woman*, for that matter?

We have those people too, who don't care, it's just all about them and what they want or what they're fantasizing about in that moment. So, it's about remaining present: "What's going on for me, right now?" Usually what's happening is that you have some kind of core belief, some value, some moral that has just been offended at such a deep level that you get that reaction. When you back up from it you can start to be rational again, but sometimes it takes a while for the brain to calm down.

There's this tiny little piece within our brain, the amygdala[10], the reptilian part of the brain, where the fight, flight, or freeze responses come from. Our brains are designed to respond initially and automatically from that place, and when that piece of the brain is stuck, it's kind of like when you put your hand on memory foam and remove your hand, and the imprint doesn't release.

That imprint can bounce back naturally, or the imprint kind of gets stuck and it takes a little bit longer to release. The elasticity depends on how deep that issue goes, and if an instant like that triggers other things. It may be something that you saw happen to Mom. It may be something that you as a man believe should never, ever be done, that there's a boundary that should not be crossed, and when you overstep that you've gone too far. It's a moral injury.

So, you try to remain present. What is it that is coming up for you? Then refrain from helping, directing, or judging it. If you've ever practiced any kind of mindfulness, if you've ever done any kind of meditation or prayer, even just sitting and thinking deeply, you know you simply observe what comes up, and that helps you remain present, that opens up the window for other things.

Grief ends up being like your fingerprint. It's unique and individual to each person. Not every path is going to be the same. Not every response is going to be the same. Yet there are a lot of similarities that we all kind of go through. Most people know Elisabeth Kubler Ross has the five stages[11], and that's usually the springboard of grief education in our world as we know it. Although contemporary grief doesn't necessarily embrace that whole-heartedly, it's important know it and how it can affect people.

It has a lot to do with your own personality and your own characteristics. It depends on each individual's beliefs. For me it was normal to participate in rituals and funerals, in wakes and celebrations of life, in prayer chains and things like that, but some cultures don't believe in anything like that. For some you have an

---

[10] a roughly almond-shaped mass of gray matter inside each cerebral hemisphere, involved with the experiencing of emotions. From Late Middle English via Latin from Greek amugdalē 'almond'. —from Google definition

[11] The five stages, denial, anger, bargaining, depression and acceptance are a part of the framework that makes up our learning to live with the one we lost. They are tools to help us frame and identify what we may be feeling. But they are not stops on some linear timeline in grief. —*Five Stages of Grief* by Elisabeth Kubler Ross & David Kessler, https://grief.com/the-five-stages-of-grief/

afterlife and for some when you're dead, that's it. So, it's about what makes sense to that individual and there's no right or wrong. There are healthy ways of doing it and if you have an idea that something is wrong or you have questions such as, "Is this as good as it gets?" that's usually a pretty good indicator of knowing you need help.

ARMED WITH EXPERIENCE and knowledge and compassion, I do love what I do. I'm very passionate about what I do. I feel like this is my calling. A soul sister once proposed we are the last to know what is meant for us. So when I realized *bereavement* was my calling, when the ah-ha moment came, it was like, *Why are we always the last ones to know, to get the memo? Duh! I've been doing this all of my life! I've been passionate about this all of my life!*

It has felt like a normal progression. I would love to say that my work has all been focused on other people because I want to be able to heal them, but the truth behind it is that in doing this, I have also healed my own grief. In doing this, I have also become an expert in my own grief—understanding how it works for me and being able to honor that authentically. As human beings, we all tend to do that. We all go through that phase of exploring and doing things that perhaps we've been told we're good at and we do it because we're good at it, not necessarily because we're passionate about it. But when we tap into that passion work, that passion piece, that can be the springboard, the catapult to become the advocate, to become the teacher, to become the light for the healing to happen.

I know now that I have always been called to teach, so when I'm going through a crisis, my number one go-to is research. I want to learn everything that I can possibly absorb so that I can understand it on some kind of level and be able to connect to it on some kind of level. When I don't understand it, when I'm not able to absorb it, things become a little more difficult for me. In going through Sergio's death, it was kind of intuitive for me. I recognized when people were not being supportive, and while that kind of shook me, I also knew enough and was driven enough to keep looking, to keep searching for help, to not just stay there. I could have gone easily into a very dark place. I could have been stuck there. There are certain losses and certain kinds of trauma that happen to an individual that can keep you stuck, like you're in quicksand—you can move but the more you move the more you sink into whatever despair it is that's there.

But going through Sergio's death, I knew enough, and I'll be honest, a lot of people pissed me off, and when I get angry, it's about a sense of justice and that always drives me. When I see some kind of injustice, I'm a change agent and I'm looking for ways to make it better, and to *educate*. With education, with knowledge, people can understand it. Let's say someone you love is dying. I can tell you until I am blue in the face about the process and the steps that it takes for that individual—what's going to happen physically to that individual, what's going to happen psychologically with that individual, but unless you are open to understand or to receive that information it's going to be lost.

If you teach somebody at their level and with what makes sense to them in their language, that's what's going to be retained. And if I can just help one person with that, that one person is going to share that with somebody else. That's what I call the *butterfly effect*. And that's my mission, just to help *one person*—one person at a time because I know that with one person, eventually, we will get to the masses.

As therapists and coaches, when we don't feel comfortable talking about grief, or when we haven't processed our own grief, one of our codes of ethics is to refer out. Well, referring out can mean losing business not to mention adding to a potential client's crisis. We all want to be ethical, but at the same time, we all work with grief. So, I teach therapists and other professionals to identify what grief is, to know what the different types of grief are, and how it is that it presents. I give them the basics so they can do basic grief work and understand the normal and natural progression of grief. I give them the information so they can recognize when it's out of the norm, what to do with it, where to go to get more information if they want to dig deeper, or how they can co-facilitate with other professionals to be able to provide support for their client, as well as recognizing if they truly have to refer out if their client or patient is truly presenting a problem that might not be in their scope of expertise. It's about building confidence, building upon the skills that they already have. As therapists, before we become interned and licensed, in our master's level courses that's constantly driven into us. So, the skills are there, but sometimes the language and personal beliefs and experiences don't clearly line up, so I help clean that up a bit for them.

I work with any professional in the healing world. It can be nurses, it can be first-responders. My current course is designed for therapists because it talks about diagnosis. It talks about recognizing those signs. However, it's applicable to anybody who does any kind of therapy or any kind of support on a professional level. It could be hospice volunteers. It could be clergy.

My *why* is to educate professionals on how to recognize and how to companion those in grief, to walk side-by-side with someone who is grieving versus taking a lead role. A coach usually takes a lead role of educating a client in what to do in order to get to the goal that they want, where in therapy it's more about educating your client but also helping them process what it is that is keeping them stuck and identifying those things that are exasperating the presenting problem. In therapy I work with a lot of trauma. In therapy I do a lot of eclectic, existential work and in coaching it's more existential and digging deep without the therapy piece.

I'm the founder and owner of LiveLifeChanged.com[12] and Compassionate Connectors. Part of my mission is creating a *culture* with professionals within the therapy/mental health field, to embrace grief care empathetically and compassionately because there is so much grief illiteracy and avoidance. I want to be a proponent, to get that conversation going, to replace that illiteracy and avoidance with empathy and compassionate connections that end up nourishing people's lives and provide alignment which is authentic to their own personal well-being.

GRIEF CAN BE all kinds of things—whether it's a job transition, death, dying, or bereavement attached to chronic illness. It can be any kind of major transition or life adjustment. It can be a mental diagnosis like depression or anxiety. And with A-type personalities, driven folks, passionate human beings, there's a lot of stress related to that, and in stress there's a lot of grief. There is a kind of thinking tied to the loss of control, and *loss is grief*, right? In my therapy practice I've served couples who have been grieving infidelity and betrayal, and other adults who have experienced a traumatic or sudden loss. In short, I help people find their way through grief. I help individuals heal their matters of their heart, mind, body and soul as they mindfully grieve and discover meaningful living.

Part of what drives me are those who inspire me. These are my children and my fellow brothers and sisters in the human race, those who are grieving, who don't know where to turn, who don't know where to get the help they need, who've never really been given permission to grieve or be vulnerable or to seek assistance.

With most people, you hear, "You just need to get over grief," or the myth that after a year or so you should be okay. With men, usually, we're told to *not cry*. Well, when you tell people, "Don't cry" or "Be strong," you're invalidating their feelings, and that sticks throughout their lives. It's looked upon as weakness, it's been looked upon as something shameful. And because people don't truly understand it, there's a misconception that there's a timeline to be able to go through grief.

I'm passionate about helping women who are struggling with complicated and pervasive grief, especially if there's trauma as a presenting factor. Sexual assault victims, you name it, any kind of loss, that's what I'm passionate about.

Nature also inspires me, how the circle of life can be seen in anything and everything. You go to the beach and see the water rolling in and rolling back. It's this ebb and flow, this momentum, and how when it's doing that it cleanses. It takes out but it also brings in. In nature I get inspired, I get recharged, I do a lot of self-care through nature. I love walking barefoot. It's very grounding. Grass, especially in the morning when it's dewy,

---

[12] http://www.livelifechanged.com

or walking on the beach, are things that really kind of inspire me. Listening to other people's stories, I feel nothing but gratitude, honor, and I'm humbled when individuals choose to have their stories witnessed, when they share part of their stories, for whatever reason, whether they just need to have that release, whether they're sharing for a connection, or whether they're sharing to educate. That inspires me. That empowers me. That drives me. In that I'm part of witnessing a difference, I'm part of witnessing a change.

We (women) do need to come together to lift each other up and to inspire each other. We're in that space where women are coming together as collaborators instead of being in competition with one another, so the mindset is kind of shifting where it's more about abundance and lifting other women up as opposed to climbing over whoever you need to, to get to the top. It becomes very empowering.

It is a lot about *paying it forward*, and that inspires me, too.

About Diane Diaz Rodriguez

Grief Educator, Bereavement Coach & Consultant, Writer & Speaker
Find out more about Diane's offerings:
Grief Support Made Easy: A Facilitator's Guide to Mindful Grieving
The Mindful Grieving Journal

www.LIVELIFECHANGED.com

Images of Diane Diaz Rodriguez in this book, © Estelle Zaret / EZ Photography

[4]

MEXICO

BY AUDREY BOLAND

> "Boundaries define us. They define what is me and what is not me. A boundary shows me where I end and someone else begins, leading me to a sense of ownership. Knowing what I am to own and take responsibility for gives me freedom. Taking responsibility for my life opens up many different options."
>
> —HENRY CLOUD, author

I'M GETTING BACK into singing. There's a contest I signed up for, and that's this weekend. Throughout the week I've been going to practice. Things are looking up. San Diego is looking really nice. I've been here since June. I have pretty much always loved to sing. I think all my sisters and I did, but out of all of my sisters I have kept pursuing it. Before I moved to Mexico I always sang in churches. I would just sing a special song, nothing serious. Well, in Mexico, this one guy just out of the blue was just like, "Are you a singer?" They wanted a female singer, and I started singing with them.

The first couple of songs I sang, I was really rough. I would just get up, sing my song, and go sit down. I was so scared! But we just kept working. I just kept getting up in front of people. Even if I didn't sing, I had to be up there with them, and I would sing or pretend like I was singing and dance. It gave me more experience with the band and being in front of people.

When I lived in Mexico City, I recorded a couple of things, so that gave me a little bit of experience with a recording studio. When I moved back again to the coast where my daughter was born, I pursued the best band in town. They had a lot of corporate gigs. They sing in the hotels in the casinos. I started singing with them in their show band and that was really awesome. I was like, *I want to sing!* But I love singing, it makes me happy.

When I came back to the United States, I stopped singing. But what's happening now, there's actually a show band who I have an audition with on the fourth, and then this weekend, there's this competition. The competition is kind of cool because I met a music manager, and this is in San Diego. He says he goes to L.A. all the time. He recruits for *The Voice* and *America's Got Talent* and shows like that. He said this weekend the contest is at a festival called the Lunar New Year. He's invited some of his friends from L.A. The winner gets $300, second place gets $150, third is $50, I think, and you get some recording time in a studio. So that's kind of cool.

I DON'T HAVE a happy childhood at all. It's just really sad. The only thing positive about it is that I'm still here. And I'm doing pretty good. I'm a (fraternal) twin. I was born in Chicago, but we grew up in Texas. We didn't end up living around our mother because between having so many children in rapid succession and, unfortunately, being married to a guy who was abusive (my father), mentally, I guess when she went down to Texas, with my grandmother there, my father's mom, the whole situation was really toxic. I guess mentally she just fell apart and she kind of succumbed to post-partum psychosis. Somehow, she moved from Texas and ended up back in Chicago.

So we lived with our father and we lived with my grandma. And our grandmother was unfortunately abusive—mentally, physically. She was like an iron hammer, and what she wanted to crush was happiness. What she wanted to crush was *me*. She was ruthless. She was not a nice woman at all. I think I realized, when I was maybe 25, that there are some grandmothers who are nice, and she was not!

I was a really timid person growing up. I hated confrontation. Family life was toxic. By the time I moved to Indiana I was about 16 and I just really needed to get out of the house. But in that time in Texas I discovered that I love music, so I started playing in the band. I wanted to play the clarinet because my oldest sister played the clarinet, but we just didn't have the money to get her clarinet fixed. So, after sitting in a band class for almost two months without an instrument I was told that if I wanted to stay in the band, I had to get my clarinet by the next day or I could play the euphonium[13] because the school gave those to students. So, of course, I decided to start playing the euphonium. Turns out I was actually kind of good at it, and I had some

---

[13] a valved brass musical instrument resembling a small tuba of tenor pitch, played mainly in military and brass bands. —Google definition

natural talent, so I stuck with it and I loved it. I started playing the euphonium in the sixth grade and I continued it in junior high. I had private lessons for a little bit, but we didn't have a lot of money, we were just kind of poor—very poor. We were on the free lunch program.

I was in Indiana and I really hated the place. I wanted to graduate early. I was just like, *Oh this is so beneath me, I am ready to move on*. What I guess I didn't realize, because I was never really treated this way, and I still didn't understand this at that point, is that I guess I'm kind of intelligent. [Laughter] I guess I never knew. I really didn't know because my grandmother said we were stupid, and our father just constantly said we were, "poor, dumb, mo-fos," but he didn't say it as kindly as that. One of the things I will never forget about my father is when we were in Texas, talking to him one time, I remember the way he was talking to me and I remember thinking, *Why does he hate us, man?*

"I didn't ask to be born," I said. I was maybe 12 or 13. I think what I meant was Why do you hate us?

And he said without missing a beat, "Well I didn't ask for four dumb mo-fos either."

I was like, Okay! Alright. That was my father. That is my father. You should quote me on that because that is exactly how I feel about him to this day.

So, I really thought I was just stupid, and I think all the restlessness I felt at that time was just a lack of being challenged. So, I managed to get back into the band—the band program there was horrible. But I'm only mentioning it because when it came time for me to graduate, I was like, I'm getting out of here. I'm going to go to school, I'm going to be an architect, and I'm going to write best-selling novels. I was accepted to Ball State University, into the architecture program. My first year was totally paid for with the FAFSA[14] and Pell Grant[15] and low-income subsidy because we were poor.

But then one day I had to go to a career fair in our school's gym. I had to interview three people. I already knew what I was doing but there wasn't an architect there. So, I interviewed a court stenographer, I interviewed some other random person, and then I was like, What the hell, and I walked up to the Marines desk. We started talking. We talked for like an hour and a half, and I was really just small-talking the guy, and he was all about it, he was like, "No, no, no we should totally meet up after school and talk."

"I can't after school today," I said. "I've got a band concert."

That's when he knew he had me. "Wait a minute," he said. "You play an instrument?"

---

[14] The Free Application for Federal Student Aid (FAFSA) is a form completed by current and prospective college students (undergraduate and graduate) in the United States to determine their eligibility for student financial aid. —Wikipedia

[15] A Pell Grant is a subsidy the U.S. federal government provides for students who need it to pay for college. Federal Pell Grants are limited to students with financial need, who have not earned their first bachelor's degree. —Wikipedia

"Yes."

"Did you know the Marine Corps has a band?" he asked.

And just like that I was like, Whoa, wait a second. The band program in Indiana was horrible. I was really just doing it because they let me touch a little bit of my soul. It really started challenging everything now because I had said for so many years I was going to be an architect, a best-selling author, I was going to design the house I was living out of. That was my five-year plan. I was set, and then just like that, this guy was relentless.

I think he was a bad recruiter and the band was so hard to recruit for, like they always needed players, and apparently euphonium players are really hard to come by. On top of that I was a female, and I think recruiters get extra points or they're not really taught how to go after females. And I just wanted to be able to play my instrument. So that's how I ended up not being an architect and not going to college, and how I ended up in the Marine Corps for four years. What I didn't plan on was that the Marine Corps was really kind of racist, unfortunately.

Around this time, around 2006 or so, racism wasn't really being talked about. It just really started being talked about when Obama was president because of all the racist slurs and comments, and a rise of police killings of unarmed black people. So, I discovered what it was like. I was the only black female in the band, probably the only black female that many of the people had probably ever seen in their lives. And I'm not stupid. I didn't talk like I was stupid. I think just meeting me challenged a lot of people's personal opinions and biases, and they still wanted to fit me in the box.

So, I was treated like I was a bad marine even though I wasn't. It was the weirdest phenomenon. They wanted to treat me like I was an idiot. They told me I was slow. Someone actually said, "Audrey, you're not stupid. I just think you're a little slow." Isn't that wild? If you know me, if you know what I write, if you ever meet me, I don't believe "slow" is what you would think. This was when I was stationed in Albany, Georgia, and when I first got to the band, I remember trying to talk to people about how I felt I was being treated and I was told, "Oh my gosh, Audrey, you need to get over yourself. It's not all about you."

Two years later, we were in this band hall and somebody called me out. They called on me to speak and I spoke, but then they got on to me in front of everybody. They chastised me verbally. By that point I was kind of used to it, but this particular time, two years later, I overheard somebody, maybe a new marine, ask, "Why do they treat her like that?"

And somebody replied to them, "Oh, it's because she's black." I really heard it, so it wasn't in my head.

I really wanted to stay in the Marine Corps because I kind of liked it. It seemed to jive with who I was as a person. I'm kind of athletic. We got to work out during the day and I loved making music. But at the end of the day, it was such a toxic atmosphere, it gave me PTSD.

When I got out of the Marine Corps, I burned all of my things. I even forgot that I had veteran's benefits—seriously! I burned all of my gear. I have no uniforms. I didn't realize just how horribly it affected me. Somebody saw my resume afterwards and asked, "Were you actually in the Marine Corps, or did you just work as a civilian with the Marines?"

"Oh, I was totally a Marine," I said. "I'm a veteran."

"Oh, you really can't tell the way your resume is set up," they said.

So subconsciously I had to go back and revamp and open myself up to other Marines, and accept it: *Audrey, you were in the Marine Corps. You had a horrible experience, but it doesn't have to define you.*

You take that horrible experience with the Marine Corps, combined with this horrible, abusive past, and I was an emotional wreck. I was severely depressed. I started drinking. I was probably an alcoholic before I was 21. I was at the lowest of my lows. But financially, I think I was okay. I was paying my bills on time, I was building my credit, I was a good Marine. I was going to work, I was doing everything I was supposed to do, but mentally I was just falling apart.

And I didn't even know it because being raised as a poor, black American, mental health isn't talked about. You get depressed, people tell you to suck it up, tell you to be hard, that, "you just have to get over it. It is what it is. It's hard for everybody." So, I just kind of thought I was ridiculous. I really did. I thought I was just dramatic. I remember trying to express the feelings that I had with who I thought was my best friend at the time, and she just kind of rolled her eyes and said I was being like a teenager. So, I bottled those emotions. I drank. When I did go dance, I would go to gay clubs. I didn't party like most women partied. I didn't go to the club and shake my butt, I wasn't sleeping around with a bunch of guys. I was just drinking all the time because being sober was unbearable.

SOMETIMES THE PEOPLE who are against you are the people who are closest to you. While in the Marine Corps, I ended up getting into Christianity because there was a guy in the band who guided me to church. Growing up in Texas, our father put us in Baptist churches. Church and God were a way of life, even if it wasn't something you strictly adhered to. And this guy in band invited me to church three times. The first two times I was getting drunk. But the third time, I went. I think I was hungover—I think the only times I was happy at that point were when I was hungover from the night before. So, I started going to church.

For the first time in my life I actually started reading the bible. I'm kind of a passionate person, and I had already experienced so much pain, I really jumped at the idea of being able to follow a plan of what I thought guaranteed happiness, that's how it was kind of presented to me. It's kind of how people present Christianity sometimes, right? Like, "Hey, you don't know who you are supposed to be, but God does. He created you for a reason." And I was so lost because of everything that had happened in my life. It was like God had reached his little hand down from the sky and was like, "Audrey, I want *you* to be a Christian."

And I was like, "Okay! I'll do it, Daddy! I'll be a Christian! I'll give you my life." It was so easy for me to fall into that and to become so extreme because I wanted, I needed to know that I wasn't terrible. I had nobody to love me, but *God loved me*. I was still very impressionable, still very vulnerable. I kind of ended up in a cult, although they would probably not see it that way. I didn't know anything about narcissism or abusive personality types, but I did want love. I wanted just one person to be all about *me*. I really needed to know that I wasn't a piece of crap, as I had always been treated. So, when there was someone interested in me, I never thought I needed to be interested in *them*. I was like, *If they're interested in me, I'll do whatever I have to, to keep that.* I was bound to end up with abusive people.

There in Georgia, at my duty station, I was absolutely miserable. I'd been a Marine for two years. I hated it. I was never comfortable in my skin. I guess I knew that I might be slightly attractive because if I walked down the street, people might honk. If an older guy ran into me, he would be like, "Hey—how old are you?" when I was younger.

"I'm like 14," I'd say.

I don't know why, but flattery meant nothing to me, it just didn't, because I didn't find myself attractive. I just thought I was an average looking woman, and stupid. I guess I had really low self-esteem. And I didn't seem to get along with people. My sisters and I when we were younger were told that we were too white. Maybe if I had grown up in another area, maybe people would have been like, "Wow! Audrey, you're smart!" Maybe they would have pushed me to go further instead of trying to make me feel shame for who I was.

But that's not what happened, you know? I was ostracized from other black people because I was too white. So I didn't want to be seen, I didn't want to draw attention to myself. I was introduced to this older guy at this church I'd gone too and had this great moment, this amazing connection. He was talking to me *like I was a person*. And for the first time in my life, I didn't feel stupid. I didn't feel like somebody was talking down to me and was being condescending. I felt accepted. So of course, I'm going to go back to that, right?

I met my ex-husband through this church group. (I'm changing some of the names for this, so we'll call my ex "Adam.") His father was incredibly abusive. He used to beat him bare-butt with a belt buckle until he bled. Adam's mom had Adam's dad committed to a psych ward—I didn't know that before we got married, which was messed up. I think I married him because he came to me and he said, "I really like you. I have some feelings for you."

"Oh," I said, "well, maybe you have those feelings now, but in two weeks or two months, somebody else will come by and you'll like them more." And I think what I really meant was *some white woman* because when I grew up in Texas, I was always keenly aware that I was black, and I was never going to be as beautiful as a white person. That's what I thought. There weren't black people on TV, and black women weren't beautiful. I mean, they were, but nobody was saying they were, or I didn't know that they were.

I remember this English class that we had, they were describing how pretty this woman was, but do you know what they said? They said she was beautiful because she was *white as snow*, because her skin was pearly white. That's why she was beautiful because she was just so freakin' white and I thought, *Well, I'm just not*. On top of that, I'm ostracized from black people. White people are the norms. I like black men, I find them attractive, but I guess I seem to be more attracted to white men, So here's Adam, here's this white guy, and he was pretty attractive.

"I'm kind of into you," he said.

So, I'm thinking, *Okay, maybe this is the real deal*. I'm in the Christianity thing because God is the right way, right? He's the high and mighty way, right? He's supposed to protect me. I fasted, I prayed. But you know what? I think when you have so many things go into your subconscious built into your world view by the time you're seven, your mind subconsciously finds ways to connect the dots, no matter what you do.

I didn't have the common sense, I didn't have the experience or the exposure before Adam. And he wasn't nice, he never was. We argued a lot, and I remember feeling like I didn't want to marry this guy. But I felt that God wanted me to do it. I was blindly following God. I wanted to please Him so bad I was going to marry this guy. *If this will bring me closer to You, if this is my path, then of course, I can do it*. You know? That's how I thought.

After the Marine Corps, we got married, and I was surprised by who *wasn't* at my wedding. It was really weird. There was just no support. I got pregnant soon after. Like the other women in this church group, I was completely committed to being a stay-at-home mom. I was scared to be a mom, I was just so lost. I had my first baby in Georgia, and I got pregnant with my second in Georgia. Meanwhile Adam was horrible to me and our "friends" at church had to have seen it, but, for whatever reason, nobody said anything. I remember telling them that Adam would tackle me.

"Well, what do you mean by 'tackle'?" one asked.

"He ran across the room with all of his strength and tackled me, took me down to the bed," I said. And this started when I was pregnant. It was really hard, and it wasn't playful. He really hurt me. I was like, *What the hell?*

"When someone is pointing a finger five inches from your face—" he said to me later. I remember thinking, *But I wasn't! I was across the room!* And I remember thinking, *Maybe it felt like it was in his face?* So, I never said anything, and because I never said anything, I guess people just thought it was true. So, I think maybe people thought I deserved it.

I still don't understand, it doesn't make sense to me how nobody took me aside and in private told me, "I'm really concerned about some of the things you are telling me." But when I told them that he had tackled me before, what they said in front of him, in front of other people at this group, was that he shouldn't do it because if somebody else happened to see it from outside, they could call the cops and he might go to jail. But nobody told me that *I* should call the cops—I didn't know I *could* call the cops. I didn't know about domestic violence. I just was really naïve, and very ignorant.

We moved to Colorado, but things didn't get better. When I had my daughter, Adam said he felt like he was going to kill himself because he could no longer demand my attention. We would eat, I would try and wash the dishes, and we would have an argument about washing the dishes. He would say things like, "What, the dishes are more important them me now?" It even made taking care of the baby really hard. And I didn't know any better, I thought this was life. You're kind of like, *Maybe this is just marriage, maybe this is just normal.* I just didn't know any better, and the screaming and the physical abuse went on.

At some point I was given a book called *Boundaries*[16]. I had never heard of "boundaries" because in my own marriage, I had never been allowed to have any. I realized within the first couple of chapters that every time we had an argument, it had been directly related to our boundaries. One time when things got physical, he knew I was upset about something and he wanted to know why.

"I don't want to talk about it," I said. He wouldn't let me *not* talk about it. He started saying things, hurtful things to draw me into a conversation, to draw me into an argument. Now we're not even talking about what I'm upset about, and he's accusing me of all this crazy stuff. Suddenly, he pushed me and we ended up having this physical altercation. It was wild. I could never figure out what caused it. I never knew that it was a cycle. But for the first time in my life I was like, *Holy crap. Maybe this isn't me. Maybe this was never about me. This is wild.*

I reached out and I told a woman at our new church, "Look, the last time you saw me I was really upset. This is what happened at home . . ." The first thing she said was she suspected maybe there was *abuse*. That was the first time somebody used the word *abuse* to my situation, and it was rocking my world because I still

---

[16] *Boundaries: When to Say Yes, How to Say No To Take Control of Your Life,* by Henry Cloud and John Townsend (Zondervan)

thought if I could try harder, we could have a better marriage, that we could have that godly life, that I could be happy. And then, for the first time, I realized, *Audrey, it's not you. It really is him.* And finally, I was just like, *I don't want to be here.*

What's funny is nobody told me to go. Nobody said, "Take care of your kids." I had two kids at the time, and in fact, people encouraged me to stay. People at church wanted us to work things out. And I had no one on my side. I couldn't divorce him because he hadn't cheated on me. Somebody actually said to me, "Well, you know what the Bible says, the Bible is really clear: Divorce is for *adultery*. So you can't leave, you need to reconcile." And that's what they really pushed for.

Looking back, I can't blame anybody, but I was young, we were moving to Colorado, I had two kids, and I didn't want to be a statistic—I would have been a single freaking mom—a *black mom*—with two kids! *A single freakin' black mom with two kids!* I did not want to be a statistic. But I couldn't stay.

I ended up getting pregnant before I left.

IT WAS HORRIBLE, because he would kind of force me to sleep with him, really like marital rape. I don't like to talk about that. But I got pregnant before I left. I don't think I even had the $50 to get Plan B[17], if Plan B was even available, but I think I wanted to. It was the first time in my life I wanted to abort. I did not want to have another kid with him. And I was scared. I didn't like my husband anymore. But I'm really glad that I did get pregnant because Abigail is the best. I mean, all my kids are, but I probably would have given up a long time ago if it wasn't for Abigail.

Adam was not happy with any of the kids, except Jonathan. And that's when it kind of dawned on me, *Oh, I see. You think with kids, I can't leave.* He actually said it to me: "I'm kind of happy we've never had money," he said, "because without money you can't leave." He actually said those things to my face. I remember being in the kitchen and he was like, "Audrey, can you promise me if we do separate that you won't sleep with another man?" I mean, none of this had anything to do with me, I was just an object to him. The kids were tools to keep me there. Being poor—it was all orchestrated. And (finally) I saw it.

I started having panic attacks. I started zoning out and I thought I was going crazy. *Oh my God, I can't live like this!* It was wild, just one thing after another. And I was pregnant. I went to a domestic violence shelter in

---

[17] Plan B One-Step works like other birth control pills to prevent pregnancy. The drug acts primarily by stopping the release of an egg from the ovary. It may prevent a sperm from fertilizing the egg. If fertilization does occur, Plan B One-Step may prevent a fertilized egg from attaching to the womb. —WebMD.com

Colorado. He was the classic narcissist-abuser to a tee. Adam told me, "If you try and take the kids away, I'll get them taken away from both of us. I have people who will vouch for me that you have anger issues."

The abuse had already been out in the open. Whenever anything got out of hand, got physical, he started getting super sweet again, crazy, ridiculous sweet. So we would sleep together again and right after he would go right back to being a complete jerk. When I was in the domestic violence shelter, I read about it, that it's just a cycle. It was crazy. It was madness. And you just can't believe that somebody is doing these things and they're acting like it's normal. You try to talk to people about it, nobody believes you. You're on your own and you think, *Nobody is going to believe me, man!*

We moved back to Georgia and I ended up going to another domestic violence shelter there. I called Adam at one point. I was away for four months and he made no effort to talk to the kids, but we started talking and I thought, *Wow, we're having great conversations. Maybe he really did change.* At that point I was still trying to do the Christian thing—*I really do want to try and work things out. He's listening to me. He's validating me*—he never validated me before!

But after I told the shelter office I was going to go back home, after I was there for only two months, Adam and I had a conversation on the phone and I just had to hang up. He started mocking me—"Oh, yes, like you're a different woman now, right? You're *empowered*, you're changed." He was seriously mocking me. And I hung up on him. I was shaking, I was like, *What the hell is happening?* I couldn't stay there anymore. I had quit my job! I was packing up to leave the next day! I didn't know what to think.

When we talked about it he apologized but clearly, he hadn't changed. He just got better at saying the things I was looking for. And I'm not stupid. He's not stupid either, right? I moved back with him, and he just slipped back into everything. I was pregnant with our third child and had no idea what we were going to do in just months when all of this came to a head. Money was already tight and Adam wasn't willing to work longer, and Adam was now in school himself.

I got back in school because I was a veteran, so going to school was giving us money. It was really difficult, actually. I had a lot of teachers who challenged my Christian mentality. I had confined myself to the idea that I was going to be at home, that my job was to take care of the kids, and I was focused on that. But people were catching on—"Oh, she's smart and bright," and it was challenging me. I started thinking about online businesses, I started thinking outside of the box in those classrooms. I took a psychology class, and in it they help you figure out your talents and interests, about mission statements, where you want to go in life, and I did that. I realized, *You know, the only thing I really wanted to do was write and sing, but I think I'm better at writing. Can I even do that?* So I started looking for ways to write.

I started looking online and I found Elance[18]. My first job was writing a book about green living, reducing your carbon footprint, writing six chapters for just $66. That's $11 for each chapter, and each chapter 1,500 words. I knew *nothing* about green living, but that was my first client. After the second chapter he said he didn't think it was going to be a good fit. I got $22. But I just kept applying. After three months, and this is crazy, I was working so much to earn money to put my husband through school, and he decided to join a D&D[19] group! He was also always playing a lot of video games.

I started getting more gigs on Elance and after a few months Adam dropped out of school. I was staying up until like 2 a.m. in the morning writing, while he was asleep. And while I didn't really apply myself at school (I thought I was stupid, anyway), the first time someone really challenged me was actually in a class in college. The fact that people don't encourage women to go to school in church is alarming, because I'm telling you, they (college classes) will make a woman *think*. I started missing classes because I was taking on so much work, but in this one class, we were talking about ourselves, and I had to get up in front of the class.

I remember being very flustered because I was working so hard and Adam was not, so I was starting to see that we were unsustainable. We had been unsustainable almost from the get-go. We needed new tires for the car one time, and we couldn't get them. The car sat in the driveway with a flat. We were living hand-to-mouth. Our credit was maxed out, and we had no emergency savings. My father sent me $25 for turning 23—but *you cannot live that way when you have children!* And I was putting the pieces together: *This is crazy, we've got kids and we're living like children. We're not partyers, we're not in high school, we're not college students, we've got children to feed. We cannot be living like this. I need to get a job*—and he's yelling at me that I'm "focused on money!" And I'm thinking to myself, *I'm not crazy, am I? We've got kids, and we've got nothing! Literally nothing! Can you even fathom that? Nothing!*

I started seeing things more clearly and being more transparent about things. I wrote an email to the pastor at our church and he wrote back to me that yes, what I was describing was a typical, abusive relationship. But the only guidance he provided was, "If he's unwilling to change, you might have to look at divorce." That wasn't very helpful because the entire time I was married to Adam, he always said one thing with his mouth, and another with his actions. And everybody wanted to believe his mouth, even while he was still beating me at night. So when I reached out to this pastor I was reaching out to whomever I could at that point, because one of the things about abusers is they *isolate*, they confine their victims to people who have accepted their versions of events.

---

[18] Elance was an online staffing platform based in Mountain View, California, United States, now operated by Upwork. —Wikipedia

[19] Dungeons & Dragons (abbreviated as D&D) is a fantasy tabletop role-playing game (RPG) originally designed by Gary Gygax and Dave Arneson. It was first published in 1974 by Tactical Studies Rules, Inc. (TSR). The game has been published by Wizards of the Coast (now a subsidiary of Hasbro) since 1997. —Wikipedia

I reached out to another friend and when I told her I was worried about the kids' safety, she told me she had seen Adam hit our six-month-old, but she didn't tell me! And my sister Amber, who was living with us at the time, had seen Adam jump on me, but if you grow up in an abusive home, you really don't know any better. I didn't know there was a word for it. She didn't either. But you hear the word *abuse* and for whatever reason that word is professional, it's polished, it's like it's taken out of the sexual abuse handbook. The more I started talking about things, the more I found all kinds of people had witnessed Adam be violent, and I still really don't know why nobody said anything at those times.

In our brand of Christian church, even when we were in Christian counseling, when you bring up that the man is abusive, you're told there is a biblical reference for it. You're told to "be more submissive" to your husband. When I reached out again to the pastor, I explained, "I don't know what I'm doing. Financially, things are falling apart. I need to work, and my husband is telling me I am too focused on money, that I need to focus on God first. Am I crazy?"

"Audrey," the pastor wrote back, "if things are really as bad as you say they are financially, you'd be crazy to not consider getting a job."

I was like, *Okay, we've got to stay together, and think outside the box.* If there's anything I'm good at, it's thinking outside the box. And it dawned on me, *Audrey, you're averaging like $400 and you're really only working like part-time. What if you could go to a place with some money saved up, work part-time, and in the other half of the time work on those businesses you're interested in?* And I'm thinking, *Yeah! If I did this whole multiple income thing, and each business only made $200 to $500 each here and there, that's still something, and if we can create a little passive income, we can eventually get ahead.*

And that was the idea that led to going to Mexico.

I TALKED TO Adam about this idea. I had studied a little Spanish already. I also thought about Peru, but Adam thought Peru was kind of far, "but I don't think I'd mind the beach," he said. "The beach and some mountains, maybe." So I started researching. I subscribed to *International Living,* all trying to figure out the best place to live. I was originally looking at an area around Cancun, but it was kind of expensive to live there and they encourage Americans to stay in the tourist parts of Cancun. And there had actually been a travel advisory because Americans were being targeted, like their drinks were being spiked and people were being assaulted and robbed. So I looked into other places.

I found out about Santa María Huatulco[20] and it sounded perfect. There were mountains. There were beaches. It was located kind of in the center of the state. What a lot of locals say is that cartels have a truce

---

[20] Santa María Huatulco is a town in the southern Mexican state of Oaxaca. It's known for sprawling pre-Hispanic ruins in nearby Parque Eco-Arqueológico Copalita, including a ceremonial center with a large stone temple and a ball court. The Bocano del

with the area, that cartels will put their families there to keep them safe because Huatulco is a relatively safe place. And that's how I found Los Playas Huatulco, which is actually getting kind of big, but it's still a lovely, little tourist location. Their main bay which is called Playa Santa Cruz gets cruise ships that house thousands of people. The cruises would go through Panama on a two-week cruise and they stop at Playa Santa Cruz for like six hours, and sometimes dock there overnight.

The local economy thrives on the tourists. But the tourists are mainly Europeans. Americans are finding it now. It's really a great place. There are parts that are third-world, but there are parts where you can go to Mexico, enjoy being in a different country, and not feel like you're in a third world. It's like the best of both worlds. It's really cheap. But I thought if we went straight to the playas we'd pay more, so I found a beach called De Felipe, in an area about 45 minutes away. I talked to Adam about it, and he was okay with it. So I orchestrated the move. And we did it!

I no longer liked my husband, but we were still trying. I still believed all things are possible through God, and Adam told me that he wanted to try. I had the move to Mexico all orchestrated and by the end of July we went. I wanted to go to Mexico with $10,000 but Adam wanted to buy a car (we bought a Ford Expedition) and go around on visits before we left, and we spent a lot of our savings. We went to Virginia, we went to Albany, New York, and then we went to Georgia and left for Mexico out of Atlanta. The Expedition was hunkered down with everything we didn't sell before the move, and because we were worried about driving it in Mexico, we left the car at Adam's mother's house and from Atlanta we flew to Mexico—Adam, our three children, and pregnant me.

We got down there with less than $3,000 and I was freaking out! I had to pay the hotel $700 to stay the entire month because I didn't have any luck finding any other place that was decently priced. They were trying to charge through the roof for places with air conditioning and hot water. Once we were in Mexico City, we took out another $600 in pesos and within two days half of it was gone, in part because Adam was tipping people like $10 and $15. We were in Mexico City for a night, and then we went to Los Playas Huatulco, then to De Felipe. We took two taxis with all of our stuff and the kids, and Adam was tipping the drivers as much as the fares. He was spending our money as fast as possible, and we were arguing all the time.

On our second day in Mexico he said to me, "Can I tell you something?"

"What?" I asked.

"I don't want to be here. I just want to go back to America." We had just sold almost everything we had to get there.

Río Copalita Museum has ceramic and jade artifacts from the site. Nearby on the Pacific coast is Huatulco National Park, with beaches, coral reefs and diverse wildlife. —Google Maps

When we got to De Felipe, I found out it was known for Playa del Amor, the "Beach of Love," and it's a nude beach. The beach is beautiful—rolling, beautiful waves and clear water you can see the fishes through—so it was an incredible place to walk along the beach and pick up the shells and whatnot, but it was kind of difficult to live there because it wasn't really kid-friendly. There are hipsters and travelers from Europe, from France, Germany, wandering people, the type with dreadlocks who make bracelets and stuff they sell on the beach and whatnot. It was so completely different from what we were used to. But it was probably the best thing for us that we were moving on, because Adam might have wanted to stay at Playa del Amor.

We were there for a month and we went on to Puerto Angel which is about 15 minutes away, but it's really third-world, there is really nothing nice in Puerto Angel. I had just gotten a nanny for four or five hours a day, but after being there for about two weeks she told us she couldn't do it anymore because the place wasn't safe, and that the kids didn't watch or listen, but I think the real issue was Adam wasn't watching the kids, and he was pretty aggressive with them, and in Mexico, that's not their culture. They *love* children.

The day after she left, Adam was really being very aggressive with the kids, and they were just being babies. I told them they couldn't go to a certain area of the house, but it wasn't really a house, it was an unfinished project that was two rooms. The bathroom was located outside, the kitchen was outside. You had to leave the house and go outside to use the bathroom, and if it was raining you would get wet. There was a house right below us. We were kind of on a cliff, so people would actually come down this hill and walk right through our kitchen to get to the house down below us. There was just no privacy.

Around the back of the house there was a lot of construction sand because they hadn't finished building or laying down the foundation. So if the kids went around the back, they could reasonably slide down the sand, several meters! So Adam and I were arguing about him not watching the kids with the danger in the back yard. We were screaming at each other. I was on the bottom of the house and he was on the top of the house. He was screaming down at me, and I was screaming up at him, pointing a finger.

And then I stopped, and I said, "I can't do this anymore."

Maybe he realized I was serious because his entire tone changed. He stopped yelling at me and came down. "Look," he said, "I'm really sorry. We can work through this."

"No," I said. "I really think we can't. I left you and you didn't see your children for three or four months. I came back. We sold everything. Now we're in Mexico, and if you're telling me that all of that was not enough for you to change, and all of a sudden you say we can work through this just because I say *I'm done*, I don't think I can believe you."

When he realized I wasn't going to try to make things work anymore, he told me, "Okay. I guess I'm just going to go back to the United States." But we had three kids and I was pregnant!

"So, what's going to happen with the kids?" I said.

The only thing he would accept was him going back to the United States without us. We didn't have enough money to bring us all back. We had $1,000 left available on my credit card, with no savings. I took $400 out and gave it to Adam and he was mad about it—He was going to leave us there in Mexico with literally nothing if he could.

The church that we were going to tried to talk to him and convince him to stay, but he wanted to go. I was going to need some kind of help *immediately,* because I was about to be there alone and I had nothing, and he was okay with that. He bought a plane ticket and three or four days before his flight, these two women said to me, "Audrey, listen. If you want us to talk to him, give us a chance. Don't come home yet, stay wherever you are, and let us talk to him."

I had exhausted all of my options. I called all of my family to see if anyone would be able to come and help with the kids. I called my sister, I called people I had served in the military with—I called anybody who might help me until I got back on my feet. I was six months pregnant at this point. In just three months I'd have a newborn. Finally, my sister Amber was going to help me, and I wouldn't have been able to survive if she hadn't.

The American women convinced him to stay just long enough for my sister to arrive. I was now *completely* out of money and it was horrible. I remember walking downtown when Adam was still there and hurrying back after a few hours because if I stayed too long Adam would lock the kids in a room and come looking for me. I had to walk down to the nearest town and use the internet café to work.

And when Amber finally got here, she was deported. I forgot to tell her you can only come to Mexico on a tourist visa for six months. When she arrived the lines to come in to the country were so long they eventually told her to get in the line for returning Mexicans and when asked she told them she would like to stay for a year, but she had no visa and they deported her. She had $580 in a bank account, so she used almost all of that to get back. I had to stay in Mexico City for the next 24 hours, and I had no money. To get back home I had to withdraw against my account.

Adam left me in a foreign country with three small children and I was pregnant. When he got back to Atlanta, he totaled our car then forged my name on the title to sell it. To survive for the next two months, I was withdrawing against my account and I was lucky I had happened to have been a veteran. I had overdraft protection up to $500. Every time I over-withdrew, I was charged $20, and that's how we survived. It was just horrible.

I started focusing on writing after that, because that was the only way we had to survive. Things didn't immediately improve, though. When Amber arrived, she put all she had into helping us that first month, and went into a deep depression, seeing how we were living, how Adam had left us there like that. I was writing through Elance, taking all the jobs I could find. When I finally took a chance and published my own story, it was because one of the clients I had really encouraged me to do it. I put off my other assignments, making several late, and took two weeks to write my first book. I felt bad about it, but really, writing that first book was what I needed. It gave me a break.

I wrote the book, and this client I had who encouraged me did the ebook formatting and everything else to help me. I had written him a book series first, before I wrote my own. He put my books on Amazon with all of the little code words. In the first two weeks, I had minimal sales, but then one day, they *skyrocketed*, and I didn't know why, but it was nice! I still get royalties off of that series. It was so wonderful. And after the release, when I started seeing how much money I was going to make in the next few months, it was *wonderful*.

I bought a garbage can, I bought a table for the kids, and we had a late Christmas. Looking back now, I think I did a really good job of keeping the kids from everything because they're pretty well-adjusted children. They're *happy*, and others tell me they see that. I couldn't really see it because I knew how much of an internal struggle was going on with me. After that money started coming in I moved into a different house and bought some furniture, and as things were starting to look up, I started to discover things in Mexico I was unaware of because I had been so focused on writing all of the time.

ONCE I REALIZED I had been married to a malignant narcissist, all of his actions started to make sense. I started reading up on PTSD and stopped feeling like I was crazy. I started trying to figure out how I could get help, because from what I could see the PTSD was unmanageable. It was little things. My kids would come and tap me, and it would feel like they were punching me. I used to think if I could just hold out a little more things would get better, but I decided I wasn't going to go through these things anymore.

I ended up moving to Mexico City and I was able to get free counseling from an American association that specialized in domestic violence in ex-pats. We talked over the phone several times a week at first. I think by doing that, everything I had experienced up to that point was validated. And I guess that's when I started to really hear, for the first time, things like, "You know, you're really smart." And that's when I stopped living in survival mode. I've been able to get more counseling since then, and sometimes you need it. I've had a lot of trauma. I needed a break. I needed to be able to care for myself. You really can't make good decisions when you are in survival mode—when all life is work, make money—because all you can think about is *that day*. You can't think about a month from now when you don't even know if you'll have the rent a month from now.

MEXICO BY AUDREY BOLAND

I moved about five and a half hours north of Mexico City, for about six months, to see if going back to the United States was worth it. While I was there, I read this book, *10X*[21], and I started adopting some of those principles. I decided what my goals were going to be, what I was going to focus on. Working on myself always includes going to the gym because I feel healthier, I feel happier, and I look good. And if you look good, you feel better about yourself.

There were times when breathing would *hurt* but I just kept waking up. And if I had the strength for that, what else could I do? You've got a little daughter dependent on you. I remember that night when I thought about taking Plan B, and I'm really glad I didn't. She's the best, and I don't know what would have happened if she was not there. At the end of the day, I'm going to do whatever I can for my children. It's been a crazy journey. I've had a lot of adversity in my life—I still do—but my story isn't over. I have my kids, and I'm a great writer. I have great friends.

My sister Arlene, when she was pregnant, invited me to San Diego, and I thought that it was time to go back to the United States. I thought about my other sister Amber and how she dropped everything to come help me in Mexico, so I wanted to drop everything for Arlene. She told me she wanted me there the next Monday.

I didn't wait. I left on Wednesday, and I got there by Friday.

---

[21] *The 10X Rule: The Only Difference Between Success and Failure* by Grant Cardone (Wiley)

About Audrey Boland

Audrey Boland is a best-selling author and professional ghostwriter.
Reach out to her today!

Visit:
www.BOLANDGHOSTING.com

[5]

HATS AND SCARVES AND STUFF LIKE THAT

by Gail Fay

"I had been thinking of the disaster as a horrible mistake, as an unscripted deviation from the happy story of the life I had been promised. But now I began to understand that my ordeal in the Andes was not an interruption of my true destiny, or a perversion of what my life was supposed to be. It simply was my life.... To hide from this fact, or to live in bitterness and anger, would only keep me from living any genuine life at all."

—NANDO PARRADO, *Miracle in the Andes*

I WAS BORN IN PASADENA, California. I grew up in beautiful downtown Burbank, California, about a mile from Disney Studios and what was NBC Studios. I was very involved in sports. I would say one thing that inspired me was athletes. I was determined to make the Olympic team and I was desperate because I was good, but I wasn't great. So, I remember thinking, Oh, maybe I could join the handball team or something goofy. But I played a lot of sports. I played soccer, softball, basketball, I ran track and cross country in high school. That was my first love. The other thing I really got involved with, I guess in the eighth grade, is reading. And writing came out of that.

I ended up being the editor of our school newspaper when I was in junior high for at least one or two semesters and had the most incredible eighth grade English teacher, Steve Campbell. He's why I know how to write. And I am convinced he is why I ended up becoming an English teacher. I mean, he was incredible. I had him as an eighth grade English teacher and I had him as the supervisor for the school newspaper. I don't know if I ever thought of Mr. Campbell as inspiring, but maybe that's the word I would use now. I went back when I was teaching eighth grade English years later and talked to him to pick his brain to get ideas on everything from grading strategies to how to communicate certain grammar tips. He definitely had an impact on my future teaching career and ultimately in what I'm doing now in terms of writing and editing.

I didn't know at the time, and again, I don't think I would have used the word inspirational, but looking back, I can say he had a huge impact ultimately on both of my career choices—I became and an English major, went on to become a teacher, and now, I'm doing editing and writing (often ghost writing). I think I also learned the joy of creating, in a way, from him too.

I didn't continue with the newspaper, but I continued reading and writing. I had a really good friend who helped me. We would discuss novels in depth. We had to turn in school papers and—this might have been his description—I started to look at the process like that of birthing a child. You've labored to get these ideas and fit them all into the right order. It was like a puzzle, and I loved that part of writing. I think that was an early seed that led to where I am now.

I went to college at UCLA and was an English major. I had no idea what I wanted to do with my English major, I just knew that I loved to read and write. During my senior year I reported on the UCLA women's soccer team. (At the time it was like a club team. They weren't like a division one team yet.) This was back in the late eighties, so soccer wasn't as big there as it was on the East Coast. I would report on the teams and write articles and that was the first time I combined those two loves, sports and writing, in my junior or senior year in college.

When I graduated from college I had no idea how I was going to use my English degree, but I was going to use it somehow. I ended up teaching PE at an elementary school for a year, and then I got an opportunity to teach eighth grade English. I did that for 10 years after that. And that was fun, and again, that was when I went back and talked to Mr. Campbell. I remembered his enthusiasm, I remembered his love for the language, and tried to impart that to my students. I'm still friends on Facebook with some of my students and they remember certain things I did way back then. So I guess it made an impact. And toward the end of that time I got engaged.

HATS AND SCARVES AND STUFF LIKE THAT BY GAIL FAY

I MET MY HUSBAND Bob working at a children's camp, and we did this together for several summers. He thought it was hot that I drove the bus, so that was a winner, and we dated for a while. We got engaged in February of 1999, and a few months later I was diagnosed with cancer. So, we were in the process of planning for the wedding and all excited and . . . that was not exactly what you'd expect that to happen.

I had continued to be active in sports. I was still playing softball, I was running, and I started having symptoms after I would run. I had a little back pain. I had what I thought was blood in my urine—which isn't normal if you're running. I kind of let it go for a while because I'm stubborn. Finally, I went and got it checked out. They ran all these tests. They checked my kidneys, they checked my bladder, but nobody ever said cancer. They didn't check my uterus because I was 32 and I was otherwise young and healthy—I was running, I was physically active, and so on, so I was kind of ready to drop it. I wasn't really good about going to the doctor, I was like, "Okay good, I went to the doctor. There's nothing wrong."

But thankfully both my fiancé (Bob) and a good friend who was a nurse, said, "You know, you really should go get a second opinion." So I got a second opinion. She did a different series of tests and found out I had polyps in my uterus. I had the polyps removed and called the doctor to find out when I could start running again. When he called back, I thought he was calling to answer my question, and instead he was calling to tell me I had cancer, which was shocking to say the least, because I'm pretty sure Bob had asked him point blank previously. He told me on the phone. I don't remember how the whole conversation went other than the fact that he said, "You have cancer," and everything after that was kind of a buzz. It was stage one, it was early, but it was shocking, you know?

That would have been May of 1999. I was 32, I was engaged, I was otherwise healthy. This was not part of the plan. Bob was living in Santa Barbara at the time and I was living in the San Fernando Valley, which were about 90 minutes apart. I think he came down the same night I was diagnosed. He stayed with friends and then it became this process of trying to figure out, Okay, well what do we do? Basically there were two options at that point with uterine cancer. Either have a hysterectomy, which we wanted to avoid because we were engaged and we were hoping to have kids; or there was a drug and it was used for something completely not related, like stimulating appetite in AIDS patients. So the available research of how effective it had been was not readily available. We knew a couple of other people who had had cancer, who had each tried an alternative therapy called Gerson Therapy, and it had worked. One had thyroid cancer and one had bladder cancer and they're both still alive today. I mean, they beat cancer by simply doing this alternative therapy.

We decided to try it, but we also knew that in someone young uterine cancer tends to be more aggressive. Gerson Therapy focuses on cleaning out the toxins from your system through organic fruits and vegetables, coffee enemas, and tons of supplements. It is very labor intensive; in fact I think it calls for 13 juices a day. Some of them were what we call green juices that included leafy greens, and one of the green apples called granny Smith apples, and then we had carrot-apple juices. I had so many carrot-apple juices that my hands turned orange, literally. The palms of my hands we're orange. And there was a special soup. And we knew that Gerson Therapy, a lot of times, is more effective with other kinds of cancer which are slower growing.

So knowing that I continued to see my Western doctor throughout the process, and they did a certain kind of biopsy. They were trying to see if it was spreading from my uterus down. The first test everything looked good. I went back three months later and when they did the test, I knew something was different. I could just feel it. I don't know how, but I just knew that something wasn't right.

So Bob and I decided to do the Gerson Therapy and we postponed our wedding. He went with me to Mexico. We stayed there for a week, and we got the training. We went in to see the doctor about the second biopsy results and found out that sure enough the cancer was advancing. My only real option was a hysterectomy, which was a blow because that's what we had been trying to avoid in the first place by doing the alternative therapy. In the meantime I found a lump in my groin, where your legs fold, and the doctors were thinking it was so advanced it had already moved down to the uterus and spread, so this was a very bad situation.

We called it the week from hell. I think I found out all of this information in one week—the diagnosis, about the surgeries and so on. They were going to do what they called a radical hysterectomy, because they thought it had been spreading. When they actually did the surgery, they discovered I actually had two kinds of cancer. In a sense it was a better situation because it meant the uterine cancer was still contained. It had started spreading to the cervix, but it hadn't spread outside. But I also had the ovarian cancer on my left ovary, which had sloughed off onto my bladder and also into this cyst that was in my groin. I had two primary kinds of cancer and the ovarian cancer was stage 2B because it had moved into the pelvic cavity area. Because of that I had to do chemo. My first thought—and I kid you not—was, I'm gonna be a bald bride. Not, Oh my gosh, I have two kinds of cancer! Bob and I still laugh about that.

HATS AND SCARVES AND STUFF LIKE THAT BY GAIL FAY

I HAD SURGERY at the beginning of February, 2000, and I think I actually started chemo towards the end of March, 2000. I did six rounds of chemo treating the ovarian cancer. I lost my hair. And one thing somebody told me—and it was the best advice I received—is take a lot of pictures. They were like, "When are you ever going to be bald again?" I am so glad I took her advice because it made it so much more fun. I mean, you already have to go through this situation, so why not make the best of it? Bob shaved his head with me. We took pictures of the two of us bald, we stuck our heads together like Velcro. We bought matching do-rags and we took pictures with those. My friends had a baby who was bald, so I took pictures with the bald baby. I mean, we just took a ton of pictures and I am so glad. That was like the best piece of advice I got.

You have to go through it, so you may wanna have a little fun with it.

Losing my hair for the first time was rather traumatic. I didn't think it would be, I don't know why. I'm not a girly girl. I don't think I was ever attached to my hair. For some reason I didn't think it would be a big deal. I had long hair—and my hair was long and it was permed (this was the late 90s, after all), and I had a lot of hair. I had it cut to my shoulders and then it just started falling out everywhere. I found it in the shower, on the pillow, in the car. I mean, it was everywhere and it was extremely traumatic. I tried to hold onto it. I got it cut to my shoulders and I then I got it cut to my chin and then I just got it shaved. It was far more traumatic than I thought it would be. But I survived.

And then, we finally got married. I finished treatment at the end of June, 2000, and we got married on October 14th, 2000. I had about a quarter inch of hair, maybe. One thing I discovered while dress and veil shopping is that veils are meant to go over hair. They do not look good if you have no hair. So my sister got me a hat (my first). I never did wigs because I was afraid they would fall off and itch and I just didn't want to deal with them. So I wore hats and scarves and stuff like that.

One of the hats I had was a straw hat, but it was more fashionable. My sister and I spray-painted it white and we took a glue gun and glued on a veil to the back of it. And that was what I ended up wearing for the wedding with the wedding dress. It was kind of cool because it was something I had worn during chemo, but then my sister helped me make it something that was better than chemo. So that was kind of cool.

The bigger loss, the one I have a harder time talking about, was not being able to have kids. The hair grew back.

Another hard aspect is when you have something like cancer, people don't know what to say. I get it now, because even though I've been through cancer, there are people who have it so much worse than I did and do. And I still have a hard time knowing what to say to them because here I am—I'm still going to the gym and running and doing all of these things, and I'm going through chemo, whereas other people can barely get out of bed. So I do understand that, that there's a sense of not knowing what to say.

I myself, I get tired of talking about cancer. But everyone is different. So if you know someone who's going through cancer, ask them, "Do you wanna talk about it, or do you not wanna talk about it?" Ask, "What's the best way I can support you?" For me personally, I figured people were gonna ask how I was doing and that's cool, but it's not the only thing I wanted to talk about. I would rather talk about the UCLA football game or the Dodgers or what that person is doing or whatever, you know what I mean? I wanted to make cancer the smallest part of my life, and I wanted to be as normal as possible.

For me that means just being as normal as possible. That means cooking dinner, going shopping, being out in public with no hair. I'm an active person. So if I have the energy to get up and go for a walk or a hike or go to the gym or go to a spin class, I'm gonna do it. It's what kept me sane, being able to still do those kinds of things. If I have the energy to do it, I'm gonna do it because it makes me feel like I'm at least a little bit in control of what's going on and it makes me feel normal. This is what I would be doing anyway. It's my way of saying, Screw you, cancer. You're not in control.

My first time around with cancer, I was just doing what needed to be done. People often say, "Oh, I admire you," or "You're so strong," or you're this and you're that, and am I? I'm just doing what I need to do to get through this. And the way I know how to get through it is by being as normal as I can. The other thing is, you're going through it anyway. Why not smile? Life is much more enjoyable if you're laughing. Plus I was married to Bob, so you know that's of course enough to laugh. The first time, when we decided I was going to do the chemotherapy, I had to have my own refrigerator for all the food. Bob went out and bought what we needed. He tracked down doctors and insurance stuff and yes, even shaved his head. Yeah, he has been amazing. One of the pictures on my desk is of both of us bald.

We took the same picture 20 years later, when the cancer returned.

GOOD HEALTH GOING in to something like cancer will help you, no doubt. I was in pretty good shape the first time around. Then as part of my cancer treatment, they gave chemo patients a free one-month membership to a gym. We got to take yoga, Tai Chi, and other classes and that's what got me back into going to the gym. I had already been active, but it was because of that that I really started going to the gym again and in between the first time with cancer and the second time with cancer I continued going to the gym. In fact I was in better shape, I think, when it happened the second time around.

Going through chemo, most people get so sick. Honestly, I have not thrown up once, and I've now done 12, 13, 14 rounds of chemo. I get nauseous a little bit and then I'm kind of tired for maybe four days and then I'm kind of back to normal. Honestly, other than the fact that I don't have hair I don't look sick. I think the physical activity helps mentally as well as emotionally and physically. I think it helps on all levels.

I stopped doing Gerson before surgery because my Gerson doctor was actually the one who said, "You should probably start eating some protein to help your body prepare for surgery." So I kind of weaned off Gerson and I've never gone back. In general I try and eat healthier—lots of fruits and vegetables and physical activity—but I've never gone back to the lifestyle of juicing and enemas. It was very hardcore, and I needed people's help. It kind of saps your energy because you're not really eating protein, so I think you're a little more tired anyway. In fact there's just so much to do with Gerson, I don't know if one person can do it on their own, honestly. It's 13 juices a day, like once an hour plus making the soup. So I definitely had a lot of help and I needed the help.

We got married and I did my regular follow up every three months, every six months, once a year. But as far as I was concerned, I was done with cancer. The major continuing thing was that we couldn't have kids. Ever since that I've had short hair because I love it now. It's awesome, especially after we moved to Florida. That was a good thing that came out of it that I probably wouldn't have ever tried, and I discovered that I love short hair.

But then one day we entered a new stage. In November of 2012, Bob and I were laughing about something and I coughed up a chunk of blood. I went to the doctor and got a CT scan. By early January they had determined that it was in my right lung, and they thought it was lung cancer.

I now had a third cancer.

I had surgery around the end of January, 2013. You have three lobes on the right lung, and they took a third of the lowest lobe. They tested it and determined it was from the ovarian cancer. It had hung out in my body for 12 years and then came back, in my lung.

I had to do the same chemo treatments, and this time because I knew the trauma of losing my hair, I cut it into a fun style ahead of time and did things I'd never done before. I put in highlights and then a friend dyed it pink and blue. Again, if I have to go through this, I'm gonna have fun with it. There's this certain feeling when you start losing your hair, like if you have long hair and you're wearing a ponytail for too long and you take it out, it feels like it's going against the grain somehow. It's like this weird prickly feeling. As soon as I started feeling that I shaved off my hair because I felt, I am not doing this again! Bob shaved his head again, because he's awesome.

This was in 2013 and I was already in the habit of going to the gym as much as I could. I went to spin class at least once a week (other than the week I had chemo), because it was normal. It helped me feel normal. I felt better physically, mentally, emotionally, and I found out from other people that it was an inspiration to them to see me in there, even though I was bald. I was doing it for me, not for them, but I think it had a side benefit for others who saw me still doing what I could. So, I went through chemo, and went back to life as normal.

I'M NOT A touchy-feely person, I never did support groups or anything like that having to do with not having kids. I didn't talk to anybody about that. I was a "stuffer," I say. I just stuffed everything, but there's only so much room in one's tank when one is a stuffer. And somewhere around 2015 I realized that tank was full. So I actually had an opportunity to go to this camp called Epic Experience. It's a free outdoor adventure camp for adult cancer survivors. I didn't think I needed it because I was already doing everything I could to live beyond cancer (that's their tagline), but going absolutely changed my life, for sure. I was there with other cancer survivors. They're based here in Colorado so we went snowshoeing and we acted like 12-year-olds. It was awesome. Laugh, laugh, laugh. It was the first time I talked to other people about having chemo, about what it's like to lose your hair, all these things I had just dealt with. To talk to these people was just really cool.

And when I came home, I decided, Okay, I've survived cancer twice for a reason. I thought, Maybe it involves giving back in some way through this organization, Epic Experience. I started volunteering, writing and editing for them. Then I volunteered at the camp. I was cooking and helping by doing all the work so the campers just had a blast. And that was amazing because when I went as a camper, I was just focused on me, and how this was awesome and wow, it changed my life. But when you go and volunteer and you watch people change over the week, it's just amazing.

I stayed involved with them, and the second time I volunteered I met a young woman who did cancer education workshops on college campuses. She'd talk specifically about breast cancer and ovarian cancer and they needed an ovarian cancer survivor to be a "facilitator" or somebody to share their story. I would've never done this before because I just was trying to make cancer the smallest part of my life possible. But after going to that camp, I realized, Okay, you survived this for a reason. So in October, 2017, I started doing that at UCLA. I traveled for the organization, the Rivkin Center. They were event sponsors and they do research specifically related to ovarian cancer, based in Seattle.

So I've now done this at UCLA, I've gone to the University of Utah, I've gone to Washington State, I've gone to USC, and we do what we call cancer education parties. It's a serious topic, it freaks people out. They don't know how to talk about it. So we try and present the facts, but in a way that's less intimidating I guess, and more fun, and allows people to ask questions. It's really cool, I've really enjoyed doing them. Hopefully I'm going to be able to continue that here in Colorado because the University of Colorado is not too far away. That was a really cool thing that came out of Epic Experience.

And now, I've just been diagnosed again in May. So here we are.

I wasn't entirely surprised. I had had a cough. One of the things we say in the cancer education workshops is the importance of knowing your body and knowing what's normal for you so that if something's not normal, you can go get it checked out. Specifically, we're talking about ovarian cancer and breast cancer. I had a cough for a long time and finally went and got it checked out, and here I was, taking my own advice. We did a series of tests—Is it asthma? Is it allergies? Finally we did a CT scan and we did a pet scan. And in May, just a few months ago, I found out I had two lymph nodes in my chest, not in my lungs, but just below my esophagus that lit up on the pet scan. I had them biopsied and they were metastases, again, from the ovarian cancer. It was shocking. It had never been in my lymph nodes. It's sobering.

Sometimes I think of cancer as being cancer with a small c, and cancer with a capital C. I don't feel like I've really experienced the life-threatening nature that I would associate with a capital C. All things considered, it's been kind of easy, you know what I mean?

It was a little shocking in the sense that now it is in my lymph nodes. Nobody has ever said the prognosis was bad or anything like that, it just was a different. This time I actually had to do radiation, which I've never had to do before, which is miserable. And now I'm in the middle of getting chemo again, and it's just a little different from the other times.

I am getting through it, and I'm feeling really good, actually. I mean, I'm blessed. I am just so thankful that I fell into this job, the ghost-writing gigs. I can schedule around chemo. I know what days I'm probably going to feel more tired, so I don't schedule phone calls for those days. And then the days I am feeling good I work more hours. Having this job has just made it easier to be normal. Not much has changed other than the days I go in for chemo. Other than that, I'm still here working and talking on the phone and editing and doing all that stuff.

I'VE HAD PEOPLE comment on my smile a lot, so I'm gonna say yes, I guess I'm a naturally happy person. I can't say that I always thought of myself that way, but I have had people comment on this more than once. I don't know if I would ever have used the word, happy, to describe myself growing up, but I think I was always positive. I don't know that I've ever made a conscious decision to be that way. It's not like the home I grew up in was wonderful. My parents got a divorce, my dad died when I was young. Somehow, I just kept going. Somehow there was something in me that knew, You have to go through this anyway. Being all morose and negative isn't gonna help. And I love to laugh. It's so much more fun. I've always appreciated people who have a good sense of humor, I've always appreciated a good joke.

For me, this is where sports came in. For me that was an outlet. So if things were crappy at home, that was my escape. Physically, mentally, emotionally, it really helped. It was a place for me to belong, even though I wouldn't have said that back then. It was a place for me to achieve. It was a place for me, it gave me all these things even though I didn't quite know it at the time, and I think that's continued through to this day. Sports, and a sense of humor, I think is huge. Another cool thing that's made this round of chemo more fun is that my sister sends me care packages of movies to watch during chemo, along with snacks, coloring books, and other fun stuff. We've also painted our toenails the same color before each chemo this time around.

And another thing for me from a young age is having a faith, having a sense of knowing, and praying, often just as a way of remembering verses. There's one I just read the other day:

> "Do not fret--it only causes harm."
> —Psalm 37:8, *New King James Version*

It helped me cope. It was praying and knowing it's out of my control, but that's okay. I can take one step at a time. It's a sense of peace. That contributes to the smile as well, at some level having the sense that I don't know what okay is gonna look like, but it's gonna be okay. It's these internal conversations with God, whether it was anger or frustration or, "Okay, let's do this," which may sound odd because at the same time, almost every time I'm at the gym, I'm in spin, at some point I'm like, "F-you cancer!" Not out loud, but in my head. So I'm simultaneously thanking God that I have the ability to do this, and at the same time I'm like, "F-you cancer!"

HATS AND SCARVES AND STUFF LIKE THAT BY GAIL FAY

Today, I am 52. I try and do spin classes once a week. I haven't been running as much, partly because right when I was diagnosed is when we moved here to Colorado, which is in a higher altitude, which makes running harder. But it's gorgeous out here, so I walk a lot. I do free weights, a lot of stretching. I haven't done yoga but I did one class before I left California and I know it would probably be something that would be beneficial. I'm in the habit of going to the gym, taking a class, getting on the elliptical, those kinds of things. And walking, being outside, it's huge for me. Nature, just the breeze. I'd say the breeze in my hair, but I have no hair, so the breeze on my face. Being in the sun, looking at the mountains, the clouds. Even now the clouds here, the weather, it's just gorgeous. I think that's helped each time, that ability to get out and enjoy it. I am thankful and I am very well aware that not everyone who goes through chemo has it as easy as I do. So I am very thankful that I'm able to get out and do that.

I have this sense that I'm still here for a reason and I can't necessarily say what it is, but I feel like, Okay, I can tell my story and maybe that'll help someone. As with the cancer workshops, in this book I can share my story. I don't know if I would say that keeps me going, but that is one thing that is energizing—sharing my story, and hoping that it's gonna help someone.

I would like to inspire people who feel helpless or hopeless for whatever reason. It doesn't have to be related to cancer. For some reason we often feel like we're the only one who is experiencing X, whatever it is. But the truth is you're not. That was one of the things I learned, and I feel like I'm still learning, is once I was willing to open up and share with people rather than trying to stuff everything, I realized I wasn't the only one. Other people experience these things as well. It may not be the exact same thing, but it's true, there's nothing new under the sun.

We have a common humanity with common experiences and common thoughts, even if at times it seems we're the only one who's ever experienced X.

So many aspects of cancer can't be controlled: if you get it, if it recurs, the need for surgery, long-term side effects, hair loss, chemo brain. My current uncontrollable is that it has metastasized to a single lymph node in my chest and now I need radiation and chemo. I've decided to focus on the things I can control, starting with my hair. I can make fallout less traumatic by cutting it short now. I can make it an adventure by choosing a hairstyle I've never tried (faux hawk a la P!nk as worn by someone with minimal styling prowess and wicked cowlicks). I can choose when to shave my head and make it a party if I so desire. Choice is a powerful thing. (Hair cutting credit: Gloria Davis) #canthurtme #cancersucks #badassoldlady

About Gail Fay

Gail Fay is an author, editor, and freelance writer.

Reach her through her website at

www.FAYWORDWORKS.com

Or email

gail@epicexperience.org

Epic Experience: www.epicexperience.org

A LITTLE KINDNESS
by Christina DeBusk

> Like a small boat
>
> On the ocean
>
> Sending big waves
>
> Into motion
>
> Like how a single word
>
> Can make a heart open
>
> I might only have one match
>
> But I can make an explosion
>
> —RACHEL PLATTEN
> "Fight Song"

PEOPLE ARE ASKING me these days how I am. I'd say I'm probably 95 percent. I'm still working on getting my core strengthened backed up, but other than that, my fatigue has pretty much gone away and I'm kind of back to me, I think.

When you donate a kidney, the remaining kidney grows in size to help compensate for the loss of the other. Until it does, it's not as effective at pulling the toxins out of your body. You also have a four-to five-inch incision that runs right under your belly button. That has to heal as well and mine is getting there. My understanding is it takes six months to a year to feel "normal" again.

There have been times where I've felt like the recovery has been super long, times when I get frustrated if I can't do something I could have easily done before. For instance, prior to the procedure—which was April 19, 2019—I was walking four miles a day. Yet, after the donation, while staying at my sister's house to recover, I struggled to walk to the end of the drive. Each time I went out, I would try to walk further than before. Just one more mailbox, I would tell myself. Just one more.

Some days I wondered if I'd ever get back to where I was before. Then I'd look back and think, Wow, okay, ease up on yourself. In fairness, it only took me three or four weeks till I was back to my four-mile daily walk. And I started writing again, for work, a week after the surgery, but only part-time.

As for my kidney's recipient, she's up and down. Most people who have chronic kidney issues and get a new kidney start to feel better; it's just a matter of balancing the meds so their body doesn't reject the new kidney but still functions the way it's supposed to. She is also contending with a disease that has now started to attack the new kidney. They're trying to figure out how to stop it from progressing and, potentially, how to undo some of the damage that the disease has already done.

To be honest, I had a hard time when asked to be a part of this book because I don't know what to say. I mean, I understand that what I did helped her, but I have a very difficult time with it being any more than that. To me it was as simple as knowing I was a match and not being able to live with myself if I didn't donate.

I knew my recipient from school as I had graduated with her brother. Plus, she was a massage therapist so, when I lived in Michigan—where I flew to do the donation—I'd gone to her a few times. Other than that, we were friends on Facebook, which is actually where I saw that she needed the kidney.

Here's the weird thing: when I read that post, I thought, I'm a match. That said, I didn't know if what I was feeling was real. My sister had donated her kidney about twelve years prior and I remember her saying she knew she was a match too, well before she was tested. So, was I really a match or was I just reliving her experience?

I talked to my sister about this and she said she went to a meeting with a bunch of other donors and quite a few of them felt the same. As a result, I wasn't totally surprised when the hospital called and gave me the news, asking if I'd do further testing.

I did the additional testing in August of 2018 and they came back and said, "Your kidney function isn't quite where we want it to be. It's okay, but it's not good enough. We're afraid if we take one of your kidneys you could potentially have problems down the road." It bummed me out for my friend, but I did feel a little sense of relief.

Part of that relief came because my husband and I were in the process of moving and I had a trip overseas planned. Since all of this was coming together at once, when they said, "No, we can't proceed," I felt I could then focus on everything else going on.

Fast forward to February of 2019 and the hospital got back with me. They said they had a different, more comprehensive test they wanted me to try, a more accurate test as far as kidney function. "Okay," I said, "I'll take the test." I did and its results revealed that my kidney function was good enough to move forward.

It just so happened I was scheduled to go back to Michigan to work at my aunt's bakery the next week. While there, I went to the hospital and did my eight-hour testing.

I would say I was in good physical shape going in, which is hugely important. I went through a few different physical tests to determine match and suitability and, again, to ensure I had good enough kidney function. This consisted of physical testing, x-rays, CAT scans—you name it. But a large portion was mental testing.

I had to meet with a psychologist. I did memory testing. I was asked to talk about my life and share how I cope with the different things that have happened in my life. This portion of the testing stressed me out more than the physical testing, but they want to make sure you'd be okay mentally after donating, and that you know fully what you're getting into.

The neat thing when it comes to the donation process is that I had a completely different team than the recipient. It was pretty impressive, actually. Nerve-wracking, but impressive.

The following week, I received word that the doctors had discussed my case and gave me the green light to donate. We set the surgery for April and, while I was excited to help my friend out, the closer the date got, the more challenges I faced.

For example, on the flight to Michigan, my plane was diverted to Nebraska because Chicago was closed. I got stranded overnight, so I pulled out my laptop to get more work done before being off. That's when I realized that I'd left my power cord in California. The next day, I managed to leave my phone charger in Nebraska, leaving me with no way to charge my two most important devices.

I was also concerned that not arriving in time for my preop the next day would delay the surgery. However, the hospital was great. "Don't stress out," they said. "We'll get this figured out."

When I finally made it to Michigan and got to my sister's house, she had no power. I thought, Okay, with all these obstacles, am I missing something? Is God telling me today is not your day? You really need to rethink this.

I was sitting and talking to my sister and kind of broke down. "Is all of this a sign?" I asked. "Part of me just wants to call the hospital and say, Screw it. I'm going back to California."

To this, my sister said, "Look, at some point you're going to get a sign. Something is going to happen that's going to tell you what you need to do."

Yeah, right, I thought, whatever. I wanted to believe her, but I didn't. There were just so many obstacles.

The next day, I drove the two hours to the hospital for my preop. After I checked in, I took a seat across from a man with a cane. We started talking about the weather and so on, kind of to pass the time, and he said, "Let me tell you my story."

"Okay," I said, and thought, Okay, here's my sign.

This man told me how he was driving a big rig, got stuck on an expressway off ramp in the snow, and while trying to figure out what was going on, his rig ended up backing over him. He told me he could see the tires coming up across his body and running over him. He told me how it crushed him internally and that it's a miracle he was even alive.

I was amazed with his story, of course, but for some reason I felt a little disconnected. Part of me thought, Okay, this is my sign, I'm supposed to be getting something from this, but what am I supposed to be getting? Is it the fact that sometimes we go through things that we don't understand and we should just be thankful we're still alive? That type of thing?

My mind was trying to process what he was telling me and, before he was done with his story, the nurse called me back for my appointment. As I was walking past him, I put my hand on his face, which is odd for me because I normally wouldn't do that to a total stranger. And I said, "I want you to know that I really appreciate you sharing your story."

"The reason I told you that story," he said, "is I want you to know that God is good." That was what I needed. That was the sign. That was the thing that I really needed to hear, I thought. God is good and I wouldn't be doing this if he hadn't walked me down this path.

When I went back to start the appointment, I was talking to the nurses, telling them what had just happened. I shared how I was having some major uncertainties about whether to proceed and this man, with his one final statement, was able to finally put me at ease.

I was in tears as I shared how much this relieved me and, soon, they were in tears as well. At the end of my story, they asked me, "What guy was this?"

As I started to explain, "It was the guy—" it struck me as odd because I realized he didn't talk about anything being transplanted, yet that was the unit he was on. Our conversation had been cut short, so maybe he just didn't have the time. So, I described him to the nurses. No one had a clue who I was talking about.

I thought, Really? Was he even real? It was the strangest frickin' thing. From that point on, I thought, Okay, you got this.

Today, it's the one story about the whole experience I can't get through without crying. It was crazy. It just put my fears to rest.

I AM A FIRM believer in God. I grew up Christian. I don't go to church much after the age of about ten, but I have a lot of faith in God because there have been so many times where things have worked out with no explanation otherwise. I relied on my faith a lot through this process.

Before the procedure, I had many fears. Fears like what happens if they take my kidney and my other one doesn't work anymore? What if a close family member needs a kidney and now I don't have one to give?

I was also concerned financially. I am a freelance writer and taking so much time off of work would be a hit. There would also be costs associated with flying to Michigan.

I had tons of fears going into this, but I just kept saying, Okay, God, if this is what I'm supposed to do, help me walk through this. And that's where the interaction with this gentleman came in.

I've also relied on God through this whole recovery. Just help me push a little further so I can get feeling a little bit better and help me know when not to push and to know that this is what I needed to do, and just help me recover. I rely on Him every day. I don't know if I could have done it without Him.

I wasn't super public about what had happened until the recipient encouraged me to share my story. She did this for the longest time, but I didn't know what to say. I still don't totally know what to say.

I understand that this is a big decision, so it's not like I would go out and be a total advocate for donating kidneys because everybody has to make that decision on their own. And it is a big thing. But she pushed me to try and be more vocal.

It's also uncomfortable for me when people are like, "Oh my gosh, you saved her life!" I don't feel that. I also don't like the term "hero" or "angel" because people have called me both and it makes me uncomfortable. I was just a girl who did what I would hope anyone would do if it was my family member. I stepped up and that's all it is to me.

That said, I do get it. I get the biology of what I did and how giving her a kidney would help improve her quality of life. I just didn't get the psychology of it. That is, until I got back to Michigan and the community she lives in—the one where I'd grown up—which held a fundraiser for her to help offset some of her costs with time off, further recovery, and all of that.

It took place the night after I got in, after I completed my last round of testing. I went, and her dad was there, her brother was there, her aunts, uncles, cousins, you name it. I was not prepared for the effect the donation had on their lives too, and that was pretty touching for me.

Yet, the main reason I was donating was because I couldn't live with myself if I hadn't. One of my final tests when I find myself in any type of internal struggle is the test of regret. Would I regret it more if I did it, or would I regret more if I didn't do it? That made it easy because I knew I would absolutely regret it if I didn't do it.

There was also one point right before I was due to fly to Michigan when I was talking to the recipient on the phone and she said, "I probably should tell you that my cousin just found out he's a match." The first thing that went through my mind was that I was no longer her only solution. It lifted that burden.

"Heather," I said, "would you rather have your cousin's kidney?"

"No, I wouldn't."

"Okay, then."

Knowing that I wasn't the only match, I felt better about myself because I knew I was doing it for the right reasons—not because I had to, but because I felt it was what I needed to do. It was a huge mental shift.

In the end, I know there's a reason for all of this, a reason I decided to donate. Of course, my main goal was to get the recipient off dialysis and give her a better shot at life, but it feels like there was something more. I'm sure this isn't the end of the role that this has played in my life. I can even see myself speaking about it someday.

Ultimately, my goal in sharing my story is to give people a glimpse of my experience to help them better decide if this is the right decision for them. It would be nice to think that I could inspire someone to take a positive action because I've been inspired by people in many different ways.

Some people have inspired me to become the person I try hard to be. For instance, just looking at the women in my life, my mom inspires me to always do for others, to be there when they need me, and to always lend a helping hand. My step-mom inspires me to follow in her footsteps and be a great step-mom to my own step-daughter. My mother-in-law (whom we just recently lost) inspired me to find the good in any situation, to smile, to laugh, and to enjoy life for what it is. My older sister inspires me to give life my all and to always seek to understand where people are coming from.

I also draw a lot of inspiration from the men in my life. My dad has always been a hard worker and has taught me a lot about working for myself. Both my grandfathers were farmers, so I understand the value of hard work.

I'm also tremendously inspired by my husband, Matt. He is constantly striving to reach his maximum potential, to always achieve more, which encourages me to do the same. There is no stopping him from doing what he wants to do and nothing is out of the question—two philosophies I work hard to keep in the forefront of my mind as I move forward in this world.

I'm inspired by people who are thought of as "underdogs," those who, by all appearances and accounts, shouldn't have succeeded but did. They serve as reminders that it doesn't matter what types of obstacles are in our way, it is ultimately up to us how far we go in life. As long as we keep pushing forward, we'll eventually end up right where we need to be.

Even people who've played smaller roles in my life have inspired me to become a better, stronger, and more caring person. Like the older man I passed in the hall at work one day who told me I have a nice smile, inspiring me to share my own compliments with complete strangers because I know firsthand now how they can change the trajectory of their day. Or the woman in the checkout line at the grocery store who let me go in front of her because I only had two items and she had a full cart, inspiring me to share the same act of kindness when roles are reversed.

Others have inspired me in opposite ways, by motivating me to avoid becoming the person I don't want to be. For instance, I've had people in my life who I've previously called friends, only to have them walk away without so much as a reason why. This inspires me to not be that way with those I cherish. I've also had people cut me off, interrupt me, and seem generally disinterested in what I have to say, inspiring me to not portray these types of traits with those I love.

I have a sweet spot for anyone who has a dream not yet met, anyone who wants to be more, achieve more, or do more but just isn't sure how (or is too afraid) to proceed. Anyone who has not yet reached his or her maximum potential yet, despite the struggles, refuses to give up. These are the people I write to in my books, speak to in my seminars, and enjoy coaching one-on-one.

The world is full of inspiration in countless different forms. It's up to each of us to recognize what type of inspiration a particular person has to offer and figure out how to use it to help us become a better person.

What's the best advice I can offer to anyone seeking a little bit of inspiration? When trying to create a better life, we have two options: make excuses or make changes. Everything we do in life is a choice that either takes us one step closer to our goal or one step further away from it. As an example, choosing to eat a salad for lunch gets you one step closer to your goal of smaller jeans, whereas eating a donut takes you one step further.

Aim to make the majority of your choices ones which move you ahead. And when you falter (we all falter at some point), don't let a lapse turn into a relapse. Don't climb the staircase partway only to throw yourself to the bottom when you stumble on a middle step. Instead, catch yourself, re-stabilize, and continue to work your way toward the top.

Remember why you want what you want, why your dream is so important to you. Keep these whys handy for the days you just want to give up because, sometimes, they will be the only things that will get you through, the only things that will keep you pushing against all of the resistance you feel being thrown your way.

And when all else fails, rely on your faith. Whether it's a religious faith, a spiritual faith, or simply faith in yourself, know that you are on this path for a reason. There are skills and traits and characteristics you have that make you a unique asset to the world. Don't deny the rest of us the privilege of all you have to offer. Let your light shine because that is what it is meant to do.

TODAY I AM a freelance writer and specialize in writing and editing content related to health and wellness, personal development, personal safety, and small business success. I also offer services as a coach, helping anyone who wants to learn the art of writing or looking for help with improving their health.

I'm also a speaker with topics that center around motivation, change, success, and—thanks to my career in law enforcement—tips for how to protect yourself in this increasingly unstable world.

Sometimes I still let my fears get in my way but, overall, I've learned the value in looking for opportunities in situations that initially appear to be obstacles. I've also learned the value of being uncomfortable, because if I'm feeling uncomfortable, it means I'm moving ahead.

I've always been a big believer that people can do little things that impact others in a big way. A little kindness can go a long way. For instance, before the kidney donation, the surgeon asked me, "What's your favorite song?" I told him it was "Fight Song" by Rachel Platten.

"Alright," he said, "that song will be playing when you come into the OR."

The day of the donation, when they rolled me in, the song was on. To me, this was huge. By doing this one little thing, he made me a person. I wasn't just an organ donor.

Through the process, there were many times when people would ask, "Are you the donor?" I know that they didn't mean anything by it, but you almost lose your identity. You become "the kidney donor." But that doctor had made me a person again, in just that little bit of kindness.

And he kept a promise, which is also big for me. But even more than that, while the song was playing, this surgeon sat down and held my hand until I was out.

With all the bad things that happen in the world, those little kindnesses are what matter most. They're what inspire me to keep going, but to be an inspiration to others as well.

INSPIRING WOMEN TODAY

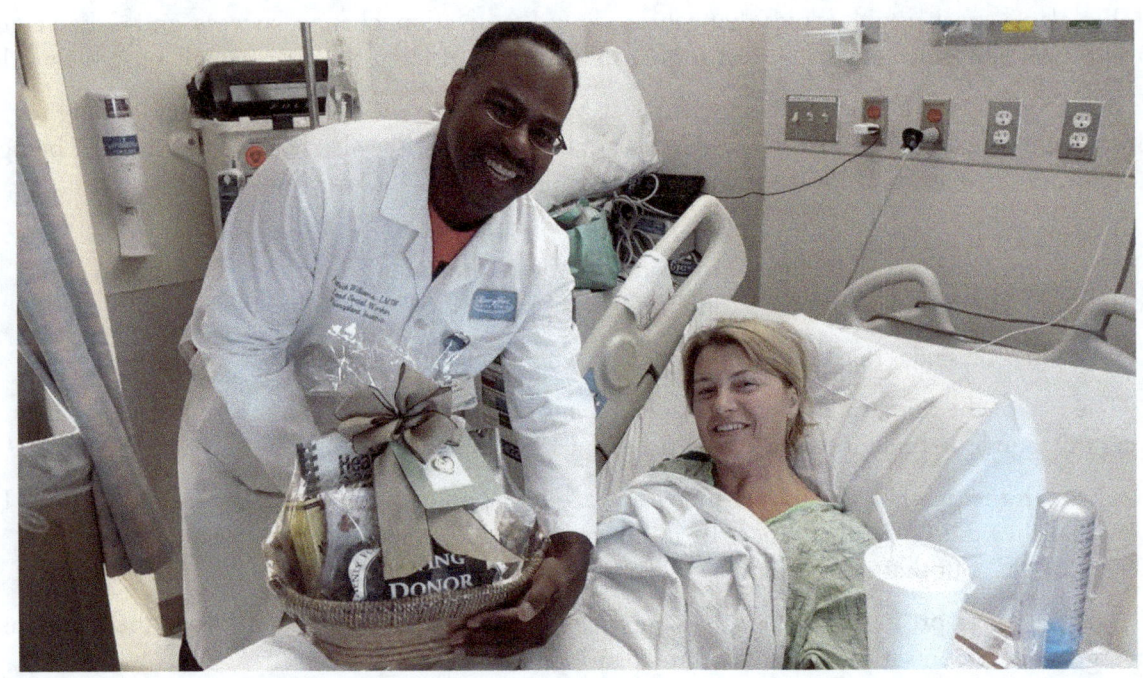

A LITTLE KINDNESS BY CHRISTINA DEBUSK

About Christina Debusk

Health Writer & Editor, Coach, and Speaker

Christina is the author of *Becoming Kidney-in-Laws: An Honest Look at What It's Like to Be a Living Kidney Donor* and other titles.

Contact her at christina@christinamdebusk.com

www.CHRISTINAMDEBUSK.com

[7]

WOMEN & CHILDREN FIRST
by Stella Ssemakula

> "If you educate a man, you educate and individual, but if you educate a woman, you educate a community."
> —AFRICAN PROVERB

I GREW UP as an orphan and was raised by a single mother. My father died when I was four years old, so I didn't get to know him. And so, all my life, I was taken care of by my mother. When I was a child, I used to watch Oprah and I followed her story. I always wanted to work on TV shows and be able to talk to people like Oprah. I used to see her videos and movies here, and I really wanted to be like Oprah Winfrey. Unfortunately, I didn't do that course. It was a very expensive course that I couldn't afford. So, I studied social sciences. There are two things here that can prevent a child from going to school. One is that they have to pay money to attend school, but they are poor. And second, there is a cultural problem. If the grandmother and the mother didn't go to school, they may see no reason for education. So that needs a culture change and telling their children, "No, we are in a civilized world. You need to go to school." There are two barriers, then—poverty but also the cultural system that some people didn't go to school, so they don't value education.

Growing up as orphans, there were four of us—two brothers and one other sister. My mother was the sole provider of every basic need. We had our aunties and uncles who would come in once in a while and bring us food, bring us clothes, and we also got some sponsorship from charity organizations. There was a project that supported poor children, and one of my brothers was supported there. And the rest of us could only be in day schools. We would walk from home to school, and that's how we had our education. During school time we would be with our mother and then during holidays we would go on and stay with our grandmother because it was so hard to buy food in town during holiday time. So, we would go to the village and cultivate food. This food (that we used to cultivate) would be transported to the suburb where we lived with our grandmother when we were in school. That's how we were able to go to school, have some education, and grow up.

I see how education can help someone make a better life. I went to school. That's the reason I can speak some English. If I didn't go to school, I wouldn't know what to do—I'd be in a village now, digging food and just being there, doing nothing, just cooking food. So, thanks to the education, I'm able to help other women and children.

I am Stella, and I'm married to Patrick. I live in Uganda in Masaka district. We have four children and I work with a project called the Women Reliance Foundation. I wasn't born in Masaka. I was born in Mubende in western Uganda, but I live in the town suburb of Masaka district.

In Africa, life is not so easy, given the circumstances of poverty. It's basically an agricultural country. The vegetation is tropical, and the main activity here in Africa that people do is farming. We grow the food and also sell the food. So, most of the people rely on agriculture for survival.

I don't have a car but we have motorcycles that you can hire and you can go anywhere. It's called boda-boda. So, you pay some fee to the person and then they take you to where you are going and they can also pick you up. So, it is the easiest and fastest transport that we use here but also we have cars to hire. If you want to go to a place that is at a distance, if you don't have a personal car, then you can use that, you can hire a car.

Most of the people are below the poverty line and most of them are children and women. The men try to ignore their responsibilities so there's a lot of suffering for the children and the women to meet their daily basic needs. Domestic violence has affected the children and the women as well.

I don't know what the problem is, but men here make the women pregnant and then do not follow up on their responsibilities. So, you find that women here are single mothers who are struggling alone and the men have ignored them. I don't say that they are so poor they can't work and support, but they ignore. It's polygamy, getting different women. Some are teenage mothers, children who dropped out of school due to pregnancy. So, they are all hopeless. And the husband is also young, not knowing what to do next and how to take care of the child. And others are widows. Their husbands died due to HIV. But most women here are married but their husbands are not able to support their families. I don't know why. I don't know the answer but it happens here and it's common.

Some men go away but some are there but they're alcoholic and have other women. So, they tend to ignore the family needs and whatever income comes in goes to alcohol and women and they ignore that the children have to go to school, have to put on new clothes, have to eat well. Such responsibilities are ignored.

So, I am trying to share the circumstances of women here in Uganda.

IN UGANDA, WOMEN are 50 percent of the total population of 45 million (2017). So, most of the population is women and children. Given my background of being raised as an orphan and with a single mother, I have this passion of helping and supporting women who are going through the circumstance that I also lived through and understand. And that's basically the background of Women Reliance Foundation, to help and support women and children so that they are in a better situation.

Part of how we do this is with micro loans, by getting support for businesses. We also do charity. We do charity to those who are totally poor and not able to run a business. And those who already have a business, we support them with financial support of what they're already doing and we also train them on how they can grow their business. We work with underprivileged women and women who didn't go to school and cannot access. So, we usually work with market vendors, those who work in the shops. And we work with women selling agricultural products, who sell second-hand clothes, shoes, and those women who work in shops and mobile money services. We also have those who work in roadside restaurants and those who hawk different products, looking for people to buy items like clothes or agricultural products like tomatoes or potatoes. Charcoal is a fuel used here for people to cook their food. We have women who also sell charcoal.

The way we started is we had women's groups where we could meet for faith-based inputs. And from those groups, we said, "We need to empower women," because one of the things that hits women here is poverty. So, that's how it came about. There was me and there were two other women who already were doing this kind of work that encouraged me and supported me to go ahead and support women who are in poverty, who are poor. We can support them to get out of the poverty that they are in.

For example, Viola is one of our clients and she sells agricultural products and charcoal. She's married with six children but the husband is not so helpful. We've had Viola through our training, teaching her how she can grow her business by not using the business money in family needs. And through the records, you see that she is progressing and making more profits because she's having more sales in her business. So, we have supported her to grow financially in what she sells but also we helped her to support her life at home because she's able now to buy some milk for her children and also buy the items that children need at home.

And this happens in our Christian community I belong to. There's a community sponsorship program that I work with two days in a week, and then in the three days we work with Women Reliance. We go to the women and follow up with those who have got the loans and also train those who will then be able to get the loans. So, that's how my week goes. So it is like three days in a week but I do it throughout the week. I also have two days with the sponsorship for children. It is a project for supporting children who are not in school or those that have dropped out of school. It works directly with the women. So, the women who are struggling so much, we get people who can donate to sponsor these children into school. These women who are orphans or vulnerable children are supported in school. It's called Impact.

MY DREAM IS more people will support us and these communities will continue to grow and women will continue to get more support and there will be less poverty. That's what I hope for. I hope people will come on board to support the women, they'll come on board to come and visit the women and see how they live and join hands and make life of these women better. The best way to do that is through supporting Women Reliance Foundation and coming and visiting us here in Africa.

Come and visit and see the women, their struggles, how they live, the life they live in, their businesses. There are those who make products also, maybe see how they can sell their products. I don't know if in your country people would buy craft, but some women make craft here and it would be good if they would get people there who would buy the craft.

I would like to inspire the children who are hopeless, giving them hope that they can make it in this life, that they can change their life. If they want out of their circumstance, something good can happen to them. And my passion lies between the two categories of people—women and children. I want to inspire women that they can do something to change their situation, not to just sit and do nothing about their lives and circumstances.

Being a part of this book is an inspiration and I'm inspired by this chance and opportunity. Thank you very much. It would be great to have you visit and I would love to meet you someday.

> "Financial inclusion helps lift people out of poverty and can help speed economic development. It can draw more women into the mainstream of economic activity, harnessing their contributions to society."
>
> —SRI MULYANI INDRAWATI
> Minister of Finance of Indonesia

INSPIRING WOMEN TODAY

No poverty is a long-term goal that can realized. Our team works tirelessly to achieve sustainable communities in Masaka by training abandoned women, widows, and single mothers in micro-businesses, connecting them to resources and equipping them to lift themselves and their families out of poverty.

About Stella Ssemakula
AND THE WOMEN RELIANCE FOUNDATION

Help our team reach its objective by donating to our work.

Find out more here: www.womenreliance.org

And donate here: https://tinyurl.com/womenreliance

Thank you!

[8]

OUT OF HIDING

by Kristina Savka

> "He only earns his freedom and existence
> who daily conquers them anew."
> —JOHANN WOLFGANG VON GOETHE

"JUST WHO DO you think you are, eh?"

My right hand was poised over the kitchen sink. In it I held an empty breakfast plate. I still had the smile from a giggled greeting to my friends, the giraffes and monkeys that lived in the bottom of the bowl.

I turned my head to face the direction from which the rhetorical question had boomed at me. I stared and I felt his eyes burn into mine, even though he was several paces away at the doorway to the kitchen. I froze, one foot planted on the top rung of a two-step stool (I was tall for my age but still couldn't reach comfortably). My knuckles whitened as I instinctively gripped the gilt-patterned edge of the plate tightly in my hand. My world seemed to slip into slow motion as I cringed for what seemed like minutes, but in truth was probably mere seconds.

"But, but Dad, what have I—?" I did not get the opportunity to ask what had brought on his outburst.

My father interrupted and his lips curled as he yelled, "Shut up, you little upstart!" He stomped toward me. The kitchen's polished timber floorboards creaked as he approached. He did not need to touch me physically—his threatening stare was enough to hold me transfixed at the sink.

What have I done? Stunned into silence, this time I asked the question of myself in all my childish naivety. My brain raced as I searched frantically for some fragment of understanding of this parental outburst. As hurriedly as my immature brain could process them I sifted through that morning's events, those of yesterday, the day before and the days before that.

Nothing.

There was not one thing in my recent conduct to which I could attribute my father's behavior. As he came closer I averted my eyes and focused on the book lying open on the kitchen table. I hesitantly said, "Look Dad, that's what I want to be when I grow up, a famous princess like that, with such beautiful dresses and jewelry and long, dark hair, and I'll marry a handsome prince and we'll . . ." I had just expressed, in my most confident ten year-old manner, who I wanted to be when I grew up. You know, that voice of innocence a more mature soul could describe in words as, *I can do and say what I want. I can be anything I want. I'm a bright shining star full of wonder, joy, anticipation, of discovery and fulfillment of all that life will offer.*

I was not that more mature person. I was a ten-year-old child, but even without the language skills to articulate my dreams, I knew my strength would, one day, make those beliefs come true. That day, with my father now looming over me, was not going to be it. My inner voice and that shining star were extinguished, shattered into a million pieces of shadowy remnants of me.

"Think you're Little Miss High and Mighty, don't you? Don't get big ideas you'll never be able to realize, kid. Life's not going to be like that. Stop living in Fairyland. That way you won't be so disappointed."

If only this had been the first harsh lesson in my young life. Sadly, it was only the latest of many scars, some mental, some more obvious, inflicted on my innocent, trusting childhood by my father. By my reckoning, it started when I was three years old. In my small world nothing made sense except the feeling of fear that something terrible was about to take place simply by the charged energy I lived in every day. On this particular occasion the physical violence was exacerbated by not greeting my uncle promptly when he arrived to visit. My father flew across the room in an angry rage and seized my little three-year-old body and started to hit me repeatedly. My uncle watched in horror, stepping in to save me and release me from my father's grip. The hell was over but the scars would run deep and the shame would linger many years to come, setting me up for the choices I would make later in my life.

I NOW KNOW what motivated my father's behavior throughout my childhood. With the benefit of adult comprehension, I can see that the man who tried to crush my childhood spirit with his negative, dismissive, and threatening behavior had, incredibly, himself become a victim of the same abuse and control from *his* father. It was his own deep, unprocessed childhood wounds inflicted on him by his father, my grandfather, which was the catalyst for his ever-more inappropriate conduct. I am not a mental health professional but, if I had to guess, my layperson's intuition would lead me to believe that my precociousness, my spirit, my confidence as a child, even from my very early years (but particularly as a strong-willed female child) somehow exposed and threatened my fathers' inadequacy in his role as father and husband.

I hold no grudge against my father. To do so would simply perpetuate the literal and metaphorical slaps on the face I suffered as his daughter. These days I see my father as a man morphed into a meek, subservient, shell of a man, totally afraid to speak his own mind or make a decision for fear of constant retribution and control from his domineering wife, my stepmother. I do however, in moments of self-indulgence, let a wry smile cross my face as I think of the idiom, *What goes around comes around.* Some call it karma.

My mother became my safe haven and I started to cling to her. She would try to console my wounds but never managed to heal them. In my naivety, I thought fixing things was a parent's job. How wrong I was. Sadly, I watched my mother fall victim to depression after years of living with abuse and slip into a world I could never reach for many years.

Earlier in my life, I saw my mother as a survivor and she would use all she knew to be okay in a man's world. Her superpowers were her looks and the ability to groom herself, to be impeccably presentable and fashionable. My mother always instilled in me a pride in my presentation and to always be ready to take on the world well-groomed. But my mother's beauty grooming led to an altogether different type of grooming. Between the ages of 5 and 15, I faced a situation even more challenging than my father's often-violent behavior. I was molested over that decade by a pedophile.

A trusted member of our community started to take an interest in me. I was flattered, even as a five-year-old, by his attention and affection for me. I have recollections of thinking how proud my mother must have felt that someone was appreciating the beautiful child she had created. That childish beauty was to exact a terrible price. My dignity, my innocence, my trust—all were to fall victim to this predator, year, after year, after year. The community to which our family belonged had an unspoken creed: stay silent—there could be no scandal. I lived by that creed in fear, suffering in silence, enduring the pain, struggling in the later years of that period with a confusion my adolescent brain could not resolve.

To mask the hurt to my mind and body, I committed to learn my mother's craft which so inspired me. So clever with her hands, she taught me to sew and to use my hands as instruments to give form, through the medium of textiles, to the creations I increasingly had swirling around in my head. At five years old I had already started to absorb her knowledge and produce simple but well-made items. As my unquenchable thirst for knowledge of all things fashion progressed, I became evermore drawn to its allure. The myriad textures of fabrics, the visual stimulation of color, the aesthetic poetry almost, of form and style so excited me that fashion became my escape, another world in which I could mask my fears.

In my teenage years I quickly used my creative power to create Fashion that simply made me hide who I was. Growing up in a dysfunctional home was so challenging at the time and I had no other tools to use to help me survive and get through things other than this amazing talent of reinventing myself with interesting fashion ideas. I would use different eras in history to become a fashion chameleon. The fashion trick had worked and I got noticed but always in a way to put focus on my talent and disguise my pain. This suited me just fine since I had already learnt from a young age that it was not okay to be me or have a voice for that matter. My traumatic childhood was the perfect excuse to hide who I was, and fashion was the perfect camouflage tool.

As I aged, the thrill of the creative process became so profound that I am not ashamed to say I became a perfectionist and I think it is fair to say that the whole fashion milieu intoxicated me. I simply fell in love with the industry, with all its component disciplines. From the minutiae of fine stitching, to the grand kaleidoscope of colors, the kinetic excitement of swirls and flounces, sometimes the sheer grace of simplicity of design, parades, modeling, I simply fell in love with Fashion. It was my first love and I have never left its embrace. More than ever it is my enduring passion and has been my profession for over three decades.

My welcome to the real world came in my forties when I started to feel how much *I was tired of hiding*. I needed to be me. I desperately wanted to just be me, to be seen for who I am and not what I could create. I needed to become truly visible for who *I* was and am today. I needed to process what happened to me and how I could come out of hiding, and feel *safe to be me*—unapologetically me!

WHEN I LOOK at old family photos, I can see that even as a baby my mother fussed over my appearance. I would come to know the discomfort for the sake of beauty was worth bearing. I grew to believe that a little pain and suffering in order to achieve true beauty was a girl's lot in life. *How I would come to rue the pursuit of beauty.*

My earliest memory of *shame* came at the age of five. In the evenings my mother would painstakingly put rollers and pins in my hair and tell me how pretty I would look, with my dark, shining curls. I would wriggle and complain that I could not sleep because of the discomfort of the rollers. They had spikes in them to hold the hair in place. I asked my mother, "How am I supposed to sleep with this in my hair?"

"Oh never mind about sleep, dear," she said, "Just imagine how pretty you will look in the morning."

With saucer-wide eyes I stared at my mother and tried to imagine what I would look like with gorgeous curls in the morning. Sleeping was truly uncomfortable but I began to understand *that to achieve beauty, pain is normal.* This was to be my motto for a long time in achieving the perfect look just to fit in and be accepted. This was the beginning of a nightmare that would last a decade when all this looking good would attract a pedophile in our local religious community and the grooming began.

No one would believe the horror that would last a decade because speaking up was discouraged and in no way acceptable for me to make any scandal in the community. So the silence and pain and confusion continued until I escaped that community finally as a young 15-year-old.

As a child growing up, witnessing my father's violent rages and irrational behavior in the home created so much fear in me. I was a sensitive child and being the first born I always felt responsible for my siblings. They would always be up to mischief, but I always ended up getting the blame and being punished along with them. My father's motto was that *if they got into trouble, we all got into trouble*. I witnessed my own mother get into trouble, being hit in a corner of a room where she could not escape for not changing my baby brother's nappy when he had wet himself. The punishment never suited the crime. We were only small children, but punishment included violence, which seemed normal in the 1970s.

This horrible homelife caused me to lose my voice, literally. The fear was so great I found myself stuttering, afraid I would say the wrong thing and get into trouble. Stuttering created extremely deep shame and caused such horrible embarrassment that would last for more than 25 years. At the time I thought, this is my eternal fate and I would never be normal. After my parents' divorce the stuttering got so bad, a psychologist (one my mother was seeing for her depression) suggested I have no contact with my father for a year. This was successful until the day I answered a call from my father and the stuttering came back. I was so horrified that all that good work learning to speak again had come undone. I realized this fear was deeply ingrained in me (It would take years to finally lose the stuttering.). My whole world became confusing. It seemed the only way to make sense of it all was to keep creating a persona I could be comfortable enough to show up in, and so no one knew what was happening.

Years later when I landed the enviable role as the online host for CHTV, a platform used to showcase business owners and their services, I couldn't believe how far I had come. A stuttering girl who felt so embarrassed to be heard, to one day be a fluent speaker and lead the conversation helping others become seen and heard.

IN THE 1970s women did not have much of a voice or the inclination to speak up as we see today, and any scandal caused by what a woman said was heavily shunned. Here is where I learnt that speaking up was not accepted and I was discouraged to create any attention toward myself in any way. The deep shame I felt from my childhood wounds would take years to heal and overcome.

It was not easy being a migrant in the 1970s. For starters, there was horrible name calling, like being called a "wog[22]." *Just another excuse to hide again,* I thought, so I changed my name from Kristina to Christine. *There*, I thought, *I'll fit in now and no one will bother me.* How wrong I was. The reality of what I had done had not yet fully sunk in because needing to be liked was huge on a teenager's agenda. I didn't yet fully understand how I had robbed myself by hiding *my name*. It would take a few years to see the folly of such an act. Luckily, I discovered my birth name was a bit more *exotic* and suited my fashion persona after I graduated from fashion college.

Hiding was becoming addictive and normal. My teenage years were turbulent. I was always dodging verbal and emotional bullets that I seemed to attract into my life. *Why me?* was always on my mind as I tried to navigate the most challenging of years trying to fit in. From as early as I can remember I was placed on a pedestal by my mother who adored me in her dysfunctional way but who also set me up to fail in the real world. I would encounter many challenges from my peers wanting to tear me down so they could feel better about themselves. I was hated and despised for

---

[22] Wog: noun Chiefly British Slang: Extremely Disparaging and Offensive. a contemptuous term used to refer to any nonwhite person, especially a dark-skinned native of the Middle East or Southeast Asia. — https://www.dictionary.com/browse/wog

being creative and always looking like I was better than anyone else, *Just another reminder of my father's word*s.

From a very early age I had learnt the art of expertly applying makeup. This medium was the perfect tool to compliment my fashion outfits and create a mask I would wear for a very long time. My skin would never see the sunlight. I was too afraid to be seen without my mask. I would meticulously spend hours getting made up in the mornings just to leave the house and be seen.

When I was 18 years old it was difficult for me to be seen physically without any make up. My first serious boyfriend would occasionally spend the night at my place on a weekend. I was so used to being this *made-up fashion queen*, I had so much fear because I had to wake up early, go into the bathroom, and put on all that makeup as meticulously as I could, doing the best job to look so natural. I then slinked back into bed, wanting to look as if I had just woken up like this.

"Hi, good morning," I said, as you do being a very insecure 18-year-old from a really painful life of abuse. It was clear I was really hiding.

"What are you doing with makeup this time of the morning in bed?" He asked.

He can see me? I gasped. *My goodness I went to so much effort to look so natural.* I must have spent an hour in that bathroom trying to make myself look as natural as I could, and yet he saw straight through it. The irony of it was that in my mind I thought no one would see or know my tricks. It was at that point the mask was starting to somewhat crumble, but it would take many years to finally be comfortable enough to not wear makeup at all and be okay with it.

THESE DAYS I'M fully okay to just be me and I laugh at the silliness of doing such a thing as I did back then. I can now see how the loss of my identity could create such a need to hide and invent something other than *me*. You can only imagine the liberation of finally removing those shackles of shame that created my need to hide in the first place. For the first time my skin breathed a sigh of relief in my late 30s after the arrival of my first child. There simply was no more time to hide.

It has taken many personal development courses to become who I am today. It took courage to speak up. It took strength to own my voice. It took resilience to survive. My journey into personal development began in my mid-20s when I started to search for answers as to what actually happened to me and why. The books on human psychology I discovered helped me to truly understand the human mind, and helped me make some sense of the mess. But it would take many more years to fully understand why people do what they do to hurt others.

This discovery was the beginning of my breakthrough. It was the beginning of understanding and compassion. It literally took years of coming out of hiding to become comfortable enough to be *myself*.

It started with accepting myself. It started with forgiving myself.

To arrive at acceptance I had to learn true self-love and what that looked like. I had been a victim of violence for such a long time, loving myself was just not on the agenda. The only thing on my mind was normally, *How will I survive this day?*

In my 40s I started to truly understand what self-love was all about. I remember looking in the mirror one day and sincerely saying to my reflection, "You are beautiful just as you are and I love who you are."

From that day it's as if someone gave me tremendous power to be me.

It was me. I gave myself this permission

I started to see my fashion skills in putting myself together as a fantastic tool, and in a whole new way. I was now using fashion as a doorway to creating my unique style to shine, and to show up being my true self, not caring what others thought or said. I was finally free to be me. I started to understand the difference between *fashion* and *personal style*. Later on, being consistent in who I was and how I showed up with my personal style meant that people could trust who I was. It became my personal brand. I didn't need to keep reinventing myself anymore. I could just simply be me.

Style became my new way of showing up and I never wore "fashion" again.

I learnt self-expression in the form of personal style is my best communicator to the world. I discovered how I was going to show up for the rest of my days and fully own it.

My style was becoming synonymous with who I am and people started to notice the consistency of who I was being.

This new way of being was so liberating!

THE FIRST TIME I found myself fully confident to own my voice, be seen, and be heard was presenting on camera in the late 1990s. I remember being asked by a producer to sell a product in an infomercial to a large Asian audience. He said my voice was golden and my energy was magnetic on camera. This was the start of my foray into the world of TV. To think this girl who couldn't speak clearly or without a stutter would become a *speaker* was just unfathomable. Yet here I was owing my voice taking up space, and allowing myself to be seen as *me* and loving it. It took a lot of courage to be me in front of the camera and *show up*. But I did it. Those years spent growing, learning, and loving myself paid off big time.

The journey of showing up live in front of others first began in 2000, in front of a classroom full of eager students willing to learn my first love, fashion design. The students gave me fantastic feedback and it was the start of me showing up and giving value and others accepting me for who I am on a whole new level. This new confidence was now my superpower. I learnt that being me was okay, and that what I had to say and how I showed up was valuable to others on their journey.

These days I take great pleasure in helping others to discover their unique style and how they will show up in the world and achieve what they are here to do. The tragedies and losses I have experienced in my past have made me into the woman I am today.

One of my biggest transformations came when I became a mother. Raising children took life to a whole new level of being me. Early in my children's youth, I asked myself, *What will I teach them? Who do I need to be?* and *How will I show up?*

My children were the catalyst for me becoming the most authentic self I have ever been in my life. There is no hiding when it comes to children. They see and know more than you can ever imagine, it's just that they may not always know how to articulate what they know but they do see you—and see all of you. There is no hiding.

Ultimately the degree of my transformation and change came from my connection to my higher power. I grew up with the idea of a loving God but the tragedies in our close knit religious community pushed God out of my life for a long time. As I navigated through life and tried to do it on my own terms, I clearly made many mistakes, seeking love in all the wrong places, chasing after things that never satisfied and messing things up along the way. I realized being open to a divine calling and fulfilling my mission here on Earth was going to take something bigger than me. In the messiness of my life, I reached out to the divine for inspiration and guidance and I've never looked back. I won't ever try to do it alone again.

Is life easier? No! But it sure is lighter and clearer as I realize that in all circumstances there are invaluable lessons for my life.

One of the most important lessons was learning the power of forgiveness which became my guiding light.

After many years being a victim of abuse, I have finally cracked the code. With divine grace I freed myself. Resilience has been my greatest tool. I have learnt to love myself on a whole new, truthful level.

I have learnt to drown out the negative voices.

I have learnt the power of forgiveness toward myself and others.

I have found my voice to speak up, be seen, and be heard.

I am a living testimony that all things work together for good for those who believe it is possible and rely on divine power every day.

We do not have to be victims of our past because the past can only exist in the present by choice. We choose if we will bring it back to life in our minds and speech therefore each day is an opportunity to renew, recharge, and refresh.

To be in the zone of flow and abundance there must be a shedding of the past, with all its weight and burden.

I live by this motto, "Let go and let God."

Written by Kristina Savka, edited by Rodney Miles Taber

About Kristina Savka

Signature Style Strategist and Camera Confidence Coach

Founder, The Amplified Women Collective

www.KRISTINASAVKA.com.au

[9]

THE HOLISTIC APPROACH

by Lisa Johnson

"Vulnerability is the birthplace of connection and the path to the feeling of worthiness. If it doesn't feel vulnerable, the sharing is probably not constructive."

—BRENÉ BROWN

O NE THING I WAS AWARE of growing up, because I've always been prone to deep and meaningful conversations, to deep connections with people and girlfriends, when I was maybe just finished with high school that caused me to go, "Oh my goodness," even before I had that rape myself, was that the majority of my girlfriends, those I was hanging out with, have had some form of abuse. You wouldn't have thought that, and you couldn't have predicted that sort of number.

This subject has been such an issue with privacy, embarrassment, shame, and all the rest of it, because it does tend to crumble somebody's confidence so greatly, it's definitely not usually something that somebody will say, "Hey, guess what? This has happened to me." But with that movement (#MeToo), it's made people go, "Well, guess what? That's similar to my story," or "I've had some aspects of that myself."

People hearing this are often remarkably surprised because they're going, "Oh my God. Well, that hasn't stopped you in your tracks," or "That doesn't look like a big worry wound we can visibly see."

In my psychology practice I'm big on supporting both physical health as well as emotional and psychological wellbeing. Many of my clients tell me, "I wish I had a physical thing that people could look at and therefore understand better what happened to me, versus just psychological stuff," because it's hard to understand or appreciate these things unless you've walked in those shoes or had similar experiences yourself.

When people do find themselves in similar places, they often say, "It wasn't until I was sitting on the couch myself that I actually understood how crumbling anxiety or depression can be, how debilitating it can be." A lot of clients I see say, "I'm so much more nonjudgmental about so many aspects in life because I've really hit rock bottom and I wouldn't have thought I could've ever gotten to this place."

Yet this is a common story when I'm working with people: "It was back when I was four," or "back when I was eight," or "back when I was twelve," and "the perpetrator was eight years older than me," or "ten years older than me." It's quite typical in the clinic. And further, "Yeah, it was definitely kept quiet," or "Lisa, you're the first person I've ever told," or "I finally just told my mother right now," or "Nobody would've believed me back then." Occasionally you do hear, "I told my mom."

Often the people I see in the clinic—and a part of the reason I see them in the clinic—is they have been *forbidden* to share and forbidden to disclose, and they don't want to upset anyone else. They know how much upset it's caused *them*, why would they want to inflict pain on somebody else, especially now that they aren't able to protect them? I mean, when they've got loving parents, they would hate for their parents to know this is actually what happened to them. And guess what? The abuse might've been perpetrated by a brother, an uncle, a family relative. How much more upsetting is that?

Survivors are remarkable people. They do remarkable, selfless things.

I've seen quite a few clients of late, too, who were preyed upon by a brother or other family member, typically a man. Some of these men end up developing into good citizens and good people in the world, so there's a real hardship for the victim now because they end up being kind of proud of these people, if yet disgusted and disappointed as well. I like to think we're at a turning point, though. It's a privilege of my work to see how the victims—my clients—can actually turn a corner with some of these people and face them or challenge them or have some sort of closure themselves.

So I was standing around this circle of friends when I was a teenager talking about this and I could honestly say *seven or eight out of ten* of my girlfriends had been abused or assaulted sexually in a significant way growing up. I was born in 1979, so that wasn't the dark ages, but goodness, it was still a pretty closed, shutdown sort of time to talk about such things. Interesting. The women and young adults who I see the clinic today are far more forward typically, and far more enabled to realize the impacts and discuss it all.

Today people speaking out is a big thing. There's a lot more gender equality. There is a lot more education and there are more opportunities in general for women today. This is why I did my master's in organizational psychology. Our workplaces are our biggest thing that can hurt or hinder us, and we need more equality, we need more health and wellbeing instilled and supported in our spaces. With that comes equality for all diversities, whether that's gender, ethnicity, or cultural diversity. Communication and globalization, in a positive sense, have moved things forward, and there is a lot more awareness about diversity across the world today. Everyone has their own story, and that's what's beautiful.

Because of my dyslexia and learning difficulties, I don't choose to read books for a hobby. I almost say "my books are people" I meet, work with, and learn from. I tend to think I've missed out in certain aspects of learning because of my learning difficulties, but I've just learnt differently. I learn through conversation and I learn through emotion. In anyone's story, if there have been factors which stop a person or which limit their ability to realize their own potential and therefore make meaningful contributions in life, that is a massive loss. And this is the point. When you work with people and support them to develop, they may be able to go out and make meaningful differences in the world, to help others more broadly, and to tune into things more amazingly. So, that's what we want to do for people.

It's still quite common for females in the world to experience abuse of some kind, unfortunately, as I did. But what also had a profound effect upon me was my learning difficulty. That, right from a young age, affected my reading, my writing, my comprehension, my ability to interact with that learning environment, and my ability to feel confident and smart and intelligent. Even in kindy (kindergarten), I was kept down a year, so I was pegged early on and evaluated as someone who would struggle when it came to learning. Certainly, in grade one, it was definitely "She's trying hard, but from that learning aspect or developmental aspect there, she's really struggling." So in terms of my self-esteem and self-confidence and where I thought I might sit in the world, I was not sure I was going to fit into a workforce or feel that I was going to be useful in the world. That sense of purpose, for me, was actually more important and more significant than any physical abuse. Every day I'm faced with challenges associated with my learning difficulties. It's a daily thing. It's not every day that I'm faced with challenges around my abuse.

But the learning issues has actually been what's made me a better person in the world, a more innovative person, and a more collaborative person, because I've realized that I can't be all things to all people and I certainly can't do all things to a really high level. But today I am considered a highly educated person. I owe a lot of that to my father. My dad was schoolteacher and he would sit with me at night and help me edit my assignments. He would sit beside me and help me understand what the question was in the assignment and what they were asking for. So we were able to work together and I did okay in school as far as my grades, but all of that was a struggle. The learning style they applied to all children never actually suited my way of learning, and we didn't have alternatives like we have for learning today.

My parents were a little bit naïve, and they sent me to a speed-reading course when I was in grade twelve. I was sitting there in the speed-reading course, and the lady who ran it said to my parents, "I think it's a little bit more than Lisa needing to learn a technique for the speed reading. I think she's actually having some significant difficulties with reading and she might have some learning things going on. How about you send her to a learning consultant, an person who specializes in that?" She then ran through a series of questions with me and she said, "Look, I suspect you have a significant learning difficulty, but, obviously, I'm not a psychologist, so go along to a psychologist."

So I went on to the educational psychologist in my final year of high school. We went through her assessment (one of which was the Child Intelligence Scale), and she said, "Yeah, look, your reading age is equivalent to a twelve-year-old." I was nearly eighteen. "And your writing skills, same thing," she said. It was woeful.

I remember receiving those results and crying—crying out of sadness, crying out of release, crying out of, "Oh my goodness. There's a significant reason why I have a problem with this. No wonder I've been trying so hard, harder than everyone else, to get through the hoops, and needing the support of my dad."

I then went along to a behavioral optometrist, and she said to me, "Apart from the fact that you have learning difficulties and dyslexia, tracking and reading along the lines is not going to work so well for you because your optic nerve on one of your eyes hasn't developed to the same amount as the other one. That makes reading *fatiguing* and I see you switching off after you've been reading for a short period of time. There's a biological thing that's going on for you as well as the cognitive aspects of things."

Again, I cried tears of relief and tears of frustration, going, "These things should've been identified when I was in grade one, or grade three, five, as they're being identified now for children."

Once it was identified it was something that could be managed somewhat. In the last part of grade twelve they said to me, "Oh, we'll actually give you extra time to finish off your assessment pieces, your exams in school," so I was able to finish my exams for the first time ever. So instead of having three hours, I had four hours. The issue is becoming cognitively *drained*. When your processing speed is already slow, your brain is already having to work really hard to get that information in. Then, to have an extended period of time, it's more like an endurance race. Nevertheless, I had more time to read and sit there and focus versus never being able to complete an exam before in my life. So that was remarkable.

My dad said to me (bless him), "Look, you're not clinically smart, Leese." This was at the end of high school. I'd managed to get into university for environmental or health science (my dad was a big greenie and I loved the environment and I loved health, so it was one or the other). He said to me, "You're not going to find that easy, Leese. And how are you going to do it? You really need to be living over there, near the university, and I can't help you with the editing, so how am I—"

And I thought, *It's alright. I'm not a natural academic or a natural learner. The system's not geared for people like me.* So it was ten years before I got to university because of all those feelings and experiences.

Yet because my parents exposed me to such diverse people as I grew up, I did learn good communication skills outside of my peers. I was really shy with my peers because of identity, sexuality, tomboy stuff, so I had an interest in connecting with people who were interested in connecting with *me*. So, in addition to very good social and communication skills, I developed an intense interest and curiosity in *people*, and that's what led me to pursue health as my profession, along with my ability to connect with people.

The *gift* of the learning difficulty was that I had to learn through other ways and means, and found anything with *emotion* easier to assimilate. If you told me an emotional story, I'd remember it. If you told me what "adjectives, verbs, and nouns are," or anything to do with grammar (rules), I really wouldn't be able to regurgitate that back to you, and I wouldn't remember the rules, either.

"Leese," you might have said to me, "this isn't grammatically correct because of this and this."

I'd say, "I've got nothing."

If you *sang* it to me and gave me some emotion or stories around it, I'd remember those rules and I'd remember those systems amazingly well. Even ten years later, I'd meet you again and I'd say, "I remember when you told me that particular story. It was significant around this and that and how that linked to your own personal story, how you discovered some abuse in the family. In fact I remember even more detail that you gave me on that, because that was interesting." That creates a holistic picture in my mind.

And that's what brought me to *complementary (alternative) medicine*. In grade twelve my parents decided to finally spend some money on these learning difficulties, so they gave me some assistance by way of an educational consultant again. She went through the basics with me—reading and writing—right after high school. Remarkable. It was just lovely to have that one-on-one attention, actually, to support me academically, even though I had no reason to use it then because I wasn't going to be going to university. But, in doing that, I found there was that *connection*.

Then someone said to me, "Go and see a kinesiologist."

"A *what?*" I said. "I can't even read the word or say it or understand it. What are you talking about?"

"Oh," they said, "they work with learning difficulties and other things. They'll be able to help you."

"Whoa," I asked, "they'll be able to get inside my head and re-wind it and tighten up things? What're you talking about?"

After about six months of persistence, I finally decided I'd give it a try. I went and saw a kinesiologist, and it was *remarkable* what he thought about my learning and the aspects to do with my brain integration. He even surmised, "You didn't crawl much as a baby, did you?"

Surprised, I said, "No! My parents told me I just pulled myself up and started walking."

"Oh, okay," he said, and he explained, "That would have neurologically affected your wiring and your visual memory and other things, and there are these different learning processes that were really not where they should've been, so you didn't have the foundational abilities for learning back then."

Kinesiology was the turning point in my life, where this stuff started to make sense and I started to have me tools and strategies to open up those learning pathways.

"I've always wanted to have somebody to take on as a trainee," this therapist said to me, "and I think I've found that person. Can you run my clinic? Can I train you up?"

I learnt massaging from one of my dear friend when I was about thirteen and loved giving massages just because I loved helping. That touch and connection gave me a point where I could nurture someone in a safe place and basically hug them and believe in them. It was great, it was legitimate, and it was really clear what it was about.

I started studying at the Australian College of Natural Medicine at the time, which was the leading natural medicine college in Australia, and started studying kinesiology and remedial massage. That's where my learning really began, because it was around something that was going to give me a future, and in some way, it was something I could help others with. So, for the last twenty years, I was a remedial massage therapist, self-employed mostly, and a kinesiologist. That was my profession.

Today, as a psychologist, we can't touch people, and we certainly can't use anything that's not mainstream in terms of approaches, so kinesiology would be like witchcraft for a psychologist at the moment. But there are a few psychologists in the world who are starting to open up their minds to alternative ways of doing things. Kinesiology taps into the system of acupuncture, so there's somewhat a base of evidence for its usefulness. So, basically, I'm a psychologist who in disguise has skills in remedial massage and kinesiology. They assist by way of my understanding of the mind and body, if I am limited to not performing them physically.

A lot has happened in last twenty years around kinesiology and there's a lot more evidence of its efficacy now. The issue now, because I've done research twice, once in my honors year for psychology and again for my master's year, is *money*. To do research and find evidence of efficacy comes down to, first, somebody being interested enough to research something, and then for that thing being testable through well-designed research. To do that well, you need money and talent behind you. So, until someone with a great deal of money who wants to do something robust with kinesiology, from an evidence point, it's going to be quite tricky for us to get it across the line.

Kinesiology today is gaining ground thank to grassroots acceptance. You only have to speak to people who have had success with it to realize this. Meanwhile, as with any other profession, there exists a wide range of kinesiologists. Some, quite rightly, focus on an esoteric and spiritual kind of kinesiology, and that's fine, because it's no different from clairvoyance and other kinds of energy work. But there exists as well a robust kind of approach, people doing a very science and evidence-based kinesiology. This is what I like about healthcare, really, is if you look at it from complementary *and* mainstream perspectives, there's something for everyone.

There's a practitioner to suit all experiences and all cognitive styles. We have just got to find the one that suits, really.

The ability to look at things from both the mainstream and complementary medicine perspectives is to see things more holistically. Healing techniques we know of from Eastern medicine have been remarkable. What I love about Chinese medicine is it very clearly states that to understand what's going on in our own body, we need to look to nature for answers. And when we look to nature, we realize nature has systems, like an ecosystem, and it has elements—fire, earth, metal, water, wood—and each element generates, controls, or influences another.

Controlling cycles, for example, demonstrate that fire has the ability to melt metal, and metal has the ability to chop wood. Wood has the ability to break down into the soil, and soil has the ability to hold and contain water. Water has the ability to put out fire.

Generating cycles demonstrate how each of the elements generates another, such as fire to earth and water to wood.

This demonstrates a difference between Eastern and Western medicine. If your daughter, for example, has something going on physically, a Western approach might suggest we go treat her with an antibiotic, that we kill it all off. An Eastern approach might ask, "What's actually going on here? Hmm . . . the soil. There's something there that's not going well. Her digestive system, her feeding center's not going well. Let's look at supporting it, let's look at rebooting it, just like if you had a garden, let's look at nourishing and nurturing to re-establish equilibrium. And then, you know what? *The body has the ability to run itself.*" And, lo and behold, it does. And that's what's remarkable, is that the body is so very capable of doing so many amazing things.

As a psychologist, I've been doing a lot of work with trauma, and *Eye Movement Desensitization and Reprocessing* (EMDR[23]) is a style of therapy that's now recommended for working with trauma patients. Fortunately for me, it's got parallels with kinesiology, but it's all evidence-based.

With any therapy, one thing I keep in mind is what I was taught along the way. I was once told, "When you're working with people, sometimes you just need to get out of the way." As health professionals, we sometimes get in the way of the body's own healing process. We need to enable the right conditions and then we need to get out of the way and let the body do what it

---

[23] Eye movement desensitization and reprocessing is a form of psychotherapy developed by Francine Shapiro in the 1990s in which the person being treated is asked to recall distressing images; the therapist then directs the patient in one type of bilateral sensory input, such as side-to-side eye movements or hand tapping. —Wikipedia

does, naturally. It's nice that I've found a modality in psychology that speaks to my modalities in complementary medicine.

But the biggest thing for me, the richest part of my own story, if you ask me, is my living with learning difficulties. They are something I have to manage daily, and they upset me daily. I have to remember, though, that the gift of it is I realize *I'm only as good as the people I'm connected with* in the sense that if I wasn't successful as a psychologist, I would be working, probably, in an administrative role, and I would be a horrendous administrator. I wouldn't be efficient. I'd have a lot of sadness. I'd be pretty internally frustrated. So, getting with a good organizational fit and getting those good working conditions that line up with my values, with my strengths, with my skills, with my natural capabilities is essential. I think for somebody with learning difficulties, I don't really have a choice to do it any other way. I don't have the choice to be a perfectionist, because I couldn't be. I'd be insane if I was a perfectionist. It's actually kept me away from perfectionism, whereas a lot of psychologists are perfectionists and amazing academic achievers. I just couldn't be one of those. So my learning difficulties have actually taken away a lot of stress because there's no point striving for perfectionism. I'm not capable of it. What I *am* capable of is what I am now doing, in my holistic approach and practice of psychology. I'm quite innovative, I think out of the box, but I need a team of people around me to be able to make magic happen, so to speak.

And now, today, where I really need to be is in front of people, helping people. Whether that's speaking and workshops, whether that's in organizational spaces helping to equip them to support and develop their staff through training and development, or whether that's helping organizations create healthier and happier workplaces, where people's diversities are embraced, where people's skillsets are embraced, that's where I need to be. It's easy for me and it's something I love and I'm good at. My best place is where I'm working with teams of people, enabling those sorts of opportunities. I don't mind what that looks like, it may be more of going and talking to masses of people and doing wellness workshops and retreats. I know my deficit is marketing and the administrative sides of things, so if I can work with people that are already switched on and ready and willing, I can do amazing things efficiently.

My research area was burnout among health professionals. I found if you're working in your area of love with the people that you want to be with, and you feel like you're generating something, there's *flow*, like a musician playing an instrument. And that's all of us want that in life.

A *better life* can be achieved by exploring your lifestyle, mind, body, and spirit holistically. I believe your health is your greatest asset and it can be the greatest teacher and challenger. Our body has an innate healing ability if it is offered a holistic range of supports and the right conditions to enable growth and recovery. Become your own friend, teacher, supporter, and believer to assist yourself in creating a better life. Access the support of others who enable you to gain a better understanding of health and wellbeing, and those who share with you the skills you are needing. Gain vital information and learn from others who specialize in the aspects that you need assistance with, and allow them to be your teachers. We are born to connect and learn from each other, and this enhances our ability to learn from ourselves.

IT'S AN INTERESTING WORLD, the world of psychology. Psychologists tend to be a little bit private in some regards, even though we know therapeutically how much happens, that catharsis you get by sharing. I'm quite an open-book sort of person, though, and this is quite nice, this cathartic process of sharing and disclosing a few things, because I definitely have not written this all down in one space before now. In thinking about this *Inspiring Women Today* project, some of those questions led me to, *Oh, okay, this is what's fueled my fire and this is what's made me quite deliberate about my pathway and quite strategic about how I've gone about it.*

In fact, that's why I am a psychologist now, because I thought it was going to be a hard gig for me getting anywhere academically, and getting any of these pieces of papers (diplomas), so the one piece of paper that I could get that would give me the most access to helping others with the most amount of respect from the mainstream world, versus being a social worker, versus a counseling degree, which would've been far easier academically. I thought, *If I'm going to do this, it's going to burn and hurt anyway, so I may as well do something that's going to take me to the highest place that I could've obtained.* So that was interesting.

As I discuss in my own book, *Balance,* I'm a believer in the influence childhood is on our adult lives, and interested then in the place I grew up in, in the people around me and what my parents exposed me to, who and what gave me my talent, specifically that deep interest and curiosity in people and diversity. So that was the start of my story, I suppose, and of my interest in people and in the environment and nature as well.

Today my greatest challenge, privilege, and source of motivation and inspiration are my two young boys. They have taught me more about mindfulness and being present than any other influence. In their eyes I find the curiosity and the openness to explore, appreciate, and connect with people and the natural environment all around us. I was fortunate to grow up on acreage and be surround by nature. My parents lived a lifestyle where we enjoyed lots of home-grown produce, an active outdoor lifestyle, and strong social and community connections. My parents were heavily involved in the markets where everything was handmade and homemade. Through this market community I enjoyed connecting with diverse people and enjoyed a lifestyle that had a strong health and wellbeing background. It was a great teacher. Today, motherhood has been my greatest privilege and my greatest teacher.

I'm still quite practical and outgoing. I still see myself as a good bit tomboy, and I've always enjoyed climbing trees and building cubby houses and all of that. So that was interesting when it came to my own identity. As much as I was very strong and had a good sense of self, there was also a lot of teasing and bullying that I unfortunately experienced because I was a lot more tomboy. And that, in effect, enabled the guy who abused and raped me, because he used that to his advantage. It helped him manipulate the many situations to happen between he and I.

But challenges can push you to think outside of the box. My own dyslexia taught me to learn in diverse ways, to ask for help, to not be a perfectionist, to use my grit and determination and passion to interact with what I wanted to learn, to be strategic with my time, to be kind and compassionate with other people with their own adversities, and to explore different opportunities. The sexual violence I endured taught me the importance of being true to myself, asking for help, having a voice, creating healthy boundaries, and the importance of validation of people with unique experience and pains.

Interesting how it unravels. Most psychologists would agree that most of us are in this space of helping others because we've had experiences or had close people who have had experiences which lead us to want to assist and help other people, and to help them understand themselves and fix themselves. I wouldn't quite go that far with myself. I actually felt like I was in a good space personally, but it's certainly about helping others for me now.

THE HOLISTIC APPROACH BY LISA JOHNSON

AS THE DIRECTOR of Asami Engagement Psychology, Lisa Johnson combines over 20 years' experience in complimentary medicine and counselling with a Bachelor of Psychology and Masters of Organizational Psychology. Taking a holistic, complete wellbeing approach; Lisa supports individuals, families, communities and organizations to enhance and enrich their most important asset, health. Lisa is available for appearances as well as consulting individuals and groups. Contact Lisa today to find out more, and to discover upcoming events and workshops.

health.holistic@optusnet.com.au

engagementpsychology.com.au

[10]

THE WORLD IS YOUR OYSTER
by Ali Pilling

"Choose a job you love, and you will never
have to work a day in your life."
—CHINESE PROVERB

"THE WORLD IS your oyster. You have enormous opportunities and choice, especially when you leave school. It's true, I have employed over 500 people in the last 30 years, especially youth, starting as an employer when I was just 22. I went to university, followed my heart, and I tapped into my interest in finance and business. I got my degree and realized I wasn't cut out to work for anyone but myself. Then, I tapped in to my heart again, this time to my true passion, which is plants. Together with my husband Rob, we created and grew our own business. So today I'm here to share with you a few tips I think will help you, not only with work experience this week but in your future.

"Let's have a show of hands, has anyone heard of Gary Vee? Not many of you. I'll warn you if you do look him up, he swears more than my husband. But he is extremely inspirational and motivational to our youth. Well, like Gary, I believe in my heart and soul that there has never been a better time than *now* to do what you love, to love what you do, to wrap meaning and purpose around what that is, and find a way to get paid for that, whether you work for somebody else or you create your own business. And that is the core message I want to seed with you today.

"I hope that you guys have lined up your jobs for next week, that you've had the courage to tap into your heart and find out what it is that you truly are interested in, and that you love and enjoy and learn more about what that field or profession or trade or career can be. That's the *aim* of work experience. It's an awesome platform to give you experience. If you find next week that it's not your thing, that you don't enjoy it, that's all good, too. Because guess what? It's good to know what you *don't* enjoy because you're not going to waste any more time pursuing that path. But I will encourage you—and I love the words of Steven Spielberg—Do we all know Steven Spielberg? Famous director? Are you guys too shy, or you don't watch movies? Steven Spielberg tells us that "our dream sneaks up on us from behind, and our intuition, it whispers, it never shouts, and you need to listen carefully, every day, to your intuition.

"If you don't know what your true passion or your purpose is now, that's okay. Because you're young, you have youth on your side. And it's no race. So, my message for you guys is that the world *is* your oyster, and you have choice and opportunity, with the courage to tap into your heart and soul, to be honest and true to yourself, and to follow and pursue your passion or your purpose.

"Who has heard of Greta Thunberg? She is creating a big-time movement, isn't she? She is purpose-driven. She is concerned about our planet. She wants this planet to be here in the future for all of you. That is an example of purpose-driven.

"If you find your purpose, something you really care about in this world, perhaps it's humanity or the planet, that is a huge advantage. If you have passion, just on its own, that's an advantage, too. If you tie your passion and purpose together, you're unstoppable. You will make a difference. You will create movements. So dream big, guys.

"And here's my *number one* tip for the future: As a business owner for more than 30 years I will tell you what I discovered: Anyone who arrives at my place of employment, at ePlants, who has an innate interest in plants, nature, the planet, or the environment, stands out to me. I can teach skills, but I can't teach passion.

"So, when you are tapping into that heart space, and you're driving to work and you really enjoy what you do, it will bring out the best in you. When it brings out the best in you, it brings out the best in you for the business as well. You'll be efficient, productive, and the business will be profitable.

"And one day, that business might be your own."

Ali Pilling
Speaking to St. Teresa High School's
"Year 10" work experience students
April 20, 2019

I'M NOT SOMEONE who's overcome huge challenges. I was born and raised in Melbourne, Australia, one of three kids in a beautiful, loving family. Life was going pretty well through my rose-colored glasses until that day came when my mum, my beautiful financially savvy mum, made the courageous decision that after many arguments it was time to leave Dad, even while we were growing up. And that was, I believe, the biggest event that shaped my life and made me who I am today. I was twelve years old and my life was turned upside down the day my financially savvy mum Cath made the courageous decision that is was time to pack up the three kids (my brother, sister and I), the family pets, and family belongings to start a new chapter of our lives without our cool, laid-back, "live in the now" dad, Lenny. I sat in the removal truck between my brother Chris and the driver, a man we didn't even know, tears streaming down my face, as we waved goodbye to Dad standing on the doorstep of our family home, the only home we knew. This was the moment of heartbreak, a heart-wrenching time of my life, a young child and her siblings being torn between two of the most important people in our lives—our mum and our dad.

The pain of leaving my dad and the security of our family home, leaving my favorite street and all my friends, set me on my path to seek financial independence and security, and to learn the invaluable lesson of building a solid work ethic through the coming challenges that lie ahead. It's these lessons I can't wait to share with people, particularly teens and families, now. I feel compelled to speak at high schools (often called "Smart Chats") to the work experience kids and others on the subject of work ethic, to show them that *they* are in control of their success. I am working on a book on the subject as well (*Live What You Love*). What pulls on my heart's strings are those people, families, those moms who are working so hard. And when you look into their lives, it's like it's all work and no play. It's just working to survive, working to live, to provide the best they can for their children. And that's what I saw with my own mum. I watched my mum work really hard to give us the best education, a roof over our heads, and the best quality of life she could give us.

So, the beautiful message I received from my parents is that life is actually about *balance*. And in today's world, it is most important to value *self*—you've got to do what you love and enjoy; you have to have meaning and a purpose, a reason to get up in the morning, a feeling of worthiness all while recognizing financial independence and financial security are critical. We can't live a life of balance if we are struggling financially. My two highest values today are *family* and *home*, and having a beautiful home for my family. We lost our home when I was a young child. That became a core driver for me throughout my life. It became very important for me to seek financial independence, security, and the financial freedom that I enjoy today. It came about for me through the strong work ethic my mum showed me, and a lot of hard work.

Then, at the very young age of 14—I remember I was awakened by this, it was like an epiphany—I wanted to get off my *mum's payroll*. I wanted to alleviate her financial burden and lessen my mum's workload. So, from the young age of 14, I worked in part-time jobs earning as little as four dollars an hour back then. It doesn't seem a lot, but it meant a lot, I've found. Working part-time when you're young is a trait of the financially successful. Warren Buffett had many jobs as a teenager, for example. It sometimes requires tough love on the part of a parent, but when you encourage, inspire, and support your kids to get out in the world to work, even when you're paid poorly (at first) or not at all, you learn new skills, you get paid to learn, you get valuable experience. That helps grow your self-worth and it helps raise your net worth because your net-worth is a direct reflection of your self-worth. It's just so empowering to get kids out there as soon as they can. So, part of my mission is to help families just like my mum and my siblings and I were.

As an entrepreneur over the last 30 years, my business (ePlants) has been the platform that has allowed me to teach kids (my own and others') foundational lessons, the lessons they don't learn in school. I've been able to use ePlants as a platform to teach them life skills and money management along with teaching them about nature and the environment. It's been very fulfilling.

I want to do that for more and more people now. I'm expanding my qualifications in my horticulture arena and upskilling so I can attract youth from all around my region who are passionate or purpose-driven about the environment, horticulture, sustainability, regeneration, growing their own food—anything that can link to my business here at ePlants. We want to offer traineeships, work experience, and apprenticeships so we can help. People think it's not easy to get a job but there's always work for those who are persistent and those who are passionate and purpose-driven. I want ePlants to be one of those opportunities.

Still in our early twenties, I was working full-time as an accountant and my husband Rob, was working full-time as a brick paver, we were earning income and pouring every spare cent we made into building our dream nursery. Full of excitement, passion, energy, determination and youth, we spent many, many years working weekends, public holidays, and any chance we had developing our dream nursery—producing stock, weeding, watering by hand, mowing, building garden beds, planting mother stock, building shade houses and so much more. Our working conditions weren't great but it was a lot of fun, working under tarps, with no power, no toilets, camping in tents, enjoying nature, enjoying each other and our gorgeous dogs. There was always plenty to do and not enough hours in the day, yet every day was so rewarding.

We decided to build a shed and to deck it out on the inside to make it our home. This meant that we could now save on rent and continue to invest every cent into our growing dream. With very little money to spare, Rob traded his expertise as a brick paver for plumbing, building, and electrical work while I helped out too by doing the plumber's book work. The small but cozy two-bedroom home (shed) we built, felt like a palace to us. We were incredibly house-proud and we loved having visitors, entertaining at every opportunity. The summers were long and hot, the second-hand air conditioner we bought from a garage sale, kept us cool. The winters were short but very cold, and the fireplace that Rob's dad made for our wedding present kept us snug and warm.

Bank loans, bank overdrafts, extension of bank overdrafts, hire purchase agreements, contra deals and incoming sales all enabled us to expand. We purchased more plant and equipment—bobcats, loaders, potting machines, trucks, delivery vans, golf buggies and quad bikes. We saw to the construction of more sheds, shade houses, propagation tunnel houses, and to the excavation of new dams, irrigation pumps, computer systems and software. Administratively we added office computers, software, and security cameras. We built pathways, driveways, and growing bays. Producing and growing our stock was of course the big one and relied heavily on labour. Part of our growth and success we attribute to making new plants from existing plants. Thank you, Mother Nature!

But one of the most difficult challenges our nursery would face would be dealing with the infrequent, unannounced flash floods. The floods would put our commitment to ePlants to the test.

ROB HAD A close eye on 20 acres of land at close proximity to our nursery. He would make several trips up to this acreage, and he would discretely pull down the real estate "For Sale" signs and hide them in the bush. He did this twice over a period of three months, until we were finally ready to make the purchase. It was a Friday night in August 2003 when we contacted the agent and made an offer at asking price, which of course, was accepted. While we waited anxiously for 21 days for finance approval from the bank, another prospective buyer emerged showing strong interest in this parcel of land. He hovered over us like a vulture, hoping that our contract would fall over, and he would have snaffled it up from under us. Our solicitor notified us that he was offering us $50,000 to walk away! We didn't! We consider ourselves very fortunate to have acquired this parcel of land, which included a three-bedroom home and provided large growing grounds for the expansion of our business, for increased levels of stock, for broadening our range and production in large numbers. We were now able to embark on a new production team, we purchased a second potting machine and took large deliveries of potting mix and supplies. This now meant that our Grays Road nursery (our original seven acres) could now be filled with stock that was ready for sale, instead of stock that was in a growing stage, and not ready for sale. The purchase of this property had a significant impact on the growth of our business. Rob has kept the damaged real estate "For Sale" sign to show and share the story to our three children with an underlying message that "Things don't just fall in your lap, you have to make things happen."

It didn't feel like work. It's like that Chinese proverb, "When you choose a job you love and enjoy, you don't work a day in your life." For many years Rob and I worked seven days a week. I'm a parent now, I'm a mother of three, and we raised our family in this environment, working side-by-side with our kids, not actually realizing how much we were teaching them. We taught them that *work is stored wealth* and that wealth comes in many forms, not just financial wealth. It's also family and physical and mental health. It's also simply just doing things.

When I look back, I believe our parents express their love for us *according to what's most important to them*. So, we as children tune into and connect with *our parents' values*. My mum showed me the importance of a strong work ethic, how your work ethic is directly tied to your success, and how success comes in many forms, not only financial. She showed me this because following the separation, my mum raised three teenage kids on her own with little help from my dad. But my dad was a cool, laid-back, living-the-now type guy, and I learned from him that life's not always about work and building financial wealth. It's also about fun, friends, and family.

What concerns me most about the world today with what we're going through with COVID-19 is that the human spirit is threatened. When you take away someone's passion, their purpose, their meaning to get up in the morning, what else is there? When you have passion, when you enjoy something, you've got your heart and soul in it. We all have a passion and a purpose and when you combine the two, it's fulfilling. I've heard Richard Branson say the feeling you get when you make a difference, when you make an impact on the environment, on the planet or in someone's life, it doesn't matter how big or small that impact can be, that is fulfilling. We should work towards that. We should encourage and inspire our kids to do the same. It's just so rewarding to step back and watch your children enjoy their waking moments doing something they love. That's one of my key takeaways as a parent. It's not just about the money and how financially well-off you are.

Any successful business has come through their challenges. It's interesting that sometimes people look at success and think, *Oh, it's all right for them*, or *Aren't they lucky? Look what they have*, and all those sorts of things. But the people closest to you or who have joined you along your journey know how hard you've worked. They know some of the challenges you've embraced and overcome. Over the years for us here at ePlants, that's included flash flooding, the threat of fires where we've had to evacuate (the police came to our nursery just in December with the recent Australian bushfires), and we've even had a nasty cyclone that did some devastation, Cyclone Debbie, going back nearly four years ago.

That was a hard time for me because my mom had Alzheimer's, my dad was very ill and passed away, and life got to be a little bit much for me at that time. I took a step back. I moved out of my home for two nights and moved into my one of my vacant investment properties. It didn't even have any furniture, I just camped out on the beach looking at the ocean for a couple of days, just to reground myself. I just took one challenge at a time and moved forward, as you do.

Rob and I, we're some of the lucky ones. We're still married. The good times far outweigh the disputes in the home, the challenges we've faced. And we've raised our kids according to the same message that my mum passed on to me.

I've expressed my love for my kids according to what's important to me, and that is financial education, financial security, and financial independence. As a result, Sammy, my young 18-year-old son, was able to go to the bank and borrow a big chunk of money to buy his first investment property. He had been exposed to all the lessons along the way, so he felt comfortable with the investment because he'd been exposed to it. Up to then, we took our kids into meetings with real estate agents, to banks—we just introduced them to all of the people that came into our life. We've always treated our kids as equals. When my parents were brought up, they were taught that children were to be *seen and not heard,* but we bring our kids up a lot differently these days. We've avoided the *entitlement mentality* and focused on *empowerment.* Sure, I'm guilty of spoiling my kids here and there. That's a privilege of mine and I'm happy to do that. And I remind them of what I'm doing. If I'm taking them on a paid holiday, for example, they know I've traveled the world and we share how tough other people around the world have it.

I believe kids are a product of their environment and their upbringing. I know my kids certainly are. In addition to Sammy, my daughter Georgie is a painter and an artist. And from my upcoming book, *Live What You Love,* I talk about my third child, Bayley:

> MY YOUNGEST SON Bayley has no time for social media, life is just too precious. It is amazing what this young 16-year-old can achieve in a day. I used to call Bayley "Get Stuff Done," but now I call him "Man on a Mission." I will find him from 6 a.m. on a Saturday and Sunday morning to dusk, dressed in khakis and work boots, camouflaged amongst his food forests and veggie gardens. It's so rewarding, watching a young man who is inspired, who enthusiastically enjoys making the most of his waking moments, doing what he loves, whether it be surfing, horseback riding, drama, the arts.
>
> What is it that *you* love to do?
>
> For Bayley, he has a love of producing organic food, composting, learning the critical importance of soil health, and learning all about the healing properties in the food that we eat. He studies conscientiously at school and like most of you, has a yearning to self-educate in the areas where he has a natural interest. Bayley also loves to share his important messages with the world by

making films. A few years ago, I said to Bayley, who was 13 at the time, "You don't need to wait until you finish school to get paid to do what you love." And at age 13 he landed three filmmaking jobs—one paying a fee of $1,200. This really ignited the entrepreneurial spirit within him. He had to work around school hours, with early morning starts and full days on Sundays. He filmed and edited a series of interviews for a business promotional video.

"Wow, Mum," he said, "I can't believe I'm getting paid to do what I love!"

Bayley has since combined his love for documentary filmmaking with his love of producing organic food and his genuine concern for the depletion of our soils, combining passion and purpose! Inspired by his mentor—film producer Lance Reynolds who produced Hugh Jackman's first film *Paperback Hero*, and has worked with the late Heath Ledger, and Jamie Oliver to mention a few—Bayley entered an educational documentary into his first international film festival (NIFF, Noosa International Film Festival) titled, *The Future of Food Production*. He proudly received an Official Selection Nomination which noted, he was the youngest entrant at just age 14.

Bayley has fully self-funded his own studio, including green screens, lighting, cameras, teleprompter, microphones, and sound-proofing. He learns the art of negotiation through meeting with his clients and selling unwanted household items on Gumtree.com. He shakes hands with his customers and knows to hold his price. Bayley creates vision boards—collages of images of the numerous short-term, medium-term and long-term goals which he sets for himself. He plans and strives to achieve them, many of which he has successfully achieved already. He pays himself first and has a handsome bank account for someone his age, with a purpose for the money that he has earned. He asks quality questions. All this led him to be the film director for all school events back in 2015. His teacher gave him a wrap in front of his classmates and said that,

> "Bayley was pursuing his passion and showing leadership qualities, which he demonstrates directing and filming at school."

ONE OF THE biggest things I had to overcome was the guilt of not being there or the perception I wasn't there for my kids growing up, that I was in the business working long hours. But as a result my kids are independent in so many ways. They cook, they shop, they budget, they're independent in so many aspects of life. They've learnt life skills they don't teach in school.

Financial wealth brings quality of life and choice. It gives you opportunities for education and life experiences. And when you get *real* financial wealth, you can give back, you can contribute. My mission is to help raise financial intelligence amongst our families and our youth. To do that, I need to connect to parents and pass on what's worked for me, and to teach them what hasn't worked for me, so they can do better, possibly. I'm writing a seven-week online program. And now that purpose is even stronger because the world needs a lot right now. We need to get over ourselves and do the work and share our valuable wisdom so we can change lives and help make a difference while people are in lockdown, maybe not having the opportunity to go out and work in the workforce.

They say children have a yearning to learn the things that they are innately and inherently interested in and that everyone is born a genius. Well, aren't you guys lucky then? You have access to the internet and a wealth of knowledge from experts in whatever field you love, right at your fingertips. The world literally is your oyster. What you can create is only limited by your imagination. And I love how young people today are creating businesses around what they love, like the couple who created a successful business by dressing their Shiba Inu dog up in designer menswear and professionally photographed it. These days, it never ceases to amaze me the imagination of the entrepreneurs who create businesses around what it is they love. How exciting for you guys, that the internet has created such immense opportunities that weren't prevalent when your parents and I were your age. Be courageous, be imaginative, and be open to one day creating a business around that thing you love.

Most importantly, I learned to value me. Earning and learning helps raise your self-worth. Between my mum and dad's separation just prior to high school and the negative comments I seemed to receive year after year from my high school teachers, as you'd expect, my self-worth needed a little raising. Self-worth is an important part of success. It wasn't until my final year of high school that I made the choice to use the negative comments from my teachers as fuel, like, "I'll show you." That's the rebellious streak in me. I learned as well to seek out the positive feedback from the teachers who believed in me, like Mr. Brown, and there were others. I recall comments like, "Alison, you have great potential," and "Alison, you appear to have an interest in finance. Have you ever thought about continuing your education?"

Today, I do believe that a business is only as good as your employees. We pride ourselves on having a great, loyal team who truly love plants. We spend many hours at work, so it is imperative that everyone enjoys their working day as much as possible. We strive for a healthy, happy workplace, leading by example, with mutual respect, shared core values, a good work ethic is a must, and our employees have a chance to grow and shine. We love to give students on school work experience the opportunity to learn on-the-job training and we are proud to have offered many youth traineeships and apprenticeships over the years to those who have a true passion for plants and horticulture. We also contribute to our environment and our planet, making homes and streetscapes more beautiful, fulfilling our customers' needs, and we love to help our local community through vouchers and plant donations.

And we put a lot of care into who we hire. I recently had a special experience with a job applicant who became a valued team member, which I wrote about for *The Green* magazine:

> . . . His name was Michael and he's a paraplegic with a hearing impairment. Michael was accompanied by . . . Ben from Job Match (jobmatchgympie.com.au). . . . I asked Michael if he knew his plants! Then from a pouch at the back of his wheel chair, he pulled out and handed me a list of botanical names of all the plants he knew, which he had personally typed out. I replied, "You were just waiting for me to ask that, weren't you?" He smiled like a cat who'd swallowed a canary! . . .
>
> The enthusiasm . . . shone through like none other I had ever experienced. To this day, I have never had anyone sell themselves in an interview the way Michael did. . . I went straight to my team and told them there was no way I could say no to this guy, "I'm letting you know Michael will be joining our team," I said. But in order for Michael to commence work with ePlants it meant the construction of disabled facilities: a new bathroom and a concrete ramp to access his work station. . . ePlants was approved for a government grant to the value of $30,000 . . . this was music to our

ears and we are all very grateful. I'd like to let other businesses know that there is government funding to facilitate jobs for the disabled.

It is with great pleasure that we now welcome our newest ePlants member Michael who is following his true passion for plants and now getting paid to do something he loves. Some say the feeling you receive when making a difference to the quality of someone's life is what we are all here for... I must say it really does feel good.

"Passion for Plants" by Ali Pilling
The Green Issue 239
https://www.eumundigreen.com.au/story/passion-for-plants-by-ali-pilling/

ALL OF US are faced with challenges. What sets us apart from each other is how we deal with our challenges. It is said that "stressings are blessings," when we handle them so that we continue to grow. I'm certain there are more challenges ahead for both of us. It's a fact of life. Some of your challenges may be similar or different than mine, but one thing is for sure, and that's that we all have them. The two-bedroom tin shed we lived in was converted into offices. The children's footprints and handprints framed on the office walls, are a sweet reminder of our humble beginnings, in growing the family business. The prints still prompt conversations in our sales office today. Looking back, even the tough times were sweet. The wealth we now enjoy we truly earned and accumulated. Looking back, I'd have it no other way.

Life happens for us, not to us. Create your own business around what it is you love and enjoy and what you're good at. And you *are* good at something. There's no doubt about it.

THE WORLD IS YOUR OYSTER BY ALI PILLING

About Alison Pilling

Coach, Speaker, Entrepreneur.

Helping parents raise inspired, financially independent kids

Ali Pilling in Mexico, finding "Live what you love" carved into the concrete steps.

eplantswholesale.com.au

HEARTS OF CAMBODIA

by Sophal Chhay Benefield

"Without Cambodia, I may never have become a mother. Part of my heart is and will always be in this country. And part of this country is always with me: Maddox."

—ANGELINA JOLIE

CAMBODIANS ARE THE sweetest people you'll ever meet. They have huge hearts and they will do anything for anyone. I was nervous about going back to Cambodia after all of these years because I didn't really know how they would see me, being an American now. It turned out they accepted me like I had never left.

My heart is still in Cambodia and I love my people, I'm so proud to be a Cambodian. I believe I was supposed to be here, to make it through the war and come to the USA safe, and I believe that these things happened for a reason.

~

MY NAME IS SOPHAL, and I am originally from Cambodia. The Cambodian way is that whoever delivers a baby gets to name that baby. My doctor named me. I asked my parents once what it means. They tried to translate it into English for me, but the translation is something like *ambition*. I did find out it can mean *cultivation*, too. Names in Cambodia are very unisex, so a guy can be named Sophal, girls too, but the letters S, O, P, and H are the most common four letters of Cambodian names.

I remember bits and pieces of my homeland when I was young, playing in mud puddles when the rain monsoon came down, other things. We lived in the countryside in Battambang. We had shacks built on stilts because there was a lot of flooding there in the summer time. In monsoon season it rains for *months*.

I remember when Khmer Rouge[24], the communist party, first came to my village. They took my family and made everybody work in the rice fields. I was so cute and adorable the army guys didn't want me to work, and they kind of adopted me. They wanted to take me away from my family, and my family was scared I was going to be separated from them. But I didn't leave them.

Even then, when I was very young in Cambodia, I had a feeling I was going to go to somewhere great, and I envisioned marrying someone like Kab, my husband.

My family and I came to the United States in January of 1982, when I was eight years old. We were sponsored by a Lutheran Church family from Maddock, North Dakota. And the story of my life and how we came to the United States is a miracle. All I can remember is that my village of Battambang was burnt down by the Khmer Rouge, by the communist army. They went into the village and tried to kill anyone they could, especially the educated and the rich. To this day, I still don't know why they tried to kill us because my village was made up of poor and uneducated people. We had nothing.

It was really late, perhaps early morning when everyone was asleep and the fire woke us up. The whole village was being burned down and we had to flee. Everyone was scattered and families tried to stay together as we ran away from the burning village—children, brothers, sisters, mothers, fathers, all trying to stay together. We were scared, but I was young and I don't really remember being that scared until later.

My mother was seven months pregnant with my youngest sister while all of this happened. We left the village with just what we had on. We did not have shoes and my two older brothers, my

---

[24] The Khmer Rouge is the name that was popularly given to members of the Communist Party of Kampuchea and by extension to the regime through which the CPK ruled Cambodia between 1975 and 1979. —Wikipedia

older sister, and my mother and father were all together when we left that night. My cousins and aunt and uncle and grandmother were behind us. There were underground mines everywhere and my father told us to follow his footsteps because he was in the Cambodian army and he knew where the mines were and how not to step on them. *That* was when I started to get scared.

We walked for several hours. I looked back and saw my cousins and uncle and grandmother were way behind. I saw that my grandmother was hurt and couldn't walk anymore. My uncle waved his hand and told us to keep going on without them. We had no choice by this time—there were guns shooting everywhere, in every direction. We saw a place to hide for a little bit, and we tried to protect ourselves from the bullets there. My father saw a rock, and he told us to bend down and hide behind the rock, but I didn't know how to bend down. I tried but I had my butt up in the air. I felt a bullet run right through the tip of my sarong (skirt). My father was yelling at me because I almost got hit! He pushed my butt down so fast!

We were walking through the forest in the heat and the dark of night. My dad took his little scarf that he had and used it to absorb water from the leaves of the jungle. That's all we had to survive on for two days. It took us that long to get to Thailand. We walked through a rice field and the leeches were attaching onto me. Everything was freaking me out—I hate snakes and worms and things like that. It was horrible, walking through the rice fields, the rainforest, with all the landmines underneath and everything.

We made it to the refugee camp in Thailand, where we had to stay at the fence, there were so many Cambodian people there, all waiting for their names to be called to get accepted into the refugee camp. Some families were separated and some got to stay together, I am not sure why. At the camp, they got to choose who they wanted in. My family was lucky, we got to stay together, and we were lucky that we got in pretty fast, maybe because my mother was pregnant.

In the refugee camp in Thailand, my mother had her baby, but the baby passed away right after being born. My older sister later said remembers when we were little she was carrying that baby in her arms and crying, and I asked her why she was crying. I didn't know that the baby died.

My mom got pregnant again in the refugee camp and had my youngest sister who was born prematurely there, and my parents didn't think she was going to live, being so premature. My mother had to stay in the hospital for several months while we were there. My parents lost many children because of malnutrition, lack of medical care, and being so poor. But the doctor promised my parents that my premature sister was going to be okay. Later on the hospital was burned down and they had to relocate all of the patients.

We stayed in theses wooden buildings with wooden bunks on top of each other with no pillows or blankets, just the empty wood bunks. There was no air conditioner or any electricity in those buildings. There had to be 300 people in each building. I remember I was always scared to go to the bathroom there because there were only outhouses. They were so unsanitary, with everyone's stool everywhere, with maggots crawling everywhere, and with the horrible stink. I dreaded going there and was scared because the holes were so far down I was afraid I might fall in that horrific hole!

After *three years* at the refugee camp in Thailand, they asked my father where we wanted to go. We had a choice of going to Canada, France, or to the United States. My father didn't care, he just wanted to get us out of there.

Then we were shipped to the Philippines for two more months. We stayed at the refugee camp there as well. They put us in a school to learn some English. It wasn't much, just the basics like how to say *yes* and *no*.

Then, they found a family who wanted to sponsor us. We finished up with the legal paperwork and we flew to the United States, to California first, and were issued winter clothes because we were going to North Dakota. This was in January and it was *cold*. My mother told me we were going to a place where they had "ice blocks" everywhere, and that made me so excited! I couldn't wait! But when we landed in North Dakota, I was so disappointed because there were no "ice blocks." I asked my mother, "Mom, you said there's ice blocks here! I don't see any ice blocks!" She pointed to the white stuff on the ground, at the snow. You see, we never had snow in Cambodia or Thailand. We only had these huge ice blocks people chiseled to make snow cones from.

We arrived in this tiny town of Maddock, North Dakota, a town of 300 people back then. The whole town came out to greet us and give us gifts. My sponsors had a home with a little backyard with swing sets and a nice garden by the railroad tracks for my parents. My sponsors took my older sister and me to a cedar chest. They told me to open it. They were watching my every move. I opened the cedar chest—I loved the cedar smell—and I saw all of these *toys*. I took some out while my sponsors helped me with some of the toys because I had never had a toy in my life! I was so happy. I fell in love with this one doll. I took her almost everywhere. I remember the only toy we had back in Cambodia was a tiny doll we made with leaves and a cloth. So the toys in the cedar chest were all new to me. Most of them were used toys, but I didn't care.

I had another vision of my husband-to-be, Kab, back then, when I was in North Dakota at the Church. There was a church group picture being taken and I heard a man's voice calling my name.

We were new there and I said to myself, *Who would know my name?* I kept hearing my name and I saw this older, white, handsome, tall man waving me to come sit on his lap for the group picture. I was not sure what was going on. Finally, I went and sat on his lap for the group picture and I was so in awe of this man. I felt his heart and his kindness and everything about him. I told myself, *One day I will marry a man just like him.* I knew in my heart, *That guy is somewhere out there.* I made a list of everything I wanted in a husband. Years later I would meet and marry Kab, who fits my list to the tee—It's crazy!

I learned English pretty fast because I was motivated! I turned nine years old in January and had my first birthday party. We never celebrated birthdays in Cambodia, so everything was so new and exciting! They put me in Kindergarten to learn English, but I was not happy because I was with little children younger than me, so they moved me to 2nd grade. I was still older than these children, I was still behind my years, but we soon moved to Wisconsin. My father wanted to be near his best friend, and he happened to live in Madison, Wisconsin. I attended 5th through 7th grades there. I was still behind my age group for school and I worked really hard to keep up and took an ESL (English as a Second Language) class to help with my English.

My father decided he wanted us to move again. This time it was to Maine. I wanted to enroll in high school there but the school system would not let me because I didn't go to 8th grade. I fought this, and I had to take a test, and I made it. I went to high school in South Portland High for two years and then went to Biddeford High School for two years. I graduated from there in 1991. I attended Pine Manor college in Chestnut Hill, Massachusetts for a year and a half. My major was in interior design. I had a dream of being a great interior designer and living in New York. That was the life I had planned, but life often takes you on a different path.

I got married to a Cambodian guy whom I have three beautiful, sweet girls with. We were young and didn't really know what love was really about. We were married for nine years and then I met the man of my dreams, Kab. Together, we found success in the United States. That too, was full of miracles, but that's another chapter of my life.

MY HUSBAND KAB and I had the opportunity to go back to Cambodia after I'd been away for 30 years. I wanted to take my husband to see where I came from. I was nervous because I am so Americanized and didn't know how my family would receive me. But going back to Cambodia was one of my favorite trips of all time.

We went to China on the first part of our trip, and then got on an airplane to Cambodia. I was so nervous. I asked Kab, "What do you think my family is going to say to me, or are they going to look at me differently?" They knew I was coming. My brother sent the message to my cousin who lived in the city, and my cousin told somebody that had a car in my village. It was a weird way to connect, but we did.

"I'm sure it's going to be fine," Kab said.

"Okay," I said, but I was still really nervous.

I still spoke my language, but not like when I left. I'd forgotten a lot of vocabulary. Cambodian people in the U.S. who still speak the language would ask me, "Oh, you don't know how to speak Khmer anymore?" I had become so Americanized. Yet, when I went there, my family was so sweet and kind. People there are not used to our lifestyle, they don't know anything else besides their own world there.

My family back in my village in Battambang have nothing to this day. There is still no electric or running water. They only have one bike for transportation. The average income in Cambodia is about $200 USD a year. They don't have material things, but they are happy. And they were so happy to see me! They had heard about me but never seen me because my father had moved to the city when he was in the Cambodian Army, where I was born in Phonm Phen.

I love to take pictures and Kab bought me a beautiful camera. It makes me happy. My favorite photographer is Peter Lik[25]. He does amazing work and we have two of his photographs in our house. He inspired me. I told myself I wanted to be a female version of him. Kab and I walked into his gallery when we were in Maui one time and I just fell in love with his photographs! I knew then that I wanted to travel and take my camera everywhere we go.

FIRST, WE WENT to Siam Reap where Kab and I toured the Angkor Wat[26] temples. It was amazing! The temples are massive.

To stand in front of these temples, I was crazy, because when I was little, I always wanted to go there. I heard about it and thought, *Oh, I want to go there someday.* If I did go there when I was little, I can't remember, but my parents say they never took me, so maybe I was dreaming about it. But I always wanted to go, it was on my bucket list. I always told Kab, "I want to take you to Cambodia, I want to go back. I really want to take you to see my family." I wanted to go to

---

[25] Peter Lik is a photographer from Australia, best known for his nature and panoramic landscape images. He hosted *From the Edge with Peter Lik*, which aired for one season on The Weather Channel. —Wikipedia

[26] Angkor Wat is a temple complex in Cambodia and the largest religious monument in the world, on a site measuring 162.6 hectares. —Wikipedia

Angkor Wat, as it's a must-see place. I'm very into architecture, art, interior design. That's my hobby and my passion. And when I saw these temples, just being there and seeing these statues and temples of old, looking at all the details and seeing so much labor had gone into them, just being in Cambodia since I was from there, it made me proud to be there. *This is my home. It's exotic, it's just beautiful in every way, everything about it.* I couldn't believe it. When you go there you feel very spiritual. I don't know how to explain it. I felt *more complete,* I felt *this is my homeland, this is what I represent.* Just everything about it, the beauty, the spiritual feeling, something in the air about it.

We had a tour guide and we took an elephant ride around the temple. We have great pictures of it all, maybe for a book someday.

I believe there are ten temples there, and we saw three of them. The faces on these temples come from Cambodian rulers of the past, the history of the kings back then, and from Buddhist and Hindu beliefs. The statues everywhere were all hand-carved by the king's army, back many, many years ago. It was so amazing, my first time there, like an honor, and so many things to look at. All around there were tuk-tuk[27] drivers, temples, elephants. Some local people live nearby who have their kids sell little items for money around the temples because they know the tourists go there.

The temples are not used today. They are restoring them. The French came in 100 years ago or so, into the rainforest here, and they're pouring money into the temples now, restoring them. A lot of pieces of the temples were stolen during wartime, along with artifacts, sculptures, and sold all over the country. Today they are asking everyone to bring these things back in order to restore Angkor Wat Temple. So, there was a lot of restoration going on at the time.

Cambodian dancers go there to pose and be with the tourists. Their costumes are very ornamented, very elaborate, very traditional Cambodian dancing costumes. They do classic Cambodian dancing, very traditional.

Of course, it's much safer in Cambodia today. When we were escaping during the war there were a lot of landmines, back maybe 15-20 years ago. There are still supposedly landmines underground, and people were kind of scared to go back to visit Cambodia because of that. But they say they have cleaned everything up. You might still find few landmines in the mountains, thought, way out, up in the hills, further north. But where the tourist area is, or where my family lives, there are no more mines, it's all cleared, so it's much safer to go. And they are getting more

---

[27] An auto rickshaw is a motorized version of the pulled rickshaw or cycle rickshaw. Most have three wheels and do not tilt. They are known by many terms in various countries including auto, baby taxi, pigeon, bajaj, chand gari, lapa, tuk-tuk, 3wheel or tukxi. —Wikipedia

and more tourists visiting each year, mostly European. The English and the Americans don't really want to go back because of the history behind the war. It brings back so many bad memories.

There are big, giant trees coming down over the temples. They carve those trees. If you look, the trees surround the temples. They planted them to surround the temples of the rulers that came. Their roots are massive. You can see the roots just crushing down on the roofs.

Angelina Jolie made the movie, *Tomb Raider* there. Kab and I took a picture in front of one of the trees in the movie. Angelina Jolie fell in love with Cambodia. She adopted a boy from Cambodia. His name is Maddox. The Cambodian New Year is April 14th, and she went to Cambodia dressed up in a dancer's outfit, so pretty.

While there I gave a woman money, and I have a picture of her praying for me, to give me good luck and peacefulness and happiness. There are all of these old ladies there. I guess they allow them to do that. They pray to the Gods to give you good health, and you give a donation. That's how we are blessed, because she is blessing me in the Buddhist way.

There were children there wearing hats, and they are the singers. Around the temples, it's kind of sad. Even in cities, all the young kids are put to work, to make money off of the tourists. So, these boys are all from the village nearby, and they are all singing Cambodian songs, and they are collecting money, to help out.

There was this one girl, I just felt my heart go out to her. She reminded me of myself when I was younger. She was just so innocent, and hardworking. You couldn't help but to help her out. I think her mom put her out there and she stayed there the whole day, trying to sell these little bracelet things for a dollar. "I'll buy the whole package," I said. "Just sit there and pose for me." At first she didn't want to, and I was like, "Please, sit there for me, I'll buy you a two packages," I said, trying to speak the language so she understood. She was just so cute. But sad in a way, because they put them to work so early.

Our tuk-tuk driver asked us, "Do you want coconuts?"

"Yes, please," we said.

We had fresh coconuts to drink out of, fresh from the tree.

After visiting the temples we visited my family. It was really special to me, because I left at a young age, and never knew my family. I knew of them, but we had never met.

WE SPENT TWO DAYS in Angkor Wat (and that's not enough time, you need like a week to see all the temples). We then took a nine-hour boat ride through the *floating village* before spending three days in Battambang where my family lives, in the village. That ride was crazy because Kab and I are very adventurous and I always wanted to see the floating village. It was amazing and crazy at the same time because we were sitting on a tin roof of a little boat with no shade!

I said to Kab, "Oh, I want to see the floating village so bad."

Kab said, "Well, we have a choice, to take a bus, taxi, or take a boat to your family's village."

"Oh, I want to take a boat," I said.

We had no idea what that boat ride was going to be like and Kab said, "Oh yeah, the water is good. I checked and they say we can take the boat. It's going to drop you off right at your family's village."

"Wow," I said, "That's perfect."

We were at the boat dock early, at 6 o'clock in the morning, and we jumped on the boat. There was already a group of people down on the bottom, and we were told, "Okay, you can go upstairs." We climbed up a metal ladder. People were lying everywhere. Luggage was in the back. As we got to the top we saw people were just lying on the thin, tin roof.

And then I said, "Where's the seat, where do we sit?"

Our guide said, "Just sit anywhere you can."

So we just kind of stood at first, like sitting up and holding onto the metal roof with a nine-hour ride ahead of us.

"You've got to be kidding me," Kab said.

I told him, "Welcome to Cambodia," and I laughed.

But as I was sitting there on top of this thin roof I loved every second of it. My camera was in use for nine hours. I took pictures of the floating village, there on the Mekong River, one of the biggest rivers, probably the main river that runs through Cambodia and Vietnam. And back then, the village was being bombed like crazy during wartime, and lot of crocodiles. They've cleaned it out and made a kind of farm area now, so there is fish living there, and no more crocodiles.

It was an amazing boat ride. The people live on the water and their homes are floating so when it rains, when the water level goes up or down, their homes go up or down with the water level. Everybody still lives very simply, you can see in the pictures I took. Fishing is the main food source. They fish right outside their homes or they go a ways up, into the deeper section of the river. The local kids get on a boat and go to school that way, like 12 kids at a time. Poor by western standards, but *happy*. That's how Cambodian people are. Very humble. We don't have much, but we are very happy and very content, and they live a simple life.

MY CAMBODIAN FAMILY has a friend who has a car, and they (including my Cambodian uncle) came to meet us at the boat dock when we arrived at my village. Kab was blown away. They had never seen me before because I was born in Phonm Phen[28], not Battambang[29], where my family and my parents are from. They recognized me because I look like my mom.

"How did they know where to meet us?," Kab asked.

"I don't know," I said, "somehow they did."

We had told my brother who lives in Pennsylvania that we were going to Cambodia. My brother sent a message to my cousin who lives in the city in Phnom Penh, and then my cousin somehow got a message to my village, to my family in the village Battambang, which is five-hour drive from Phnom Penh, so somehow they knew that I was coming, and going to Battambang took a boat ride. So, they got a friend who had a car and went to pick me up at the dock. And the minute I got off the boat, they recognized me instantly.

My Cambodian uncle who was picking us up told me, "I knew it was exactly you, because you look like your mom just so much, getting off the boat." So they picked us up and took us to our hotel, which was in the village, in Battambang, and they *never knew that a hotel existed there*.

"What is this?" they said.

"It's a hotel," I said.

"Why are you here?" they asked.

---

[28] Phnom Penh, Cambodia's busy capital, sits at the junction of the Mekong and Tonlé Sap rivers. It was a hub for both the Khmer Empire and French colonialists. On its walkable riverfront, lined with parks, restaurants and bars, are the ornate Royal Palace, Silver Pagoda and the National Museum, displaying artifacts from around the country. At the city's heart is the massive, art deco Central Market. —Google

[29] Battambang is a city on the Sangkae River in northwestern Cambodia. It's known for colonial buildings such as Sala Khaet, the former Governor's Residence. Battambang Provincial Museum has artifacts from local Khmer temples. Nearby, Phare Ponleu Selpak is a circus and performing arts school for underprivileged children. North of the center are the ruins of Ek Phnom, an 11th-century pagoda with sandstone carvings. —Google

"We are going to stay here," I said.

"No," they said, "you're going to stay with us!"

"Oh, no, we already paid for this and everything," I said. It was a nice, little resort of a hotel.

"Oh," they said, "well, bring your luggage with you."

"Why?"

"Because it's not going to be safe here."

I said, "No, no, it's okay. They are going to take care of my luggage."

"No," they said, "bring it!"

They didn't know this world existed, yet it was only ten minutes from their home. They didn't have a car or any transportation (a friend with a car was helping them that day), they'd just walk or bike. So they didn't go very far from their village or explore their little town. "Wow, that's crazy!" Kab said.

We did finally drop our stuff off at the hotel and we went to my family's house right after.

A BOY SAW US coming, because we had a car. He was on his little bike, and he knew that some Americans were coming. My husband Kab was only the second American who has ever entered the village—another American guy married to my other cousin in Canada came to visit that village before. So, this boy saw us driving in and he followed us to my aunt's hut. She lived in this little place, and he just sat there looking very scared. He wanted to come in so bad, but he was too shy. I kept looking at him. I think he was scared by Kab. He was so skinny, I felt bad. He had no shirt, his nails were all dirty. That picture is of a very authentic Cambodian boy.

In the village, right away my cousin asked us if we were thirsty. I said yes, so he climbed up a coconut tree and got us some fresh coconuts to drink. I thought that was cool and authentic. We met my dad's half-sister. She was wearing a white blouse. In fact we met a group of ladies who remembered my parents because they used to live there. And that little shack where we met was where they sit, and where they sleep. She and my other aunt who lives in the same town, are about ten minutes from each other by car, but they hardly get together because this is too far. They only walk, you know, or use the bike that my uncle has.

I have a picture of my cousin doing dishes, outside, with those big barrels filled with rain water. That's the source of water we have there. They collect all the water in those big barrels and keep it through the years. Every year, April, May, June is the rain season. So that's their source of water. And sources of food are very, very minimal—just fish and chicken sometimes. Beef is really, really rare, and only if the year is an abundant one. You can get pork once in a while, when you get to the city. I have a picture of my cousin in the kitchen, that's where they eat, by an open stone fire pit thing, which they cook on. No refrigerator.

The pictures with my family and Kab with the kids are from my village where my family lives. The children in the photographs are orphans and they live there at the school. There's a picture I took in my village, of my cousin climbing up a tree to get Kab a fresh coconut, and another picture of Kab with a big smile, drinking. In another picture I have from my village, there's a husband and wife, and they're standing there trying to figure out what they doing, trying to figure out what they want to do with a fishing trap. That's very common. There's a photo of little houseboats, and most people live full time in these. There might be people in there, sleeping.

One photo shows garbage. It was taken in one of the dirtiest areas we went through. All these kids were all naked, and just jumping in the water and playing, swimming, and this whole side was all garbage. And, they are happy. I remember similar things like that when I was younger, playing in the river. In my photo, though, this is kind of disgusting. But lots of people were there in the river, washing, bathing, and then they were swimming while there was a poop floating also.

THIRD, WE TOOK A TAXI from Battambang to Phonm Phen and I took pictures of what I saw along the way. It was a five-hour taxi ride—our crazy taxi driver! He was going so fast! The pictures of the market and monks walking (there were monks walking everywhere!) are from Phonm Phen.

I met my cousins in Phonm Phen. They own a convenience store in another town. My cousin's wife was wearing red, in my pictures. My cousin took me to go and meet them. And they were just so happy to see me. She gave me a picture of her daughter who was going to school in Phnom Penh, who was in her early 20s, and she told me, "Please find a husband for her. You know any nice American husband-guy? We need a husband for her, she is going to college."

Over there Americans are known for being rich, and that everybody who lives there is wealthy. So I told her, "You have no idea what the United States is all about. You think we're all rich and wealthy. Some of us are, but most are not. We work hard for money, and we have so many things we worry about." I'm very forward with everybody, but I don't think they fully understood.

We went to a dinner that had a show, like a traditional Cambodian dance show. I sat at a table with tree lilies, a very popular Cambodian flower, while the dancers performed on the stage. It was a dark night, very hard to good pictures. We got a lot of shots of the dancers though, which is great because I loved the dancing, it was beautiful. These ladies wear traditional costumes and coming out of the dark, made for great pictures.

Our trip ended there.

THINGS IN CAMBODIA seem to be getting better. In my family's village they are getting a paved road in the next few years, and they are super, super excited about that. So things are going, but still way behind than everybody else in the world. They still don't have phones or mail in the village, but in the city they do. There, they have phones and computers and they work in offices.

They don't celebrate Christmas, but they do celebrate New Year's. There is a big holiday in the fall, in September, a celebration called *Pchum Ben*[30]. You pray to your ancestors who have passed away. You celebrate their deaths and try to speak to them through spirits. And then you go to the temples and pray for health. We bring lots of food. It's a big, big celebration, almost like our Christmas.

Of the few memories I have of my homeland, Cambodia was and still is *beautiful*. The Cambodian people will always be in my heart, they are such a sweet people. For those of us who left Cambodia for similar reasons, I believe our hearts are always calling us back, to where our ancestor's souls rest.

We want to go back and discover more of Cambodia. That first trip was to go back and see my family and where I grew up, but now I want to *discover*. There are a lot of beautiful beaches in Cambodia and other places there I haven't seen. And my family here in the U.S. is keeping in touch with my parents and my brothers in Cambodia now, both by mail and phone. We write to them once in a while, like during Christmas and things like that, and we send them money.

Kab and I have traveled a lot. We have been to Ireland, Hawaii, Australia, New Zeeland. Europe, Greece, Turkey, Spain, Africa, China, we went to Tahiti in June, and Cambodia is the

---

[30] . . . a religious festival that has been practiced for centuries. Families and relatives gather at pagodas to offer food and prayers to dead ancestors and making merits to save themselves from bad karma. . . Pchum Ben or Ben Thom is a Buddhist celebration that is observed for the dead loved ones. It is observed for 15 days, with the first 14 days being called "Ben Touch." People go to local pagodas and throw rice balls, light candles and listen to monks chanting. —https://www.khmertimeskh.com/539511/the-significance-of-pchum-ben/

most beautiful, most exotic place you will ever see. It's very different, very exotic, and it takes you back a thousand years, when you go there.

I can't tell you what it is, but I guess ever since I was little I've felt someone is watching over me, leading me into paths in my life, taking me this far, being there as I do the things I've done and gone to the places I've gone. I was never afraid to work and stand up for myself and I've always had that dream in my head, that faith in my heart, that everything will work out. Since I met Kab, he builds me up. He lets me be me and loves me for who I am. He makes me feel I can do anything, and he even likes my stubbornness, that only I can decide what I do with my life! He has my heart, and I keep a heart in Cambodia. I always will.

About Sophal Chhay Benefield

Sophal is available as a keynote speaker!
To find out more and make arrangements, visit
www.INSPIRINGWOMENTODAY.com

[12]

INTENSIVE CARE
by Claudia Frustaci

"The world breaks everyone, and afterward,
some are strong at the broken places."
—ERNEST HEMINGWAY

I FOUND MY tumor just two years after Mikey was born, on Christmas Day 2004. It was a very aggressive form of breast cancer, growing so rapidly that it went from zero to a 1.5-centimeter tumor in one year. Even though it was a stage one tumor and there was no metastasis (a positive thing, and we have to look at the positive in everything), it was a grade three tumor, the type that often comes back. They operated and started a very aggressive form of chemotherapy followed by radiation in 2005. That lasted until May 2006. I had a year and a half of chemotherapy treatments. I not only battled the actual tumor, I had to fight its rapid growth. The tumor grew aggressively because I have the HER2 gene, which multiplies cancer cells at a rapid pace.

I was fortunate enough to be a part of a recently approved study that allowed Herceptin injections to be administered to early stage breast cancer patients who had the HER2 gene. It was always given to those with metastasized tumors, and thank the Lord, they approved it for me, because here I am, all these years later. Five years after this whole ordeal I opted, for health reasons, to have my ovaries removed, which pushed me into early menopause, on top of still taking chemotherapy drugs to this day.

Not very long ago, I had chemotherapy injections on a Tuesday and on Wednesday I went for a two-mile walk, but by Thursday I could not get out of bed. I felt like aliens had taken over my body. I was in bed around five or six in the afternoon, and I had the television on. I looked over at the TV and I thought I was dreaming. Melissa Etheridge was on stage, and I don't know what show it was, but when I looked at the TV she looked into the camera and I thought she was talking to me.

"Hang in there," she said, "because it is going to get better."

I was shocked, because I swore she was talking just to me. She had just survived cancer and her hair was still incredibly short. "To all of you," she said, "who are in bed right now, filled with chemotherapy, hang in there. It's going to get better. Keep fighting."

It was an incredible moment, it was very surreal, and it made a real difference for me. It fascinates me that she touched my heart right there and then. I was fighting for my life, and she had just fought for hers. The bond is not through her music, the bond is not through her celebrity status. The bond is from one human being to another human being, and through that moment, through television, she made a difference for me.

—From Claudia Frustaci's upcoming book, *Frustaci*

INTENSIVE CARE BY CLAUDIA FRUSTACI

MY GRANDMOTHER ON my mother's side, my Hungarian grandmother who was still alive, she passed on April 20th. And, obviously, we're in the middle of COVID. And this woman here, I have many citizenships. On paper I have a Hungarian one too, but I don't have a valid Hungarian passport. I have an Italian and an American one. I don't have a Hungarian. Now, all the borders are closed, no one can fly, and unless you're a Hungarian citizen, you're not getting into that country, into Budapest. Due to the funeral, I petitioned to the police in Hungary, filled everything out in Hungarian, that I needed to come home to bury my grandmother. So, they approved it. I sent it to the New York consulate for an official translation of the document. I went to New York to pick it up. Two days later I went back to New York City and I got onto an airplane.

I flew via Amsterdam to Budapest and with that document I just waltzed into the country. I was even absorbed from being quarantined. So, as an American citizen I got out, and I got into Budapest. They didn't take my temperature, nothing. I got in and no problems whatsoever. I walked in and Americans are not allowed in Europe as of July 1st. Trump closed it for the Europeans, then the Europeans shut the Americans out. Meanwhile, while I was in Hungary, I went to Italy twice. I drove. Door-to-door was only a 10-hour drive. So, I went home to Lake Cuomo for a few days. I needed to take care of something for my family, and I thought, *This was easy.* It was all green lights, no borders, no nothing getting there. A week later, I took eight of my friends and we all went. We did Lake Cuomo, we did Milan, and we did Venice.

At first, they canceled my August 8th flight home, I don't know why, but they rescheduled me for August 21st and I came home to the U.S.

Things have changed drastically, and I have a clarity I haven't had in years. My three months away in Budapest and Italy were an "eat, pray, and love myself" kind of a time away, a time where I sat back and watched my life. I realized all the things I've been doing that I have to stop doing. I felt like I was swimming against the current for so long and then finally crawled to shore, climbed onto the riverbanks, and then staring at that river, told myself, *I'll weather any storm whether it's a hurricane, a snow storm, a tornado, whatever you want but I am not jumping back in those waters. Those tornadoes and hurricanes and snow storms will pass but jumping back in and continuously swimming against the current, it's going to drown me.* And with that clarity, I've realized a lot of things. I realized the strength I have.

People don't recognize if they're strong or not. It's kind of hard to see it in yourself, whether you can weather storms, what you can do with the slaps that life gives you. Whether it's fighting cancer alone or dealing with challenges in marriage, there's a lot we sometimes go through. My jewelry line is a nice part of my life and I'm still doing that, but it takes so much energy and effort right now, I'm just selling it here and there or giving it away. And I'm finally realizing what I'm actually very good at, what my strengths really truly are and I'm focusing on those now.

My *relationships* with people are truly incredible. I can make anything happen if the connection is right, with the right person. It's an energy thing, in my job, in sales. I never could see it before. I'm engaged with clients. I enjoy giving so much. As a volunteer I give to the ICU, to the cancer center, and to oncology pediatrics. I've gotten really involved with Georgio Armani the past few years. I'm working with some incredible professionals. They have helped me see my strengths by giving back to the community and engaging and connecting with people selflessly to the point that *they're actually helping me.* It's hard to put into words. They're actually helping me heal and become a better version of myself even through tough times. And this is mainly from volunteering, it has nothing to do with money. A lot of this is dropping what I'm doing to help someone else.

I have to work for a living like we all do, but I know that if I could, I would just give back. It brings me so much joy and it puts such peace in my heart, like nothing else. And the way I can create a relationship with someone is probably the key to my success, even at work, being able to survive even through COVID. Many of us have had to reinvent the wheel, well, I started doing *spatial consultations*. People tell me their issues and I ask questions. We close the conversation and next thing you know they put an order in for skincare—but it wasn't the intent to sell, it was just the intent to educate. So, by not expecting monetary compensation in return, by just doing it because it's something I love doing, it's coming back to me, without even realizing it.

So, I realized my ability to create personal relationships with people is my strength—the way I take care of them, the way I listen to them, the way I take the time to respond, the way I engage with them, that's my strength. And realizing that has also made me realize my strengths when it comes to my job, how I can now focus on sales by using a different approach.

It's gratifying to help others, then getting that phone call not even three or four days later saying, "Oh my God, Claudia, thank you so much. You just saved me," or when you give selflessly to Mass General Hospital, in the Pediatric Oncology Department. They wrote a letter to corporate Armani that made an executive cry on the runway because I took an initiative, didn't tell anyone what I was doing, and I created a bracelet with different beads representing different colors for different cancers. I donated them to every mother of every sick child I worked with. I didn't tell Armani, I didn't tell anyone. We gave them away as gifts for that day. This was on top of the annual event I always support. I never dreamed someone from Oncology Pediatrics would write an email to the vice president and to my executive. It circulated within like brush fire. Every executive got it, every CEO got it, everyone read it because it was shared. It was very hard to see all these sick children. This is not something easy to do but I realized *I'm strong and I can do this*. And there are a lot of us who help at the cancer center, not just me.

In another example, at the ICU in Milford Regional Medical Center, these people are literally fighting. Healthy nurses are not just injecting you with chemotherapy, they're amazing, they're kind, they're there for you. These nurses today in the ICU are risking their own lives to save us, and even bigger reason to give back to them—*God forbid you or I or anybody should ever end up at the ICU*. Through COVID, these people did not just sit at home collecting extra money. No. These people ended up working even more hours, longer days, jeopardizing their own safety to save other people. So, I initiated a program by myself. It *always seems like you cannot make the time or the money to help*, but that's not true. We can. Some people choose too and others don't. I choose to. So, I self-financed and I donated 180 kits. They took me forever to put together, but I did customized facial kits and had them delivered to the ICU.

From that I made a friend who is one of the head nurses at the ICU. When I was in Europe she kept writing me, saying, "I can't wait to see you again. I can't believe how much you've done for us." The products I gave them were all high-end products. So, I knew that they would have good results. Everybody raved about how amazing they were. And it made me feel good that I made them because the masks everyone has to wear right now wreak havoc on people's skin.

How I got started volunteering at the ICU was very fortunate. Being a local business owner in this town for 20 years, I reached out to the head of nurses and I received a message back one day that said, "I hear you are going to distribute facial kits to the ICU. If there's anything we can do to help please let us know."

I wrote back because I didn't want to just drop them all off and trust they'd make it into the right hands, trust they'd be appreciated. I said, "I'd like to come in and make sure they make it into the hands of everyone working in the ICU. I don't want them just put it in the employees' lounge where everybody can take them home for their daughters, their mothers, their aunts, their cousins." I was working 10, 12 hours a day, in fact 20 of them would take me more than half a day. You have to measure them out in cups and then label and explain them, it was just a whole process. I said, "This is for the first responders and others there at the ICU, even the cleaning people. Give it to them. They're in the ICU wiping the floors. They're risking their own health. Give it to them. Just don't leave them for employees to take it home to their mother or a cousin or daughter. These are for the front line people."

This wasn't the intention, but you have no idea the business I'm getting now from having done this—in fact I wasn't planning on getting any business out of it. That's not why I did it. It didn't cross my mind because we couldn't do facials anyway, we couldn't touch people. We were closed. So, it wasn't done thinking we were going to get clients from it. It was done solely to give back. But this landed me a great position in cosmetics. They were incredibly impressed by this. It caught their attention and they said, "Claudia, you've stepped out of the box to make this happen and we need more people like you on board." So, I might be starting a full-time position in sales, where previously most of my job was working with people from the neck up, touching them near their eyes, their nose, their mouth. So being in sales and not having to physically touch people right now, it's something that I'm considering because I cannot afford another shutdown, I'll be honest, and I also cannot afford to get sick.

All these things have led to a lot of good, and all because I care and I put time into it. And it all helped me recognize I really enjoy *people*. I was doing it because it's normal for me to give back, and all in the sadness of losing my nana. I'm blessed she lived to 99 and I had her in my life all these years. My nana had two children. Her youngest died when she was two and my mother was five. She raised my mother as an only child, and as her grandchild, I was her everything. I've been going to Europe at least twice a year, even three or four times a year because I was self-employed.

So, a couple of weeks ago on August 28th, I sat on her tomb and I realized after all these years, there's no more Nana, who was like a mom to me. There's no more house. There's no more business. The entire legacy has just come to an end. And it was a slap in the face, let me tell you, a big one. I could not stop crying through my ten-hour flight home, it hurt so much. Even to this day it takes my breath away. It made me realize everything will come to an end, but what's not going to come to an end is what you leave behind—your teachings, your kindness, your positive impact. People are not going to remember you for what you did for a living or how much money you made, they're going to remember *who you were* and *how you made them feel* and *how you changed life*.

Everything comes to an end. Even legacies come to an end, but you have got to leave something behind for the next generation. All the greed and the selfishness and the money, none of that really truly matters. Instead, it's now more clearly about how I want to live the rest of my life, who I want in my life, and who matters. People were *upset* with me, that I spent almost three months over there, taking care of family business. So, I just laugh at it. A year ago, I would have been devastated that people though that of me. Now, I laugh. And that's the big change.

HI CLAUDIA. I wanted to express my sincere appreciation for all of your amazing work with the children and families at Friday's Flashes of Hope photo session. It was an honor and a privilege to have you as our make-up artist for the afternoon . . .

For families undergoing the often emotionally and financially exhausting process of cancer treatment, the last thing they may be thinking about would be scheduling and paying for family pictures; oftentimes, this is a time-consuming and expensive undertaking. However, through Flashes of Hope (https://flashesofhope.org), families are given access to free family portraits which have been greatly appreciated and incredibly rewarding to the children and families we treat. Parents have been deeply moved by the photos of their children preserving images of their smiles, endurance, dignity, and hope. For many, these powerful photos serve as reminders of the journey the child and family have endured and overcome, and for some of the children photographed by Flashes of Hope who do not survive, these images are truly treasured. These stunning portraits capture each child's unique personality... be it characteristics of independence, courage, or playfulness... allowing each child to step out of the shadow of his diagnosis and providing the opportunity for self-expression.

I have had the opportunity to speak with a few of the moms photographed last week, and they all asked me to convey how incredible you made them feel through your talented artistry, your kind personality, and the beautiful gift which you shared with each of them. I know that these moms are unable and unwilling to set aside any time for themselves. The sacrifices that they make for their families are unimaginable, and having the ability to be pampered for the afternoon is truly a gift that they will forever treasure. One of the moms told me that she really wanted to go out for a date night with her husband because she felt so beautiful after spending time with you! Her little guy was staying overnight in the hospital for his chemotherapy, but her time with you enabled her to be in the moment and feel good about herself! Another mom shared with me that she could not remember when she had looked THIS GOOD!

Claudia, you may remember one of our teens who was hoping to use a picture taken that day for her school photo. While her peers and classmates were together enjoying the beginning of their school year, she was many, many miles away from home receiving life-saving treatment. I know that she will look back on this day and remember being made to feel like the very talented, compassionate, and beautiful young woman that she is.

Thank you does not seem enough to convey my gratitude for all of your kindnesses with us on Friday. It was a pleasure having you as part of our team, and I am very hopeful that we will be able to work together again when Flashes of Hope takes place at the Mass General Hospital for Children Cancer Center.

Wishing you all the best!

Warmly, Heather

Email from Heather Peach, MS, CCLS
Child life Specialist
Massachusetts General Hospital

CONTACT CLAUDIA TODAY!

www.CLAUDIAFRUSTACI.com

[13]

KEYS OF LEADERSHIP
by Betsy Jordan

"Our deepest fear is not that we are inadequate. Our deepest fear is that we are powerful beyond measure. It is our Light, not our Darkness, that most frightens us."

—MARIANNE WILLIAMSON
Return to Love

"My coach would read this quote to me whenever I got backed up and stressed out about doing something I was afraid to do. It was always the fear of my light not my darkness . . . It still is some days."

—BETSY JORDAN

EVERYTHING I LEARNED about being a good human being, I learned from the way my father disciplined us. "Okay, go wait in your room," he would say. I hear all these stories about kids being abused and that sort of thing but this is how it went in my family and with my dad. So, I was a little kid, and he would sit on the edge of the bed so he wasn't towering over me or hollering at me, nothing like that. He just said, "I want you to tell me what you did wrong."

"Why do I have to tell you?" I'd ask. "You sent me here, you already know."

But he wanted me to *say* what it was so there was no misunderstanding, no confusion about it, and so that I didn't walk away wondering.

And then he would mete out the punishment, which in those days was a spanking. These days it might be a timeout or something non-corporal, but it was meted out right there and then. Afterwards, he would say, "Okay, now tell me what you're going to do differently." I didn't get to file a continuance, I didn't get to wait two days, I didn't get to wait two minutes. I had to tell him right then what I was going to do differently to avoid making the same mistake. And then he would say, "Now, I want you to know I always love you." And whether I was still mad at him or not, it didn't matter, I was still hugging him as he walked out the door. That was it. It was over. He never brought it up again. He assumed and trusted that I was going to do something different.

My father was raising *leaders*, he wasn't just raising children. He had an expectation that we were not going to just be *his kids*. We were going to be doing the best we could. The message was really strong. He trusted that I would know what to do next.

Today, my brother and sister and I all talk about how we would have rather had him spank us than talk to us because that meant we had to be accountable, and we then had to be creative and come up with different solutions—all of those things that are missing in leadership today.

WHEN I TELL MY STORY, it's not because I'm wounded, but rather it's because I'm *not* wounded, and because I can see the comparisons between good parenting and the not-so-great parenting I see in my friends or in people I see who are sharing that an abusive thing happened to them. I have had things happen to me, but because of my strong sense of self, which was instilled in me by my parents, I have been able to go through and make my choices based on being happy in the world, or doing something that was a contribution because there's a gift in just giving.

I'm not minimizing anybody else's pain, not at all, but it didn't take me having a particular pain to know that there are *ways* to handle challenges. And it wasn't because I was a great kid, it was because I had great examples. And I did, all over my life.

I grew up in a very small, southern village, Mt. Gilead[31], North Carolina. And I like to say that, because it definitely took *a village* to raise me! That vibrant town was the birthplace of people like

---

[31] Mount Gilead is a town in Montgomery County, in the Piedmont region of North Carolina, United States. The population was 1,181 at the 2010 census. —Wikipedia

my grandfather, who was instrumental in organizing the National Association of County Commissioners. I remember him as quiet, loving, and kind. My father, Bob Jordan[32], was on the organizing committee with William Friday and Julius Chambers, all North Carolina men who were instrumental in organizing the UNC Board of Governors and contributed to the birth of the university system in North Carolina. Julius Chambers was a strong leader, and a strong advocate for human and civil rights, and he was also born in Mt. Gilead.

My father became Lieutenant Governor and at the time had enormous power and reach. I was always touched by his humility. He is described today as the most unselfish leader the state has known. It's fantastic to hear your father described like that. He remained active politically all his life, aiding the Democratic Party in our state, even while at the helm of the family business, Jordan Lumber Company, a manufacturer/wholesaler of southern yellow pine lumber. My father always said, "Mount Gilead is a great place to raise children and pine trees." The land has been good to him, and to me.

My mother was involved in the Methodist Church and we were both actively involved in youth fellowship. She was on the Duke Divinity School Board of Visitors, and became an advocate and board member on the Methodist Home for Children. She was a public school teacher and always carried her worry about her students.

Being born to *leaders of leaders* was inspiring, and my parents expected to raise leaders, which they did with a lot of love and fun.

I was inspired by my aunt, who was really more like my big sister. She was one of the first female basketball players at North Carolina State. She was a much better ballplayer than I was, and she took those skills and raised four very fine children. I've never known someone with better organizing skills and just through sheer willpower, she gets things done. She's a very sweet person.

And her husband has inspired me as well, who with love and faith and much grace, is a survivor of pancreatic cancer. Through his faith, belief, and the power of prayer by a large community of support, he has clean scans today. He's a miracle. My aunt's support of him and their family during that time is a wonder to me.

My own battle has always been an internal one. As a southern belle to a family of means, resources, power, and leadership, it's a challenge to remain grounded and true. To be authentic

---

[32] Robert Byrd Jordan III (1932 – 2020) was an American politician who served as the 29th Lieutenant Governor of North Carolina for one term under Governor James G. Martin and who unsuccessfully ran for Governor of North Carolina in 1988. —Wikipedia

and not be either overly humble (pride disguised as false humility is not appealing) or overly prideful, and yet to offer what I've been shown and blessed with, that takes *gratitude*. I've always known about gratitude bringing great things to the world, and to me. I've always understood the power of love and understanding. I've listened to the still small voice. My challenge has been in expressing it in the face of other perceptively more powerful people. I believe it's honed my courage muscle to be able to speak truth, even when it was unpopular to do so, among powerful people.

Carolyn Mayes coined a term she uses called *wound bondage*. There are a lot of people in this world who bond over their wounds. And there are a lot of people who are very wounded but bonding over those wounds presents the problem of *outgrowing those wounds*. What if you outgrow your wounds, what happens to that bond? All of a sudden it feels like you're not connected anymore. I'd rather people be connected on their *wins* than their wounds. So, how do you share your wins and how do you overcome the idea that you shouldn't share your wins? The thing to do is to celebrate our wins. If we continue to pick at the wounds, they don't heal. Some people stay in relationships for years which are based on their wounds, and when they don't outgrow them, things don't get better.

It goes along with the fact that *what you focus on expands*. So if you're focusing on the wound, what's happening? You're looking at the past, at what happened back there. And that means you're going to go in a circle, if you're in a boat (as a metaphor), looking at the back, and you're probably going to run into stuff.

But when you're focusing on where you *want to go*, it's more likely you're going to get there. All these affirmation-type phrases became cliché because they're true. "Shoot for the moon and you'll land somewhere among the stars," and also, "What you focus on expands." It doesn't mean you ignore the fact that you're walking around missing an arm, you need to know that you're missing an arm so you can do something about it. What this says is that you *focus* on the *solution* rather than the wound, but you do see what those things are which are lacking, you've noticed them.

That's exactly what my dad was teaching me, right? "Notice that you did this thing which was not good. Now we're going to give you a consequence. Life has consequences. So, pay the consequence, pay the price." A lot of people don't want to see they made a mistake because they don't want to pay the price, when instead we need to look at what we are going to do differently so we don't make those same mistakes. What we focus on is the solution. Back there with my dad, I didn't leave the room without having some solution, at least one. He didn't have to agree with it, but he never judged it, as long as I *had a solution*.

People will blow off advice sometimes not because it's good or bad but simply because in the process of getting it they are made to feel doubted and not trusted. This happens with parents all the time, and here's the thing—It's not just parenting, it really is about leadership because I'm seeing leaders not wanting to admit "I made a mistake and I have got to pay the price for this." It usually only happens after somebody has shown such a bright light on the mistake that there's no way they can salvage their reputation because they stuck to their guns, not told the truth in the first place, and they've not been accountable. As they work to *not* pay the price, the stakes get higher, and the price get higher.

But let's say somebody *is* accountable and they *do* pay the price. In that case, you can't stay stuck in the mistake, you have to have a solution to move forward as part of the entire handling. If you do remain without a full solution, you're motivated by guilt and that's no good, it's not productive. So, you choose a new solution, and can possibly move on.

A lot of this is understanding I've gained from observing this, and my experience growing up, so that when I see a politician or any leader, for that matter, amidst a mistake, I often feel frustrated. I want to say to them, "Come on, just admit it. Get it over with. Pay the price. Come on, dust yourself off and then get back out there."

Transparency leads to value. I mean, it's there and everybody else sees the poop on the sidewalk. There's a balance to be had with transparency and privacy. And I think we haven't yet seen all of the invasions of our privacy that we're going to see because the invasion of our privacy conversely has not been very transparent. In general, transparency is a good thing, especially when balanced with a healthy dose of privacy.

And I'm not running for office, by the way.

But these are facets of leadership—transparency, responsibility, as is being part of a team. I was talking to my sister years ago and she made the comment, "It would be difficult for me to hire anyone who had not played on a sports team." I thought about that and I understood what she meant because of the things that you learn when you've got a common goal and you need to play on a team and you want to use the best of each of your teammate's skills to win the game. I think that's why we have so many teambuilding workshops and things like that in corporate America. I played team sports all the way through school, so I took that for granted, I thought everybody knew that kind of thing, but they don't.

I've gone through a couple of divorces, and I've learned from those. Building a *team* makes sense in that regard. There are things I took for granted, and I knew it all along. I have wondered, though, when I see people who have trouble with that concept of taking things for granted, of not seeing marriage and other things as being a part of a *team,* and I have to assume many people just weren't educated in that way. So, it's not that I have had a charmed life and silver spoon because it's not that, it's that the bumps on the road just weren't quite as steep for me. There's something to having an expectation that things aren't going to be easy but *I will be able to handle that*. I guess expecting the unexpected, expecting setbacks, is also a part of leadership, along with being calm and having a way of dealing with these things.

If you don't feel you've had significant hardship, it may be the way you look at things. I'm amazed when I speak with women with similar experiences where one feels traumatized and the other shrugs it off, doesn't see or feel it was traumatic at all, never crossed her mind. It just may be a matter of perspective, of how we were raised, and so on. I have had someone being sexually abusive to me, but I saw that as *his* problem because I certainly wasn't going to spend any more time with that person, right? It was also educational in terms of how other people reacted to it around me. There were then situations later in life where I was able to interrupt that kind of behavior. At my first job, one of the first things that happened was the regional sales manager had women mud wrestling with cake batter, and this was a national company. He got fired.

I was like, "Oh my gosh! It has gotten to this point. We've got to do something about it." And it was actually the men driving the train, who decided we were not going to be this disrespectful, and at the time they understood because they wanted more women in sales.

The experiences I've had led to these little victories. I've always been fortunate enough to be able to take care of myself in the sense that if somebody was stepping over a line, I would just say "You're stepping over a line here. I'm not interested in this." That becomes more difficult if you're in a position of having to be instinct-deprived, where people would argue with you about your opinions instead of understanding and trusting you to be able to make sound judgments in your life.

My parents were interested in raising good and productive adults. I was expected to be able to handle things. I was driving a boat when I was 12, pulling my siblings, waterskiing. We were given a lot of responsibility and we handled it pretty well. We knew we'd get into big trouble if we didn't, and the big trouble was not that we were going to get beaten. It was we were going to be given a talking to, directed to finding solutions for our bad behavior. And what kid wants to do that?

It was all a part of raising leaders.

And part of *leadership* is *service.* A favorite Bible passage of mine is, "From everyone to whom much has been given, much will be required; and from the one to whom much has been entrusted, even more will be demanded." (Luke 12:48). So be it.

I can go on and on about people who inspire me—Reverend Vern Tyson and his son Tim, who is the author of *Blood Done Sign My Name* and a professor at Duke University. They have been instrumental in the Moral Monday Movement, and I know them both as extraordinarily loving people and friends. I've known Tim for most of my life. There's Harvey Gantt, former Mayor of Charlotte who took on Senator Jesse Helms and has been an architect of much improvement and involvement in Charlotte. When I ran for office (North Carolina House of Representatives), the questions he asked both inspired and made me anxious, the flip side of anxiety being inspiration and excitement. He asked the hard questions, the ones that needed answers. Substantive and relevant. There's of course Deepak Chopra, who inspired my writing with his teachings on the psychophysiological origins of disease. There's Lori Todd and Rob Katz whose work with the Legacy Center has been the cause of hundreds of transformational leaders in the world.

I'm inspired by my siblings. We always have each other's backs. My brother expanded the lumber mill, making it the fastest small log mill in the world. And his leadership inspires his coworkers every day. It's a company of excellence due in no small part to him and his creativity. My sister carries on the mantle of the family within the Methodist Home for Children and through her kindness and loyalty continues to inspire me to be greater.

I'm inspired by my daughter, whose funny, quirky take on life—through her love of all creatures except cockroaches, oh, and crying babies—will change the world, or at least one piece of it, either in the world medical community or perhaps in Africa, Switzerland, or perhaps in the USA. Wherever she decides she will make a difference, look out! She will.

Yet in a more general way, the people who inspire me are heart-centered leaders They are people of great compassion and courage. And they are often the still, small voice in the darkness.

Today I am speaking, coaching (as an executive entrepreneurial coach), and writing. I'm selling the online *Turbo Coaching* system and the opportunity for licensing, patents, and proprietary techniques. I coach transformational leadership with people who are on the cutting edge, cultural creatives. These can be political entrepreneurs, artistic entrepreneurs, spiritual entrepreneurs, and coaching entrepreneurs. And I'd like to inspire young women and men, who are the torchbearers of tomorrow.

So, you see, to whom much is given, much is expected. There is no *try*, there is only *do*. And yes, Yoda is my soulmate.

What you focus on expands. So focus on what you'd like to see expanding in your life. Take action toward that vision daily with urgency. See possibility when you are challenged. Remain committed to that vision even when you don't feel like it. And trust yourself, even when those around you are afraid and doubtful.

About Betsy Jordan

Leadership Coach. Speaker. Author

www.BULLSEYECOACH.com

SCARED AND SACRED

by Michelle Hubbard

"*Fear is excitement without the breath.* Here's what this intriguing statement means: the very same mechanisms that produce excitement also produce fear, and any fear can be transformed into excitement by breathing fully with it."

—GAY HENDRICKS

MY STORY IS about a shy, quiet little girl who's done a lot of different things, and lost them all at the age of 65. Being paralyzed by terror, thrown into an abyss of the unknown and depression, I chose to create a new life step-by-step. I share this with you to tell you, *Don't give up on yourself. In fact, be more. Be a bigger, shinier version of yourself.*

Turns out this is what the journey of life is all about.

I was born in Glendale, California, into a pretty traditional middle-class upbringing. I thought everybody's family was like ours. The bottom line was we were there for each other, and home was the place I could return to, get fed, and feel as safe as safe can be. It was not any religious upbringing at all. My dad was raised Southern Baptist but my mom kept religion out of the home, so we formed our own thoughts. We were encouraged to not be controlled by a corrupt church, that sort of a thing, which I think was good.

I was the older of two girls. I was the shy, quiet one, and a protective big sister. As a kid, I loved the beach. I loved Sunday outings with my family. I loved coloring and doing color form kits and playing Barbie and baby dolls.

At age nineteen I wanted to break free of family, I wanted to be on my own, I wanted to be out and about in life. I married a man from Lebanon who needed a green card. He soon cheated on me and beat me. That lost its appeal after a couple of years, so I got a divorce. During that time I attended and graduated from law school. I worked in law as a legal secretary, and then as a paralegal. I took the bar seven times and failed. So I stayed working as a paralegal and did the inside work of the attorney while he went out and did the outside work.

I became burned out on law when my best friend, an attorney 30 years my senior, turned 65 and was moving to Hawaii. He invited me to join him. My heart broke at leaving my parents, sister, and nephews, but this was a chance for a new beginning, and I said yes. We married shortly after moving.

Hawaii was far away, and coming back to California twice a year didn't seem like quite enough, sometimes, but living in a magical place like Hawaii was an opportunity to reinvent myself, to discover new ways of being me. I was curious to see what new parts of me would emerge and how I'd include them. While there I sold real estate, and I started doing college admissions consulting. I decided to explore my love of writing and wrote a fiction novel for teenagers titled *Sour Notes*. It deals with self-image and other teen issues. In fact, I felt like the only talent I had was writing, and I enjoyed it. I was a member of Romance Writers of America, I was even president of our chapter at one point. Published author Penelope Neri-Neary lived in Hawaii then and was a part of our group. She and her publisher created a popular series of books called the *Goosebumps Books*, kind of scary books for teenagers. Penelope had done a Hawaii version, something like *Hawaii Chillers*, and because of the success of that series, the publisher wanted to do another, like a Hawaiian spinoff of the *Sweet Valley High* books, called *Diamond Head High*. Penelope Neri-Neary would write the first book and other authors would write other books in the series.

Oh God, I would love to do that, I thought. I was alive with creativity and stories flowed into my head, so I submitted two stories and one of them became *Sour Notes*. It was reviewed as being the best written and it received good reviews. The publisher lost interest, though, and it never went beyond the three books. I purchased the rights to *Sour Notes* so it could be a stand-alone book. I believe the story of a Hawaiian young woman in high school is more relevant than ever because it's all about facing body-image issues and learning to love ourselves as we are.

I took advantage of an opportunity to use my editing skills, and became a law and graduate school admissions consultant with Kaplan TestPrep[33]. I wrote two other books, one on law school admissions and the other on getting into grad school. I was very successful in getting applicants, particularly those who were older with LSAT, GMAT, or grades in the lower ranges into colleges, including top-tier colleges, often with scholarships.

There came a point when I thought of retiring from Kaplan, but I didn't want the special clients I'd been assigned to falling through the cracks. I wrote my books on personalizing the law and graduate school application and gave the same advice in those books that I'd been giving my clients. I also made videos of the same information. To my surprise, clients reached out to me and rather than retiring, I still offer admissions consulting. I knew I made a helpful difference, and I knew I could organize what I did and how I did it. I had an outline I would share with my clients on how to write their essays in a way that brings out specifics and makes a unique impression, turning their application into a *person*, not paperwork.

My journey into myself was, more and more, calling me to own my spirituality. It got to the point where I started thinking about my future, and my family in California more and more. I decided I wanted to become part of a spiritual community. That's when I found Unity[34], and began the studies of Unity. I was going to become a Unity Minister. At this same time, I began Leadership and Transformation (LAT) training with Gay and Kathlyn Hendricks of the Hendricks Institute.

There came a moment when my church changed, my marriage changed, LAT training was changing me, but of course it was really *me* who had changed and was continuing to change. I knew intuitively I was moving back to my family and California before I even knew I wanted to leave Hawaii. The leadership and transformation training was in California, my family was in California, and I got the intuitive that, *You're moving back to California.* My only problem was *how the hell am I going to support myself?* I had no idea *how*, but that was what was going to happen, even if that meant working at Target.

And this all happened at age *sixty*.

---

[33] Kaplan, Inc. is an American for-profit corporation that provides educational services to colleges and universities and corporations and businesses, including higher education programs, professional training and certifications, test preparation and student support services. —Wikipedia

[34] Unity, known informally as Unity Church, is an organization founded by Charles and Myrtle Fillmore in 1889. It grew out of Transcendentalism and become part of the New Thought movement. Unity is known for its Daily Word devotional publication. —Wikipedia

When I moved back to California, I found most of my family, already established in their own routines. I had some admissions consulting work, but not enough to support myself. I applied for many jobs, but never received a response. My coaching business did not take off. *Am I going to live in Glendale near my dad*, I wondered, *or am I going to live in the Ventura area where I spent a lot of my childhood with my grandparents, and where my sister has a condo?* The condo had become vacant just as I was making the move, so I moved to Ventura, about an hour-and-a-half away from my dad, and where my sister lived. I came over with some money from my divorce and ended up buying the condo, which was a very wise financial investment. I began applying for jobs and began establishing my leadership and transformation coaching practices, and I continued with the admissions consulting. I thought these were going to be the first steps of the rest of my successful, solid life.

The admissions consulting dried up. It's somewhat economy-driven, and when the economy is pretty strong people are often no longer interested in secondary doctorate-degree education, which were the people I was working with to help get into school. Meanwhile, property taxes and home expenses were adding up, and my savings evaporated. The coaching thing didn't take off, either. Nor did any job at that point, actually (not even Target).

A FEW YEARS LATER, there came a morning where I was lying in bed, and I found myself in the fetal position, unable to move. *Why don't I just stay here*, I thought, *until I die?. If I get up I'm just going to start using utilities and I'm going to eat, and I don't have any money coming in, or at least not enough. Why don't I just stay here and go into "the big sleep?"*

At that moment my cat, Charlie, jumped up onto the bed and meowed at me. He was hungry, and I heard the *life* in that. *Well*, I thought, *somebody wants to be alive. He doesn't know anything about money, and he's got the will to live, so I don't know how I can deny him that.* I didn't feel it in myself, but I realized from my work in the Leadership and Transformation training that I was in the grip of fear. I was terrified. I was stuck, frozen, I couldn't move. I was terrified I would never be able to survive financially at my age.

I remembered one of the things to do when the grip of fear has you frozen is *move*. What can you move? The only thing I could get myself conscious enough to move at that moment was my fingertip. I moved it. I could feel myself starting to breathe again—my breath had been so shallow. I could feel my belly start to relax a little bit. So I moved other fingertips, and I moved my ankle, and I could feel myself coming back to some version of rational and I looked around. I was still in my beautiful townhome, in the pretty room I loved, with the cat who wanted to eat. And I decided, *Okay, I'm going to keep going.*

And I did.

I still had the vision and the tools I'd put together when I moved back to California and wanted to start my coaching business. I realized my focus was going to be around being *scared*. That was what I had been living in and was still continuing to move along in. I realized I wasn't alone in being someone who feels really scared. I started working on *Scared AND Sacred*, a coloring journey book that combines the tools I'd learned during my ministerial training with my Leadership and Transformation training. As I was writing the content, I kept making the typo of "sacred" instead of "scared." I realized I was being *nudged*.

I had come to learn from my own journey with feeling scared that when I was willing to let the fear flow though me, as slowly and as painfully as it took, the space that it opened up was really an opportunity for me to step more deeply into my own soul, to step more deeply into that sacred essence, that Christ consciousness, that intuition, luck, or whatever term there is for who and whatever we are besides just five senses and three dimensions in time and space. And I realized that being in that space provides intuitive guidance and wisdom, that it opens up possibilities and options that my fevered, panic-stricken brain couldn't come up with otherwise.

The next journey becomes trusting being in that space, that there, things can be somewhat easier. It's an absolutely bizarre, foreign, strange, undoable concept to those of us who have been gripped in the panic of *how the hell are we going to survive?* But it truly can be this kind of supported space, where even when you are alone you know there's something out there, something has your back, something is on your side, something is holding your hand.

In the space of my next journey, I ended up losing my home. I ended up filing bankruptcy at age sixty-five. I've chased after money, pushed myself to "make" money, and been so unsuccessful that I had no other choice but to put my heart's calling first instead of money. This shy, quiet, little girl is now a woman who speaks on transforming after divorce, as an older woman, when everything seems very scary. I also teach other shy, quiet ones how to speak up and stand as *leaders*. I do spiritual counseling with directors of nonprofits, business owners, men, women and teens on being themselves and feeling scared and standing strong. My admissions consulting books, coloring journey book, and *Sour Notes* are all available at Amazon and Barnes & Noble, and before the pandemic I'd begun doing book signings. It was a dream I'd never imagined could come true for me. I have talks I do and I have workshops and classes I teach. I do some individual mentoring. And that's where my focus is. My website, www.ScaredANDSacred.com, offers tools and videos and more.

I still get scared sometimes, I even have panic-struck mornings where I have to remind myself to wiggle and breathe, to get myself out of bed. But I can see where things are opening, where they are shifting and changing into something that's going to end up being the next step for me, that's going to end up being a safer, more solid step than any of the others I've taken before.

I don't know what's going to happen with my business, but my faith is stronger than ever in the goodness of what's in that sacred space of being willing to let the fear flow through me instead of being in its grip.

My latest book, which is a workbook, is called *Scared AND Sacred*. It's a therapeutic adult coloring book, and I use it in my speaking and trainings. The drawing are by my younger nephew. And this is the focus now for moving forward. I've been speaking a lot lately, using Scared AND Sacred as a guide, and gotten really great responses in terms of being a great speaker, of what I have to offer being so interesting and helpful. Initially, I spoke to several optimist clubs to a great response. I've been speaking at Soroptimist, which is an international group that has local chapters. I cancelled two book signings recently at Barnes & Noble stores because of my dad, through a recent crisis, but Scared AND Sacred is my heart, it is my passion.

I believe in oneness with all, including the Creator of all. I believe that's a very sacred and holy experience that we live. I think that our purpose is to most fully and completely and happily become our own unique self. I don't know who judges development or what the standard for that would be, but in my belief system it's becoming our own unique *self*, existing in this sacred spiritual place, in the dimension of time and space, flesh and blood.

Impact equals income, so you can be someone who does drugs and beats up women but is supremely talented at basketball and make an insane amount of money to do with whatever you want. You could be a Kardashian who has a big butt and dresses in pretty clothes and sleeps around all over the place and make a big impact and make a lot of money and be able to do whatever you want with it.

But it also means you can be someone who does really good work for others, and at the same time ensure you and your body are getting everything you need.

Right now I'm beginning the scary journey I wanted to start ten years ago, and become a Unity Minister. I'm accepted to ministerial school and am very excited. I have no idea where this next evolution of me leads, but I do know that in the sacred space of allowing, my fear can be included, and all things are possible.

About Michelle Hubbard

To keep track of what Michelle's up to
check out her websites or contact Michelle at

scaredNsacred@gmail.com

www.SCAREDANDSACRED.com
www.LAWADMISSIONSCONSULTANT.com

[15]

AUDACIOUS

by Lauren Clemett

"You deserve to be well known, well paid, and wanted."
—LAUREN CLEMETT

I'M VERY FORTUNATE to be living in Australia, which they call the *lucky country*. Being a Kiwi, I also call it the *lucky country*, living in the "West Island," because you've got the North Island and South Island of New Zealand. Australia, to us, is the West Island. Australians don't like that but we New Zealanders, we Kiwis think it's funny. Kiwis and Australians have a largely competitive nature, a little bit like Canadians versus Americans perhaps. We call it the *trans-Tasman rivalry,* because the Tasman Sea sits in-between the two countries. We have this thing between Australians and New Zealanders. We blame each other for things we nicked off each other, which is quite hilarious.

There's a dessert called *pavlova*, for example, which is made of eggs and sugar and it's got cream and fruit on top of it and it's delicious, and there is a ongoing debate as to which country first invented this dessert. Of course, it was definitely the New Zealanders, there's no question. Then there's Phar Lap[35] who was a racehorse that the Aussies have claimed for themselves. There's Russell Crowe who neither country wants to own, which is fine. And there's Crowded House[36] which is an awesome Kiwi band, along with a number of other bands who have a mix of Australians and New Zealanders, and no one can decide who actually owns them. We've all been brought up in this fabulous environment where we are highly competitive, where we are great sports people and we love to meet each other on the sports field. Today, I am really lucky to be living in Australia but I was born in New Zealand and it will always be home and I still call myself a Kiwi.

New Zealand is a very small country, right at the bottom of the world. My parents emigrated there from England, *Ten-Pound Poms*[37] they were called, the idea being you were given ten pounds to get on the ship and sail to another country. Emigrating from England, they looked at Canada, Australia, or New Zealand as their three options, and they chose New Zealand, because my dad fell in love with the Hauraki Gulf, Aucklands Harbour, and he loved sailing in his hometown of Poole, Dorset, England. My mum was a florist and my dad was an engineering draftsmen. Quite creative, both of them. They quite adventurously, jumped on a ship and sailed for a number of months, eventually getting to New Zealand and settling down in Auckland. They were a lovely couple from the south of England who'd been brought up in very Christian households and then decided to start a new life; traveled to the other side of the world; and ended up in a place where there was an interesting language.

I remember my mother saying to me, when they first moved to New Zealand, she had to write her address down on a piece of paper because if anybody asked her when she was out, "What's your address? Where do you live?" she would have to read what the words were because the address was *Wakakura* Crescent off of *Ngataringa* Road (Devonport, Auckland) which are two

---

[35] Phar Lap was a champion Thoroughbred racehorse whose achievements captured the Australian public's imagination during the early years of the Great Depression. Foaled in New Zealand, he was trained and raced in Australia by Harry Telford. —Wikipedia

[36] Crowded House are a rock band, formed in Melbourne, Australia, in 1985. Its founding members were New Zealander Neil Finn and Australians Paul Hester and Nick Seymour. Later band members included Neil Finn's brother, Tim Finn, and Americans Mark Hart and Matt Sherrod. —Wikipedia

[37] Ten Pound Poms is a colloquial term used in Australia and New Zealand to describe British citizens who migrated to Australia and New Zealand after the Second World War. —Wikipedia

Māori[38] words, the language spoken by New Zealand natives, and they were introduced to a whole new culture in New Zealand.

What I love about New Zealanders, is that the culture there is really integrated. The Māori culture is a big part of our lives. And there's the All Blacks[39], of course. Everybody knows the All Blacks with the haka[40] or war dance they have before they play. We talk about our whānau[41] which is a Māori word for family, and having lots of *kai* or *kaimoana*, which is seafood. "You're gonna have some *kai* with the *whānau* on the weekend."

So, a lot of the language and a lot of the culture is actually part of the way of life still today in New Zealand, which is lovely. And while I think the integration there is much better, I certainly don't think it's yet equal. I think, certainly, the Māori people still have a lot to fight for in New Zealand, but it's certainly a lot better than a number of other countries, including Australia. I believe that around the world we are struggling with inequality. I remember having lots of Māori friends and Māori boyfriends and how families would just integrate. There was never any question about the color of your skin or what denomination of religion you were or anything like that. It's a lesson perhaps we need to teach more to other countries.

New Zealand is probably well known as an untouched country. There wasn't a hell of a lot that anyone really cared about down here. So, we could just get on with it. We weren't invaded, although the Māoris would say they were invaded, definitely. There were definitely world wars, definitely lots of people died, and there have been injustices in terms of people trading beads and blankets for land. All of that definitely happened. There was good old Captain Cook, for instance, the disastrous man that he was. Everybody still thinks he's awesome but I think he was a bit of a pirate. Yeah, interesting place with an interesting history.

But now, we're living in Australia. We've jumped the ditch, my husband and I, and been here ten years, which we did it for the weather, which is a really simple, straightforward reason. It's like Florida in the U.S., perhaps. We lived in Wellington, New Zealand, and we remember the nice

---

[38] The Māori are the indigenous Polynesian people of mainland New Zealand. Māori originated with settlers from eastern Polynesia, who arrived in New Zealand in several waves of waka voyages between roughly 1320 and 1350. —Wikipedia

[39] The New Zealand national rugby union team, commonly known as the All Blacks, represents New Zealand in men's international rugby union, which is considered the country's national sport. The team won the Rugby World Cup in 2011 and 2015, as well as in the inaugural tournament in 1987. —Wikipedia

[40] The haka is a ceremonial dance or challenge in Māori culture. It is performed by a group, with vigorous movements and stamping of the feet with rhythmically shouted accompaniment. —Wikipedia

[41] Whānau (Māori pronunciation: [ˈfaːnaʉ]) is a Māori-language word for extended family. —Wikipedia

days there, when on rare occasions it *didn't* rain, whereas now in Australia, on the Gold Coast, they're all nice days. It rains in New Zealand much more than it does in Australia. If you've seen photographs of New Zealand, it's a very green country, with beautiful mountains and beautiful forests. That's because there's a lot of rain, especially in the South Island. They've got lots of hydro dams in New Zealand because agriculture is a big thing there.

The biggest industries in New Zealand are milk, cheese, butter, lamb, and beef. After that it would be tourism. They've had a real problem where the country's in a big mess from an economic point of view. They don't have as many resources as other places. They have a little bit of oil, but nowhere near as many natural resources as Australia. They certainly don't have the stuff on the ground like they do in here—the minerals and the iron ore, for example. The wealth in Australia is extraordinary compared to New Zealand.

The big difference between New Zealanders and Australians is New Zealanders were pioneers. People wanted to go there to start afresh. So we had great mixes of European and Māori and Pacific Island culture, where people were starting new lives with a very big sense of community and fairness.

New Zealanders are also well known for their ingenuity and innovation. For example, when *Lord of the Rings* was filmed in New Zealand, there was lots of brand-new technology created. New Zealand is so far away from Hollywood studios they had to develop all of this awesome telecommunications ability and everything else they needed to try and make it all happen. That's one example, and they have had lots of similar innovation, whereas Australia was settled by convicts. People didn't want to come, they were sent here. In New Zealand it's all about pioneering, in Australia, the undercurrent of the society is *mateship*. It really is about standing up for your mates. And that goes way back. Apparently, the history is that when a convict used to act up, instead of punishing the convict, they'd take the convict away, punish everybody else, and feed and bathe and wash and care for the convict, then send them back in. Of course, the other convicts didn't like that. So, they themselves decided, "Well, they're actually trying to get us to fight with each other and we're not going to let them do that. We're going to stick up for each other." And that just kept going through the whole culture of the country. The early settler really challenged the old fashioned English system of classes and teamed everyone together as mates.

Racial tension still exists here. I mean, I can't name one Aboriginal friend and I've lived here ten years. I don't even know whether I've really met many Aboriginal people and I've lived in and traveled this country a long time. There's definitely a distinctive divide here in Australia. The culture hasn't been as integrated in Australia as it has in New Zealand, not yet. The difference, I guess, is that the Aboriginals were almost hunted to extinction here and even today the death rate from suicide and drug abuse and the numbers of young Aboriginals in detention centers and prisons is massive compared to Europeans. That's something that Australia really hasn't handled well. They only really apologized to the Aboriginals of the country maybe 15 years ago and they're still not on par. So I think Australia is actually still quite a racist country, just based on many people's opinions. Most "good, old, true-blue" Australians will call Aboriginal people "lazy," "no good," "drunks," and so on. And it's just a real lack of understanding of the culture. It makes it difficult and I wish it was different.

In New Zealand for example, Maori is taught in schools. We have a Maori and an English version of the National Anthem. That doesn't happen in Australia yet. And the trouble with it is that there are so many different Aboriginal languages and tribes. They have started adding a "welcome to country" at the beginning of sporting and community events and they did a good job for the most recent Commonwealth Games which were held on the Gold Coast and have started including some local words like "jingery," which means *hello* in the local dialect. But of course, that only works on the Gold Coast. Compared to New Zealand (NX), Australia is an ancient country, so it's more difficult to get everyone together on the same page, but worth trying, I think.

It is interesting, how each culture has its own DNA. There's a pioneering spirit in New Zealand. There's mateship here in Australia. When you look at England, it's all about class, it's all about which level you come from—the upper class, the middle class—and you don't move out of your situation—that *Downton Abbey* thing. America is all about liberty. It's all about the right to bear arms, to have your opinion, and to be free. The class system in India is even more disgraceful because it seems even more ingrained that if you're born a beggar you're doomed to always be a beggar. If you're born into a particular caste that's wealthy you don't mix with those "lower" than you. The Chinese have a different culture, where it's all about the future, it's all about working hard now for the generation that is going to be there after you. It's not about *your* life, it's about your children's-children's-children's-children. They plan well ahead and you can see that with the way they buy into places like Australia.

So how did it all begin? In 1968, I was born in a little place called Devonport which is beautiful. It's right on the harbor in Auckland which is the largest city in New Zealand. My dad worked for the Navy. My mom was a florist. She used to work in the city. They had their three daughters and we grew up on the beach. It was fantastic, a beautiful place to live, just wonderful. And then my dad and my mum moved around a little bit. We ended up moving to a little place in the middle of nowhere called Huntly, which was cold and damp and by a river but the community was fabulous. I started off going to school there. Then we moved to New Plymouth which is an interesting place, a town on the edge of a volcano which is slightly active. We got lots of earthquakes and even get a bit of a puff of sulfur from it. From there we moved to a little place called Hunua, In South Auckland.

These were my formative years I remember the most because I was between the ages of about 6 and 15. In Hunua my dad ran a YMCA Camp. And it was an extraordinary place to live. Every week of the holidays, about 360 children would arrive on buses and spend the week with us. They'd go home a week later and another busload would arrive. It was awesome to live in that sort of environment. We had acres and acres of land and bush behind us. We used to go disappear up on the bush and build makeshift camping areas (called *bivys*, short for bivouacs) and have just a huge amount freedom. We had motorbikes and pet sheep and horses and it was really a great place to live, it was fantastic.

In my last year of high school, we left the camp and moved to another part of the country, to a small town called Marton, which according to most is in the middle of nowhere. My mum and dad ran a conference center and I hated it. It was probably the most unsettling time to be a teenager, having to move to a new town and make all new friends, trying to finish school and fit in. As soon as I could I moved back to Auckland and set up my own life. I've always been creative, always drawing, constantly painting, and involved in anything to do with photography or art. I just loved it because I was dyslexic, so I really struggled with the reading and the writing and the math and the rest of it whereas the painting and the drawing I loved. So, I wanted to be a graphic designer. I put myself through college to do that and then was offered the chance to go overseas and train for the first job that I got out of college. I jumped at the opportunity. I was sent off to England where I was going to train for a couple of weeks, which is where my mum and dad came from. So, the whole thing sort of went full circle. How ironic!

So I ended up as a young 20-year-old back in England, the country my parents had left, for a couple of weeks' training and I loved it. Loved the travel. Loved the training. Actually, I remember when I was younger, I wasn't interested in much else but I liked the idea of being an air hostess. I think it was the travel that interested me, in getting around and getting out of the country, so I loved the training in England. I got to see my grandparents and some of my extended family who lived there, and when I came back to New Zealand to continue working for the same company, I had already decided, *That's enough. I want to go travel.* I had a taste of it, and I had dual passports, which made the decision even easier. I was (and am) a New Zealand citizen and an English citizen as well because of my parents. So, I could jump around between the two countries, no problem at all. So, I sold everything and went.

Most New Zealanders of my age group ended up doing what we called an "OE," which was an *overseas experience*. Most of the time they're about 18 months to two years long because that's the length of the working visa that you used to be able to get to go to Europe, the plan being that after a year or two travelling, you came home and settled down in New Zealand. But I had decided, *I'm going to ditch everything.*

It's really quite liberating when you get to a point where you've got *no keys left*. You've sold your car, you've got rid of your flat, you've got no keys to anything. I didn't have any furniture. I had a backpack and a bit of hand luggage. All my other stuff was in storage and even then it was stuff I didn't really need, anyway. It's quite liberating to get to that point where it's just you and your backpack, and that's it.

In England I was lucky to work for some awesome advertising agencies. I started off as a receptionist even though I had a graphic design qualification. I was good talking with people, so they liked having me up front, which was great. It goes back to my YMCA days, to the camp days where I was happy to talk to anybody, 360 different kids every week. In such a situation, you're going to be quite sociable, aren't you?

I ended up working with printing companies and advertising agencies. I worked for a timeshare company. Having an OE (or gap year as many call it) is very much about having an experience, not about building your career. It's about doing what you want. So I worked behind the bar in the First and Last Inn in England which was right down at the bottom of Cornwall. I did all sorts of different things. I went and lived in Spain for a little while with my boyfriend's family and helped them run a rock-climbing business there. I travelled quite a bit over there. Loved traveling in Europe. Went skiing in Switzerland. All sorts of fabulous things. Lived in caravans and spent most of my time drinking the money I was earning in vodka and having a very good time. It was awesome. Loved it. And the two years turned into five years. So, I ended up staying because I had an English passport.

The freakiest time was when I realized how far away from home I was. I was working in the First and Last Inn. I was pouring pints of beer for the English in the pub and at the halftime of the FA Cup final (which is a soccer match, of course). I decided to telephone my dad back in New Zealand. My dad loved soccer. He's always been a big Liverpool fan. So I knew he would be up in the middle of the night in New Zealand, whereas it was the middle of the day in England. I ran across the road and got into a phone box—which in those days was this glass thing with the wind whipping underneath. It was freezing cold in Cornwall, and I was speaking to my dad on the other side of the planet. He was up watching the FA Cup final, the same as I was, and that feeling of being so distant from my home and from my family struck me. I could have been anywhere really, and it seemed so far away for us to be experiencing the same event on opposite sides of the globe.

Eventually I went back to New Zealand and settled down to have a family, New Zealand being a very safe place to make a home.

And it was in New Zealand where I decided I should probably start a career. *Enough of this messing around business,* I thought, *What is it I really want to do?"* I got into publishing. I worked for a couple of magazine publishers as the production manager. I got to know a lot of suppliers from that, which was great. I've always liked building good relationships with people. In fact some of the relationships with our suppliers I still have. I can still ring them up and have a chat, and that's awesome, years and years later.

I then moved to Wellington from Auckland and discovered the world of advertising. And I really was at a bit of a loss there. I didn't know what to do and I started applying for jobs. You'll never get a great job in advertising that's actually advertised, which is the weirdest thing ever. You actually need to go there, knock on the door, sit down, and talk to people. Take your CV with you and get to know the people. I ended up getting a job in a little boutique agency as the production manager for a couple of years. I was producing television, radio, press, direct marketing, the works. Internet didn't exist back then. So, it was all very much billboards and so on. Direct marketing was a big, new thing because all of a sudden we could get more *data,* especially as the internet really started to deliver. We knew the home address of people and about things like loyalty cards for shopping, so we could get the data of where people were spending their money and what they were buying. We then created these amazing campaigns to tag people on their shopping behavior and we were sending things to their homes in the mail. It was more than just coupons, we were actually selling people with personalised pieces of direct marketing, anything from feather dusters to fence posts and coffee cups that changed their image when you poured hot water into them.

I left that little boutique agency and ended up working for some of the big boys. I worked for Clemenger BBDO as a production manager, still doing all that amazing stuff, turning the ideas of the creatives into reality, working between the graphic design team and the suits, putting it all together, making sure it was all delivered—TV ads, radio ads, direct marketing. It was great. Then I worked at the Big Kahuna (which is Saatchi & Saatchi[42]) and absolutely loved it, loved the place, loved the culture, loved the people, loved the clients they had, the type of work they did. I mean, they were winning so many international awards. Saatchi in Wellington was probably within the top ten creative advertising agencies in the world when I was there. Kevin Roberts, who became

---

[42] Saatchi & Saatchi is a global communications and advertising agency network with 114 offices in 76 countries and over 6,500 staff. It was founded in 1970 and is currently headquartered in London. ~ Wikipedia

the head of Saatchi Global, wrote the book *Lovemarks: The Future Beyond Brands,* and later moved to New York, was our boss, and we were surrounded with world renowned, award-winning talent.

That was the level of people I was working with, truly creative people. They would do extraordinary things. One day I came to work and someone had invited a graffiti artist to completely repaint the whole carpark. Another day the creative director came in and we realized he had both of his nipples pierced. One day somebody had just run a marathon that morning and then came in to work. There were always these weird, bizarre things that would happen because of these creative people. It was the era where the best campaigns were written on the back of a coaster in some sports bar. Sometimes we'd go out for a long lunch and a day later we would all emerge and get back to work. It was extraordinary, a really, really awesome place to work. I came back from England in 1995, and this was the late 1990s. The advertising world was so interesting back then.

People were starting to realize that the media—TV, radio—was a big part of advertising and the agencies started to sell their souls. They would almost do the creative work for free just to win the client, knowing they'd make their money on the backend through the media sales. It was expensive to get on the peak TV shows. But back then TV was the biggest thing, before the internet. I remember when the final episode of *M.A.S.H.* aired, there was nobody on the streets. Even the crew had finished filming and gone out to have a last drink together, and there was nobody else out in the cafes. They were all home watching the show. Can you imagine that? Since when did the whole country or even the whole planet stop to watch something?

Those days are over. All of the production I'd been doing—all of the reprographics cameras, film to plate, all this technology—disappeared in a very short space of time. Computers became the norm. You could Photoshop stuff, you didn't need to use a photographer. All of these things happened to make things "easier and faster," allegedly. And now, of course, we've got such fractured audiences. We've got podcasts and webinars and blogs and all these other awesome things that are out there. We've got *social* media. We've still got TV and radio but we're so fractured as to where we pay our attention these days. To get a global audience for anything, you have to be a big celebrity or a big event for that to happen.

By the time I moved to Australia I was ready to get *out* of the advertising world. I had met my husband, Graeme at Saatchi & Saatchi when I was a production manager there. My boss at Saatchi's was going back to England to see family, and she'd arranged for someone to take her place while she was away. That person happened to be Graeme. One day I saw this guy arriving for a meeting with her. He had a purchase order book, which was like a cheque book for an advertising agency, for another agency called Redman Advertising, and another purchase order book for his own company, Graeme Clemett & Associates, and then while he was there, he had a meeting with Nicola, after which he was given a purchase order book from Saatchi & Saatchi.

Who is this guy? I wondered. How can he have open checkbooks for three different advertising agencies? How does this work?

Graeme was due to come and take Nicola's place, but he worked for these other agencies as well so he needed someone to take *his* place while he came down to Wellington and did Nicola's job. He approached me.

"Look, would you mind?" he asked. "What do you think? Would you go and work for one of these other agencies while I work here and run the office?"

"Yeah, sure," I said. "It will all work out."

Saatchi & Saatchi used to have a fabulous bar inside the agencies. Half of the bar was dominated by a huge coffee machine which made a proper and professional cappuccino. and the three of us sat there and worked out how it was going to go.

I was contracting to Saatchi's and I started contracting to Graeme to go and work at this other agency as well. And it worked out. We sort of swapped roles. By the end of it, we decided, "Well, why don't we just keep doing this?" I ended up working for Saatchi's and Redman and Graeme in different agencies, being contracted as the production manager. I'd drive to Hamilton or Auckland or he'd drive to Wellington. We'd debrief each other after one of us had arrived on what work was going on in each other's agency and then part again and then run each other's offices for a couple of months. In my own defense, I would turn up and Graeme's desk would be a complete mess with Post-It notes everywhere, and he would turn up to my own clean desk with everything organised and ready for him to take over where I had left off. These things showed us the need for *systems* and *processes*.

I remember working my first week at Redman in Hamilton (which is an awesome little city in the middle of the Norther Island of NZ, which they call *cow cocky country*, or farming territory). We were the production team for this agency and worked on these multimillion-dollar campaigns for amazing clients. At the end of the day we'd open the door to go home and a tractor would drive past. Hamilton is a really interesting place. It's in the middle of nowhere really. It's just farming and a river, but travel just a couple of hours in either direction and you've got Taupo, which is great for fishing, Rotorua, which has a hot springs and the mountains for skiing, and Raglan, for surfing and beautiful beaches. On the weekends Hamilton would empty out, but during the week they'd all come back and work. Great place to live because it's really close to get to these great things and use to be relatively cheap to live there. I came up with the tagline for Hamilton once. I did send it to the council but I never heard back. It was, "Hamilton: It's Close to Somewhere Interesting." I don't think they liked that one.

As we became aware of the need for systems and processes when we swapped agencies to run, we wanted to have the same level of service from our production manager even though it was a different person. So, we did things like make sure there was a work-in-progress system in every single agency. (We've still got one we use, even now.)

Thankfully, today there are fabulous tools. We use the "Monday" online project management platform. All of our jobs are in there, our templates are in there, we have progresses there, anything that's happening, invoicing—it's all there in one place. With that we have the ability for someone to come and go. It's not based on a person having to do it all. There's a system in place so nothing's missed. If I fell over tomorrow, the company could still run, the business would still continue on. What was ingrained in both Graeme and me was as entrepreneurs you're only as good as the systems and the foundation of the business you've built. If it's all based on *you* and what's inside your head and your capabilities, it's not a business. It's just another job.

Unfortunately we lost a rather large client one year and I decided to leave working with Graeme and get a job. I was very fortunate though, and managed to find an opportunity to do maternity coverage as a brand manager in a corporate setting for AXA[43]. I didn't know until I got the job that AXA was a sponsor of the Rugby World Sevens Series[44]. So, I ended up being the brand manager for a very big event in New Zealand with 60,000 people attending the biggest party and sports event of the year. Rugby of course, is a *big* thing. All these teams come in from overseas. I got to meet teams from Australia, England, Fiji, and South Africa and I was in charge of delivering the project as the naming rights sponsor, which was a real highlight for my career, being a brand manager for such an awesome event.

I was given a quarter of the previous two years' budgets because, unfortunately, when you sponsor a big event like that (which requires something like half a million dollars to sponsor it), you've then got to find *another* half a million dollars to leverage the sponsorship because you've got all the branding, advertising, and marketing that's going to happen to leverage the event. By the third year, there was no money left. It had been spent it all in the first two years. So, I had about a

---

[43] Axa S.A. is a French multinational insurance firm headquartered in the 8th arrondissement of Paris that engages in global insurance, investment management, and other financial services. ~ Wikipedia

[44] The World Rugby Sevens Series is an annual series of international rugby sevens tournaments run by World Rugby featuring national sevens teams. ~ Wikipedia

quarter of the previous budget and they still wanted to see results—even better results than the previous years. It was good in a way because they had already established much of what was needed in the previous years, so I suggested we focus on delivering the best results possible for brand awareness and cut back on anything that didn't achieve that. As a result, *I increased the brand awareness from that event by 15 percent with a quarter of the budget*. Normally, a change of *two* percent is awesome but 15 percent is a big deal. So, that was pretty cool and I'm very proud of my success there.

They asked me to stay at AXA. I had an awesome boss there. She was fantastic, the head of marketing, Ruth Colenso, amazing woman.

Much as I was tempted to stay on, I said, "No, I've got to go and do what I need to do,". I wanted to open my own advertising agency, and I did. Graeme and I were together having gone through World War II, World War III, World War IV—whatever it was with our own families because we both were married when we met, and we both had small children but we decided we wanted to be together. Our children were both two years old at the time and the advice we had from our councilor was that if we did this while they were little, they would grow up not knowing any different. So, my family divorced me for a few years. They didn't like the fact that I had an affair and had gone off with my boss. It was just horrible times, and yet, *the best thing we ever did*.

Our kids have grown up as amazing young women and both of our exes have gone on and settled down. My ex-husband remarried and moved back to Spain and Graeme's ex lives in NZ with his daughter now in university. Our kids are awesome, both daughters are now 19 years old. One is at university and one works for us, which is very cool. Really, really cool girls. We don't get to see much of Graeme's daughter, unfortunately and it's really sad because we'd love to spend more time with her, but we moved to Australia (she did too for a while) and it's not easy to get back and forth to New Zealand while we are running businesses.

When opening your own business, you've got to have the right people around you. I always wanted my own business. I actually attempted a number of businesses in my first marriage and it felt like I was doing all the work and my ex-husband was just riding along on my coattails. But now I had Graeme supporting me.

"Yeah," he said, "let's do this. I'll be there for you. We'll look at how we can finance this. We'll work together on it."

It was much more of a partnership. So, I opened my own agency in Wellington and it was very successful. It was an agency focused on baby boomer and senior marketing, which was ahead of its time. We had lots of finance companies, we had medical, we had insurance, we had all sorts of fabulous companies that wanted to tap into that growing aging market and we loved it. A few of the creatives who had worked at Saatchi's had been made redundant because the agency was downsizing so I was able to employ the guys I had previously been working with there. They used to come in as freelancers, so right away, I had this awesome group. I had great relationships with all the cool suppliers and TV companies and printers and they all loved working with us. It was a great time to have an agency.

Then 2008 happened[45]. All of my clients disappeared because the financial industry and the superannuation industry just died, died on its ass. It got to a point where we went, "You know what, do we really want to be doing this? Do we really want to be in an industry where it is so cutthroat and it is so leveraged on the economy?" because marketing, branding, are the first things that go when budgets get tight. When disaster strikes (like COVID-19 just now), people stop spending on PR and advertising. Shouldn't, maybe, but they do.

So when we moved to Australia, I thought, *If we're starting fresh, what are we going to do?* I looked at personal branding because I was getting into coaching and mentoring people and I saw a massive growth in the services industry, where people were exiting corporate and starting up their own business but had no idea about how to position, brand, and market themselves.

And that's never going to change. You're always going to need someone to help guide you through whatever is happening with your business, whether it's good times or bad times. I'm an entrepreneur at heart. I've got great, positive role models as parents who both worked and had a family at the same time. I enjoyed a great background, and I am married to a man who is a through-and-through entrepreneur. He was probably one of the youngest managers of a multimillion-dollar business in New Zealand in his 20s. He had something like 50 staff. He's very organized. He used to be a first five-eighth in rugby (a first five-eighth is the guy who stands at the back of the pack of 15 guys, watches what's going on, and pushes the play where it needs to go). He played for some of the top sides in New Zealand before he got too scared of the big Polynesian boys: "This is so dangerous," he told me, "I'm going to get killed." So he got out of rugby and into tennis! He's got that ability to look at a business or a project and to plot where it's going to go. Doesn't always work. I mean, you have your fair share of failures and we've been on the brink of bankruptcy and all sorts of stuff in our lives, but we're constantly looking at how can we can improve.

---

[45] The Great Recession was a period of marked general decline observed in national economies globally that occurred between 2007–2009. The scale and timing of the recession varied from country to country. ~ Wikipedia

He's been the best business partner and life partner you could wish for. And now, in the last year (2019), the best thing that's happened to me is I found an awesome new business partner, Annette. I've had my fair share of business partners who just didn't work at all, or were liabilities financially, or caused lots of stress, but my new partner in business is a stand-up comedian (seriously). She's awesome. She's an ex-journalist. She's not as entrepreneurial as I am, she's more of an employee, so she's learning the entrepreneurial world and doing a smashing job of it. She's just a complete Trojan, with an incredible work ethic and so many talents and skills I lack. We always have a bit of fun between us because she always wants to do these things and I go, "That's not really the way you do it but let's give it a crack!" And she's so positive. She has a good community spirit. People love her, whereas I'm much more of, "Look, let's push through and get this done! I actually don't care so much about your feelings." I'm totally on the business. We bounce off each other really well. So, *The Audacious Agency* was born and that's where we are today, sitting in the Gold Coast of Australia working together and having a ball.

At the Audacious Agency, we talk about ourselves as the *self-promotion experts*. And self-promotion, to a lot of people, is a dirty word. People don't like to think about promoting themselves. They think that that's an awful thing to do, but as Annette says, "There's no place in business for modesty." In business you've got to get out there and be your own best cheer squad. You've got to support yourself. So, we help entrepreneurs who are really sick and tired of being the world's best-kept secret to boldly stand out from the competition, which is really cool. We love to see them gaining more confidence and starting to charge what they're worth, and they become the sought-after specialist. That's our thing.

We've been referring work to each other and working together, Annette and me, over the last four years on the Stevie Awards. We've been taking women to America, going to New York, and encouraging women in Australia and New Zealand to enter the international awards. It's been amazing to see the journeys of these women, and to see the self-development and improvement in their sense of value. These women so often underestimate themselves—that *imposter syndrome*. It's the funniest thing. When we work on the awards, we do an interview with each woman, then write their award and send it to them for them to read through and approve. And so often we get an email back going, "I think you've sent this to the wrong person. This isn't me."

"Yes, it is," we say. "This is just us storytelling and putting into words what you've actually done."

"Oh, are you sure?" they say. "Are you sure this is me?"

And then they go and stand on that world stage and they *grow*. There's this huge sense of accomplishment as all of a sudden they realise that an independent panel of judges has said *you're worthy of an award* and they go on and they do these amazing things. Incredible. With the Stevies, we're very fortunate. We get to tell these incredible entrepreneur's stories from around the world, which is great.

TODAY, GRAEME AND I am are at the point where we've got grown-up daughters (making us "empty nesters"), so our plan is to be of no fixed abode. We spend quite a bit of time in Thailand and love it. we also love the States, love going to New York, Boston, and Washington, was looking forward to Las Vegas for the Stevie this year which has become a virtual event because of the pandemic, love Los Angeles, looking forward to getting to Florida. I just love the travel and Graeme hasn't been to Europe yet, so that's definitely on the plans. Our idea is to travel for six months of the year, running our business from wherever we are. That might be Thailand or Cambodia or Vietnam or America or England or whatever it is. Digital nomads.

I'd be quite happy to not own a property and just be traveling. Our old business partners, a fabulous couple in Melbourne, here in Australia, told us once that as that as soon as they'd finished a holiday, they were planning the next one, and we liked that advice. So, when you're head-down, bum-up in business and you're working so hard, you've got to have this light at the end of the tunnel, for your own sense of mental wellbeing. So that's now also become our plan.

People say to us, "So, you're going on holiday for a month?"

"No, we're just going to run our business from a different part of the world."

I love that aspect of being in a place where you've never been before, and that feeling of walking around a corner or down the road or into a place and experiencing it for the first time. Just love it. Looking forward to doing more of it. We've got to *do* things in life, don't we? I always say that—especially for women in business—you have the most amazing gifts and talents that the world needs. So important that you don't hide them away, that you get out there and show them. And I always say you do deserve to be well known, well paid, and wanted, and I say that because women have these incredible stories but they so often don't share them. So, it's really important you get out there and shine.

About Lauren Clemett

www.THEAUDACIOUSAGENCY.com

INSPIRING WOMEN TODAY

Mt. Elbrus, Russia , Summit 3 of 7

[16]

CLARITY

BY BELINDA JANE DOLAN

"Technique and ability alone do not get you to the top; it is the willpower that is the most important. This willpower you cannot buy with money or be given by others... it rises from your heart."

—JUNKO TABEI

THE WORDS THAT no daughter ever wants to hear: "Sweetheart… I have cancer." Four devastating words that changed my life and that of my little sister's forever. Four small words that set me on a powerful pathway that allowed me to turn the destructive nature of grief, loss, and suffering into a powerful way to positively impact the lives of millions.

As I write this I'm in Melbourne (Port Melbourne), which sits right by the ocean. If I were to head out into the vast blue ocean that I see in front of me the next large land mass would be Antarctica. I am however blessed to live in the beautiful Sunshine State of Australia, overlooking Mount Coot-Tha in Brisbane, Queensland. In three or four hours I'll be on a plane, back home to beautiful Brisbane and leaving the fresh Antarctic breezes behind me. I haven't stopped working and traveling since I started as a young woman, inspired by adventurers and fueled by the fact that those from "disadvantaged" backgrounds should never let their circumstances hold them back.

Living around the world has definitely added to life's colourful tapestry and the stories could fill another few book chapters.

Travelling around the world all started in teenage years when I took a quantum leap and spent the summer as a camp counselor in East Troy, Wisconsin, then going onto to travel the East Coast of the United States. From the charismatic characters from all around the world at the camp, to the bullet holes in the windows of Dunkin Donuts, to the stories of people going missing on the Amtrak train and living on Jelly-Beans, there was never a dull moment in the summer of 1996, it was life-changing, actually.

I recall returning back home through the airport. My mum was still alive at the time, came running up to me with one of her amazing hugs (she really should have won an award for the best bear hugs in the world).

"Belinda, she said, "You're never coming back."

"What do you mean?" I said.

"I know that you're meant to be somewhere else in the world," she said. "You're not meant to be here, and this is just the start of something amazing."

She was so right, and those words were a catalyst to *dream big* and to know it's possible to achieve whatever we put our minds to. It's our responsibility to do so, regardless of our backgrounds.

Epictetus, the Stoic philosopher, reminds us that we have chief tasks in life or *"ta eph hemin, ta ouk eph hemin."* It's our responsibility to distinguish between what is our responsibility and what is not. It is for us, and us alone to determine our pathway in life. We truly only have one life and it's often those moments of clarity in life that are the sign posts reminding us of our direction. If I look back on life so far there have been four major moments of clarity that I chose to act upon which have sent me on a trajectory to use those adversities to fuel the fire to make a difference.

I WAS BORN in England, and whilst most of my childhood was spent there I always knew that I would spend my life elsewhere. What many don't know about my journey is that it started a little differently. I was born disabled in both legs with *equinovarus bilateral telepes feet*. For me it was a congenital deformity of the feet that occurs in approximately 1:1000 births. Decades ago the treatment was very different, casts were placed from the toes to the upper thigh with metal bars in-between them, with physical therapy up to five times a day. As I grew older I wore ugly, brown, leather calipers, then surgery to cut the heel-cord, and casting and splints for years. It became apparent from a young age that I wasn't going to let anything stop me and I even wore holes through many plaster casts as I shuffled around on my bottom because I couldn't walk. Much to the dismay of the doctors, I never sat still and was always active.

I have vague recollections as a young girl around eight years of age at a hospital appointment with the surgeon with my legs dangling over the edge of the treatment bed, full of dreams and ambitions of being an athlete, only to be told by the surgeon that I needed to *reconsider* those goals as I may never be able to walk properly again let alone run, climb mountains, and attempt world record "Australian first" adventures.

I recall thinking even at such a young age, *You tell me I can't, just watch me!*

Despite being left with limited mobility, chronic pain, one leg visibly smaller and weaker, regular injuries, and a routine each day to ease the pain, I have made the choice to carry on, to run ultra-marathons and climb some of the largest mountains in the world. Being born with a disability was outside of my control. What I do now and in the future is within my control. I have the ability to use these challenges to show that anything is possible, we just need to want it badly enough and be willing to work hard each day to make it happen.

> **"Falling down is not a failure.**
> **Failure comes when you stay where you have fallen"**
> **—Socrates**

This is why I choose not to dwell on being born "disadvantaged," because "disadvantage" is relative. There are many who will never walk and that suffer far more than I have so I consider what happened to me as a blessing. It made me stronger and now seems like it was an advantage because when I stand on top of Everest in the near future I will have travelled there as a result of hard work, by never giving up, and because I chose not to listen to those who said that being an athlete was impossible.

One thing I have learnt over the years is those we consider motivational or inspirational have often had challenges or trauma to overcome, they've encountered some pretty tough stuff and they don't want anyone else to ever feel like they did. I suppose the global mission to create the happiest workplaces (and people) came from those tough childhood experiences, the experiences through life and from losing my mum (my best friend) to breast cancer. If I, along with those around me can create positive, happier, and flourishing environments, then it provides opportunities for those who sometimes don't realise the greatness they have within.

These types of experiences have shaped me, and ultimately the obstacles we face are a reminder that we are not defined by our challenges, in fact they reveal who we truly are. Marcus Aurelius the Roman Emperor and philosopher wrote, "Just as nature takes every obstacle, every impediment, and works around it, turns it to its purposes, incorporates it into itself, so, too, a rational being can turn each setback into raw material and use it to achieve its goal."

I do believe we have to each "fall one thousand times" to learn how to get back up again. We all fall, and I've learnt that it may hurt temporarily, but when you get back up again there is an amazing world out there, and you can't let people or things get in your way.

Very few people know the hardships I've been through because it's not something I publicize. However, as I have grown older and having worked with some of the most successful and well known leaders, athletes, charitable leaders, researchers, and presenters, a common theme amongst them all is that they have faced and overcome tremendous hardships.

There were times growing up when we had very little but it's taught me money isn't everything. During a very cold winter I remember looking down at my mum's hands one day and her knuckles were bleeding due to severe cold and the fact that she held multiple jobs, one of which was sewing through the night, turning the harsh fabric pillow cases inside out. A pair of gloves would have been two or three dollars? But she chose to give us books and pens for school, a pair of running shoes for our sports, and to put food on the table. I recall my mum's shoes used to be by the front door. I looked down at her shoes one day—they perhaps cost more than a few dollars—and saw a hole in them. It was bitterly cold, in the depth of winter, with deep snow. They were old flimsy shoes, because again, whatever money she had, she either spent on us or gave to others.

"Oh, sweetheart," she said, "I'll be okay. Everything is going to be fine."

"But Mum," I said, "there's a hole in your shoe and it's snowing outside."

"Oh, don't worry," she said, "Go and get me a piece of cardboard." And she took a piece of cardboard and she put it in her shoe.

That memory is etched in my mind forever, and one of the many reasons why I do what I do—to honor her memory, to say thank you for putting cardboard in her shoe and the sacrifices she made so we could have the opportunities she never had. Whatever she and my father did they made sure we had more than they did. She went without meals so we could go to school and to practice (We used to get free education and music lessons but you still had to pay bus fares and food.). I do what I do so others don't have to go through those hardships. The stories I have from my childhood drive me and motivate me to be stronger. We are given two arms in life, one to lift ourselves and the other is to reach back for someone else who may need it.

IT'S AMAZING HOW our journeys in life are so powerful if we use them as lessons. Before University I decided to become a police officer. The goal was to become one of the first female police chiefs, as back then there were limited female officers. I saw the best of society and depths of depravity. I had to deal with rapists and murderers, corruption, pedophiles, drunk drivers, and being badly assaulted on duty made me reflect on whether this journey was truly creating happiness. Being violently assaulted by a drug addict wasn't quite the career highlight I was expecting. However, I discovered this part of the journey was only the beginning.

I've seen the very dark side of life and the hardships people can go through, having gone through some myself. I never want anybody to feel like that or go through those things, so if my story or anything I've learned saves someone else the pain, the heartache, or the trying 100 times to succeed on attempt 101, then it was worth sharing the story.

> **"In every person there is a sun.
> Just let them shine."**
>
> **—Socrates**

As life's journey began to reveal itself several years after university, life took an unexpected turn. We had a trip planned to travel around the world. Weeks before we were due to go we found out Mum had cancer. That decision to stay took no consideration whatsoever; it was a given we stay and we fight, and that was to be my mum's biggest and last fight of her life. After surgery, chemotherapy, radiation, and countless medications and prayers in November only a year after she was given the first "all clear," our world was shattered once more.

I remember the day so vividly, our mum, our best friend, walked awkwardly down the stairs of my home which was most unusual for her as she was always so bright, so effervescent, and so full of energy, she had an inner spark that lit up a room. I shall never forget the way she looked at me, with an expression I had never seen before. She uttered two simple but devastating words: "It's back."

Despite being fit and strong and only in her 40s, undergoing multiple surgeries to pin the bones where the cancer had invaded, and the removal of the affected breast and lymph nodes, the cancer had returned and this time with a vengeance, spreading rapidly and relentlessly to her organs and brain. After fighting the fight of her life once more, she could take no more. The following year she closed her eyes and I said my last "good night Mummy," and kissed her for the very last time. I made a promise to her to continue the work she had completed as a counsellor and to make this world a happier, more joyful place to be; to give more than I take, and to never ever give up on my dreams. Even in her passing she was one of the strongest, most courageous, and beautiful souls. Not a day goes by without me thinking of her.

It was during the darkest times as she was growing more and more sick that I met my now husband, my best bud and the man that has stood by me through the roller coaster of life. Despite not being religious, I always maintain he was an angel sent by my mom, and I am eternally grateful that I didn't move overseas earlier as it would have been a different journey, a journey I could never imagine without him. I wasn't meant to go on an around-the-world trip, I was meant to stay and be with my mom, and meet the man who has been a rock and so much more for almost 20 years.

I recall a conversation with my mum at a young age reminding me to get a passport, an education, and a driver's license: "They're your tickets to anywhere in the world, to do anything you want," she said, and I think that's where my dreaming big comes from. How right she was.

The journey to focus on happiness really started from that last moment I had with Mum in the hospice where she passed, although at the time I didn't know that overwhelming grief and loss brought with it moments of clarity and became a catalyst for change that would take me around the world. I did end up travelling around the world and moving to New Zealand, then to Abu Dhabi, Dubai, then Al Ain, and in-between home to Australia. We have lived in Qatar, Oman, Turkey, Greece, Sweden, and Cyprus. The journey now continues, living and working in some of the happiest countries in the world as part of my PhD research and our work. All of which could fill many more chapters of a book.

From being pushed off a mountain by a herd of 200kg yaks on the way to Mount Everest Base Camp to getting lost in a desert, a car accident I should never have survived, and whilst out running, inadvertently being caught up in a civil uprisings, to bombs exploding near Hagia Sofia where we stood only days before, to lone running through the Outback of Australia, the lost city of Petra, and nations such as Beirut, regions in Africa, and Nepal, it has been quite a journey.

Things happen for a reason, don't they?

I wouldn't be the leader I am today if it were not for the lessons; I wouldn't know the joy of supporting others if I hadn't had untold sadness and innumerable adventures.

I wouldn't be blessed to be a part of the *Inspiring Women* project with the phenomenal women who are a part of it. I consider it all a blessing, even if it was in disguise at the time. Hopefully there might be one or two people who don't have to walk around with holes in their shoes or get sick or do any of the terrible things people feel they have to do to escape the struggles of life because of these stories in *Inspiring Women Today*.

And I'm hoping that one or more of the amazing women in this project will change lives. Perhaps it's you who is reading this chapter on a plane, seated next to a beach, or as a bedtime read, who realizes that you can dream big, you don't have to think small and you can have the life you choose and deserve. Being part of this project has been a great reminder that life can be a little different than you planned, it can be beautiful and it can also be very tough. The plan to be a neurosurgeon or sports medicine doctor didn't quite work out as planned for me but it hasn't stopped me taking the challenges and turning them in opportunities and now running multiple companies across the world.

> **"The impediment to action advances action,
> what stands in the way becomes the way."**
> **—Marcus Aurelius'**

From kimbling in a warehouse to pay my way through college to setting up my first fitness and wellbeing company when I was twenty whilst at university and holding down a full-time job, the consistent and driving force has been the ability to give back, by serving on boards and committees around the world volunteering with the National Breast Cancer Foundation, Heart Foundation, Special Olympics, Teaching English, and raising thousands for causes such as the Australian Cervical Cancer Foundation and Mental Health Charities.

One thing that has factored all through life is that we all have the same twenty-four hours in any one given day, it's how we use it that matters.

Epictetus in his teaching wrote:

> "Every difficulty in life presents us with an opportunity to turn inward and to invoke our own inner resources. The trails we endure can and should introduce us to our strengths. Prudent people look beyond the incident itself and seek to form the habit of putting it to good use. On the occasion of an accidental event, don't just react in a haphazard fashion: remember to turn inward and ask what resources you have for dealing with it. Dig deeply. You possess strengths you might not realize you have. Find the right one. Use it."

I've worked in the Middle East running the "first-of-its-kind" training and education facility for Emirati women, training them to be the doctors, scientists, and engineers of the future. At the time there was and still exists no other education facility like it in the history of the UAE. We did very early-stage robotics and AI (artificial intelligence) and all over ten years ago. Working with young Emirati women and building a powerful enablement model led me to work with leaders in the field of education, science, health, and technology. Some of the young women are now leading the way in industry and government, early career scientists, doctors, and engineers as a result of the institute. Next, I moved to Al Ain (a small city near the Liwa desert, where the founding father of the UAE, Sheikh Zayed bin Sultan Al Nahyan lived) and heading up science and technology summer school projects for young men and women, a project that was years ahead of its time due to the forward thinking leader Dr Abdullatif Al Shamsi. Having worked on multiple organisational development projects with him and the team, several years of working in such a fast-paced, high-impact environment with eye watering budgets has opened my eyes to broader horizons and generated a quest to develop excellence in companies.

After moving back to Australia and heading up the national training and development project, it was time to establish something that would create a movement, a global impact, and something so powerful as to deliver on that promise I made to my mum almost two decades ago.

> **"Don't seek for everything to happen as you wish it would, but rather wish that everything happens as it actually will —then your life will flow well."**
>
> **— Epictetus.**

After sixteen years of corporate and business experience it was time for some real clarity. This time in the form of establishing the Clariti Group. This came out of a need to focus on how we can create "Gross National Happiness" to increase the mental and physical wellbeing of all of our citizens. If we can have Gross National Product as an economic means of measuring success, then why can our nations and businesses not be measured further on the wellness and happiness of its citizens? With the deterioration of the mental health of our nations increasing there has never been a more important time.

Over the years I have worked with, consulted with, researched, and interviewed some of the best companies in the world who nurture their teams, placing them at the centre of their operations. I have also witnessed toxic, dysfunctional, politically ladened, and damaging companies destroying their company cultures, their reputations, and negatively impacting the lives of so many. We have all had an experience at least once in our lifetimes where we left a company due to the poor culture, toxic environments, and leaders who were just too damaging.

If I have learnt anything over the years, it's been that your team should be at the core of what you do. The realisation that some organisations were treating team members like commodities, like the pens and paper, almost disposable, was a sad reality of some modern-day organisations. Whilst happiness is not a commodity it cannot be chased nor should companies use happiness for nefarious reasons. Imagine a world where people could live at least one percent happier, that they could go to work in safe and enjoyable spaces where they could flourish. Now times that by ten or twenty percent, and that's our goal.

We set about shifting the narrative to "people over profits" because life is simply too short and too precious not to. That's not saying companies shouldn't and can't be profitable, quite the opposite. Our global mission is placing the mental and physical wellbeing at the center of what companies do so they can flourish as an organisation both economically and in relation to the wellness of their team.

Happiness is one of the most searched for terms on the internet. For many, it's illusive and coveted.

Victor Frankl wrote, "But happiness cannot be pursued; it must ensue. One must have a reason to 'be happy.' [...] As we see, a human being is not one in pursuit of happiness but rather in search of a reason to become happy."

In 2013 I set about gathering some of the most remarkable humans to build a global company that changes the nature of work as we know it. A special mention to Ana Tonkin, another inspirational woman who was with us for the first seven years of Clariti Group and is one of the most remarkable women I know. People come into your life for a reason and can change your whole world. What a blessing it is to know her and call her a very dear friend.

With global happiness reducing and unhappiness at work increasing, the U.K. now has one of the highest rates of unhappiness in the workplace, closely followed by Canada, Australia, Germany, and is 4 percent higher than in the U.S. Our rates of mental illness around the globe are now at all-time highs and it's time for change. Health and Safety Executive's Labour Force Survey showed recently that over 15,000,000 days were lost over a 12-month period due to reported mental health problems caused or worsened by work, such as stress, depression, or anxiety. I cover this in my first book, *Chief Happiness Officer* launching in 2021, and in the ongoing PhD to raise awareness, and most importantly to set benchmarks so that moving through 2021 we can redress the balance and reduce the mental health across our nations.

Growing disengagement within the workforce doesn't have to continue to escalate. So we decided to be a part of the solution. Our mission is simple:

HAPPY TEAMS = HAPPY CLIENTS = SUCCESSFUL COMPANY

Clariti is now an eighteen-time award-winning organisation creating peak performance, flourishing cultures, leaders, teams, taking organisations from good to great. The amateur scientist in me loves taking the science and translating it into real world learning that makes a difference. After years in development, last year we launched our Certified Chief Happiness Officer program. Our aim is to have a Chief Happiness Officer / Chief Wellness or Joy Officer in every company in the world, using areas such as positive psychology and neuroscience to educate and bring peak performance and the science of happiness into focus for each and every company in the world that wants to benefit from it. What has been most inspiring in our work is the way it gives back. For every coaching program, for every Chief Happiness Officer or consultancy project we put a child through school or a woman into business.

In 2022 we are looking to work with ALLKND and its founder Milly Bannister (whose board I sit on) to provide the Brain Pilot program into schools. Brain Pilot is a mental wellness literacy program that attempts to save lives, given that in Australia our number one cause of death in people aged 15-44 is death by suicide, all of which are preventable and actionable, and it is a charity very close to our hearts. Our work provides opportunities for our team to earn a living and give back in the most unique ways.

It's amazing, to work with people to allow them to understand they have unlimited potential (and it is unlimited) by helping them understand the brain and how it impacts our ability to perform. We're only limited by our self-limiting beliefs. It's like climbing Everest. People attempt it and people fail. People die on the mountain too. Yet it's possible to climb Everest, and everybody needs to find their Everest. They need to firstly find it then climb it. For some people it might just be getting out of bed in the morning, and that's okay, and for others it might be much more. It's about finding your goal, *your* Everest, finding your why, finding what drives you. For some people it could be having a family and for some it could be battling a disease. It doesn't have to be enormous, but it has to be something that keeps you focused. And when your brain starts playing tricks on you (throwing up barriers), you should have the coping strategies and tools to overcome those challenges. I get excited about the science of human behaviour and peak performance, translating the science and making it real for people

This is something I discuss further in my book, *Find Your Own Everest,* launching in 2022/2023.

Let nothing come between you and your goals.

Even back when I was five years old, in calipers and shuffling around on my bottom, nothing stopped me, so I am in no way phased by what we have ahead us in our global movement to create the happiest workplaces in the world. Nothing is going to stop me—not even the metal rods and bars of my leg calipers cold stop me!

As for my own personal and actual Everest, if I think back to age fifteen, I had a "vision board." I put a picture of Everest on there. A s a young family we sometimes had no money and no food, so how the heck was I ever going to be able to climb Everest? I had no idea, I just knew I was going to do it. I travelled around with that vision board until I lost track of it. Then, not long after my mum passed, I was reflecting on preciousness of life. I asked myself, *What can I do that's so insanely crazy it defies human logic?* I decided I would do the Seven Summits (and now I'm going to do the Grand Slam as well, where I ski to the North and South Poles). If I can do it, I thought, then anyone can do it, literally anybody, because it's all about putting your mind into what you're doing and you can achieve anything.

As I write the final part of this chapter there is also a top secret first Australian Woman adventure planned for 2022 which is going to be the most demanding physical challenge of my life and bigger than any ultra-marathons I have run and any mountains I have climbed. It is going to take everything I have and more to make this a reality with great coaches and sponsors and with 12 months of training, hard work, and commitment ahead. My motto remains the same, "Dream Big. Aim High and Never Give Up."

People are often intrigued with the journey to the Seven Summits especially given my disability at birth, and I can honestly say it's been a life-changing ten-year project that has been several decades in the making, from the "stroll" up the first summit, Mount Kosciusko in Australasia, to climbing Kilimanjaro. The second of the Seven Summits was one of the most life-changing of all. I discovered a project by a woman named Mama Lynn called The Light of Africa, and the children there absolutely stole my heart when we visited to deliver books, toys, and clothes.

Some people come into your world and change it forever. Mama Lynn and the children of Light in Africa definitely did that. From the moment I met Joey, Margaret, Mama Lynn, and all the children, I knew I had to do more. I met many children there, but two beautiful children in particular, Margaret and Joey, caught my heart and changed my life. Margaret was an albino, African child. If you don't know what happens to albino children in Africa, it's quite terrifying. They are hunted for their limbs, which are cut and removed and often sold to witch doctors.

The Light in Africa is now located in Mererani in Tanzania, the only place on earth where the rare gem Tanzanite is found, which is just as precious and lucrative as diamond, coal, or gold. Mererani is the source of a 300-million-dollar-a-year industry, yet 30 percent of the 200,000 people who call this place home survive on less than a dollar a day. Every day, 4,000 child miners between the ages of 8 and 14 risk their lives in poorly-constructed mineshafts for barely a meal a day. This forces many women to subsidise their income through prostitution. Children are also compelled into sex work in order to survive, a common story for many mothers and daughters in this area.

I will never forget how when first meeting Margaret on my first visit to the home, she gave me the most adorable hug. She looked at my skin and could see that we were almost the same color. The look of delight on her face. I couldn't speak Swahili, but I saw this acknowledgement in her face and when she spoke I had someone translate for me.

"We're sisters," I said to her.

"White sisters," she replied.

The curious look on her face transformed into in the most beautiful smile.

At the time I first met her, Margaret was safe in a protected area. She's not there at the moment, unfortunately. Her family asked for her to go back to the farm. The children are often put in homes because the parents can't afford to feed them, but when the parents can afford to feed them or the children are old enough to work they're taken back out of the home and sent to work.

The second child I met was Joey. He was the most beautiful little boy. He had just been brought to the home when I arrived and I remember speaking to Mama Lynn about him.

"We've just had this little boy brought in," she said. "He's very, very sick and he may not make it." He was basically dying.

His father remarried a younger woman so he could have more children, however they couldn't deal with Joey because he was very sick. He had cerebral palsy. He was visually-impaired, possibly blind. He was also hearing-impaired, possibly deaf, so he had been left in a goat shed to die by his family.

Now, I don't have children, and I'm not very good with children, but Mama Lynn simply handed Joey to me. "Hold him," she said.

"Okay, now what do I do?" I was holding him but my goodness, I had no idea!

"We'll put him in his stroller," she said, "and we'll feed him."

He didn't have the strength, so I held up his tiny head while Mama Lynn fed him. She had around a couple of hundred children and had to go and deal with a visitor, so she left me with little Joey. I held his head as I dipped the spoon and fed him. I talked to him, cared for him as though he were my own, and even if it was for only a day, this little boy was going to be showered with love after years of neglect and suffering.

"You're the most amazing, strong, young boy," I said, unable to know if he could hear me. I continued holding and talking to him, "You're going to grow up and do something amazing. You could be an engineer, you could be a pilot, you can be anything you want to be. As much as it's tough now, it's not always going to be like this." I continued to talking to him.

His eyes flicked toward me and he started smiling just as Mama Lynn came over.

"He's smiling," she said. "It's the first time he's smiled since he's been here."

"It might be wind," I said. "I think that's what babies do."

"No," she said. She looked at Joey and looked at me and said, "It isn't wind."

There were many defining moments in that first trip, especially those with Margaret and Joey. My life was changed forever by spending time with them and I knew I had to do more, whether it was one percent or ten percent of my time, it didn't matter, I knew I needed to do more. I wanted to use Clariti Group as a vehicle to positively impact lives of "one million and one people." And that's what we're doing now through our programs, through giving back. So every time, for example, people buy my *Chief Happiness Officer* book, they'll buy a *brick* or support a project. "Buy a book, buy a brick" is part of our One Million & One charitable project to positively impact the lives of one million and one people globally in our lifetime. Of course, that's not exact amount! It's an arbitrary number we chose because we wanted to dream big. Along with partnering with Stella (featured in this book, *Inspiring Women Today*) and Patrick from the Women's Reliance Foundation in Uganda, we have the honour of supporting a woman into business for $150 dollars. This grassroots micro-finance project is impacting the lives of hundreds of women and their families, allowing them to find work that is safe and sustainable to feed their families.

We also partner with Uganda Kids who came to us through a connection we were working with, Paul Fyfe and his wife Sue, to support children into school and we can't wait to do more over the coming years.

We do what we can with what we've got. The more work we secure the more we benefit others and that's what drives me to work harder. If you look on the Giving Back page of the Clariti Group website you'll see photographs and videos from many of these and other projects.

Getting to know those children over in Tanzania and learning their stories changed my life—some of the most horrific stories, children dropped into latrines, pit toilets, and left to die. I met a young girl whose family couldn't afford a wheelchair so her grandmother had to break the bones in her legs and elsewhere in her body so they could compact her body and put her in a crate used for oranges just to carry her. She was one of the courageous young ladies I met the second time I visited two years ago when we delivered four suitcases full of much-needed supplies

A lot of people are reluctant to get involved because they don't know how. *How can I possibly help those people in Tanzania, Uganda, or the youth of Australia?* My reply is that it's *little things* that can make a difference. It might just be a drop in the ocean but drops create ripples and ripples can create a tsunami of change, they really can. We do have to start with the little things, and sometimes it's the little moments in life that take your breath away, sometimes it's a smile.

What I've have learned from all of this is that you can't pour from an empty cup. You have to be strong emotionally as well as physically and you have to be financially able to give if only a little time or funds. I don't mean you have to be a multi-millionaire, but you can't continue to give if you have nothing yourself. You do need to choose who you support, otherwise you'll quickly be exhausted. I receive a lot of approaches these days and you sometimes have to learn how to say *no*, which is always tough. Whenever we can give time we will always do so.

CLARITY BY BELINDA JANE DOLAN

The Seven Summits journey has taught me that YOU REALLY CAN achieve anything you clearly set your mind too. I didn't think I'd make it to the top of Summit Three of Seven, Mount Elbrus in Russia, after becoming very sick, and actually, I *crawled* up sections of it. Thankfully, there was only me and my guide to see my crawling in the snow. But the crawling doesn't matter, falling down doesn't matter, getting sick doesn't matter, it's the story that you tell yourself in order to get back up again that matters. It's okay to fall to crawl and shuffle. Never be afraid to admit you failed or fell.

I suppose there's a spiritual element in everything I do. We have one life (depending on your religious beliefs) so you have to live it. Today, this moment is our only guarantee. My mom died in her forties. She had to leave my sister at the age of fifteen. So, we never know what's around the corner. Living a fulfilled life is vital. I know that when I go to the grave I'm going there in bandages and duct tape! I'm not going perfectly preserved, I'm going to the grave with scars both emotional and physical, the broken bones, the surgeries, the torn ligaments and much more to remind me of the adventures. Scars are beautiful reminders that we are alive. This is your life and it's about making sure that you live it. You don't have to undertake crazy adventures to truly live and love, you could pot plants, you could find a cure for world hunger, you could knit, but whatever it is, do it with passion and commitment.

I wish for everyone who has reached the end of this chapter to know that you are capable of so much, you have greatness within, and let no one ever tell you that you can't or it's impossible.

When we meet again in the next chapter, or book, or at an event or reach out and connect, I would love to hear how the book inspired you. When I finally get to the summit of Everest, I can say I did it, and I want you to also say the same, that you found your own Everest and you climbed it.

Because anything is possible.

Dream big. Aim high. Never Give up.

Love and adventures,
Belinda Jane

Written by Belinda Jane Dolan, edited by Rodney Miles Taber.

About Belinda-Jane Dolan

www.CLARITIGROUP.com

clariti GROUP

Belinda Jane Dolan
CEO & Board Director

(07) 3435 1539
belinda@claritigroup.com
www.claritigroup.com
claritigroup

OUR MISSION:
" Creating the Happiest Workplaces on the Planet "

PRE-ORDER NOW!
LAUNCHING DECEMBER 2020

INSPIRE WOMEN TODAY

VISIT www.INSPIRINGWOMENTODAY.com and JOIN OUR EMAIL LIST for special author and publisher events, offers, new releases, opportunities for beta readers, and to be a part of launch team events.

And NOMINATE the next INSPIRING WOMAN to be featured in upcoming editions of this series.

If you enjoyed *Inspiring Women Today, Volume 1*, one of the best ways to support a book is to share it with others.

- Please share on your preferred social media. You can link your post(s) to www.INSPIRINGWOMENTODAY.com.
- And few things help more than leaving useful, honest review on your preferred retail platform.

WOMEN / FUTURE CONFERENCE

Women Future
CONFERENCE

NOVEMBER 1–5, 2021

REGISTER TODAY!
WWW.WOMENFUTURECONFERENCE.COM

"Some people only ask others to do something. I believe that why should I wait for someone else? Why don't I take a step and move forward? When the whole world is silent, even one voice becomes powerful."

—MALALA YOUSAFZAI

. . . and for Fallon

www.ingramcontent.com/pod-product-compliance
Lightning Source LLC
Chambersburg PA
CBHW080612300426
43661CB00144B/902